Texts in developmental psychology

Series Editor:

Peter Smith
Goldsmiths College, University of London

ALSO IN THE *TEXTS IN DEVELOPMENTAL PSYCHOLOGY* SERIES:

THE CHILD AT SCHOOL
Peter Blatchford and Anthony Pellegrini

ATTACHMENT AND DEVELOPMENT
Susan Goldberg

Forthcoming:

AGEING AND DEVELOPMENT
Peter Coleman

Friends and Enemies

Peer relations in childhood

Barry H. Schneider
University of Ottawa, Canada

A member of the Hodder Headline Group
LONDON
Co-published in the United States of America by
Oxford University Press Inc., New York

First published in Great Britain in 2000 by
Arnold, a member of the Hodder Headline Group,
338 Euston Road, London NW1 3BH

http://www.arnoldpublishers.com

Co-published in the United States of America by
Oxford University Press Inc.,
198 Madison Avenue, New York, NY 10016

British Library Cataloguing in Publication Data
A catalogue entry for this book is available from the British Library

Library of Congress Cataloging-in-Publication Data
A catalog entry for this book is available from the Library of Congress

ISBN 0 340 73208 3 (hb)
ISBN 0 340 73209 1 (pb)

1 2 3 4 5 6 7 8 9 10

Production Editor: Anke Ueberberg
Production Controller: Fiona Byrne
Cover Design: Terry Griffiths

Typeset by J&L Composition Ltd, Filey, North Yorkshire
Printed and bound in Great Britain by MPG Books Ltd, Bodmin

What do you think about this book? Or any other Arnold title?
Please send your comments to feedback.arnold@hodder.co.uk

To my doctoral students

Contents

List of figures and tables   ix
Preface   xi
Acknowledgements   xiii

1   Theoretical and historical roots of peer relations and research   1

2   The importance of peer relations   17

3   Where does social competence come from?   37

4   Peer relations and success at school   73

5   Defining social competence   89

6   Techniques for assessing children's peer relations   109

7   Relationships at the dyadic level   129

8   Peer relations of children with atypical patterns of development   149

9   Cultural differences in peer relations   163

10   Cultural imprints on children's friendships   183

11   Facilitating children's peer relations   191

References   209

Index   249

List of figures and tables

Figures

2.1 Implicit models concerning the link between peer relationship problems and later maladjustment

3.1 Causal links discussed in developmental literature

4.1 Six mirrors of the classroom

6.1 Sample rating-scale sociometric measure

6.2 Remote observation of playground behaviour

11.1 Social problem-solving model

Tables

2.1 Longitudinal studies linking aggression during childhood with long-term adjustment

2.2 Longitudinal studies linking shyness or withdrawal during childhood with long-term adjustment

2.3 Selected studies showing that friendship is linked with children's concurrent well-being

3.1 Studies linking parenting with childhood aggression

3.2 Studies linking parenting with childhood shyness

3.3 Studies linking parenting with children's popularity, peer acceptance, friendship, social competence, or sociability/leadership

4.1 Selected studies showing that social interaction with peers is associated with higher cognitive abilities or better academic performance

5.1 Personal and behavioural characteristics of popular children

5.2 Personal and behavioural characteristics associated with rejection by peers

6.1 Cooles used in an observational study of the social play of young gifted children

8.1 Studies since 1975 on the social acceptance of children with mental retardation by their peers without mental retardation

8.2 Studies since 1980 on the social acceptance of children with learning disabilities by their peers without learning disabilities

8.3 Studies since 1980 on the social acceptance of gifted children by their non-gifted peers

11.1 Studies of the long-term effectiveness of social skills training with children and adolescents

Preface

It was with both delight and trepidation that I accepted Peter Smith's invitation to prepare a volume on children's peer relations for the Arnold Texts in Developmental Psychology. I took up this challenge because I had often searched in vain for a comprehensive text to help me introduce my own area of research to students in courses I have taught. The assortment of excellent chapters and review articles I assigned them failed to provide a coherent presentation of theory and research on children's peer relations, or of their practical applications. I have found that students without extensive background in the behavioural sciences particularly need an integrated overview of the field.

In addition to providing the teaching resource I felt was so lacking, I had several main objectives in mind as I wrote. First of all, I wanted to convey to both the beginning and advanced students the historical, social and intellectual context that has stimulated the scientific study of relationships among children since its inception. It is important to me that students appreciate that the questions asked by researchers and the methods researchers use are vitally intertwined with the history of ideas and with the socio-political currents of the times and places in which the research is conducted.

My second goal was to foster an appreciation of the profound commitment to empirical science that has characterized research and practice in children's peer relations since the days of its pioneers. To accomplish this, I have provided a more thorough review of studies than one typically finds in textbooks other than those intended for students at the most advanced levels. I hope that readers find the experience of perusing the results of series of related studies a satisfying one. The concise tables, free of jargon and technical detail, should facilitate this task. I would not have done justice to the empirical traditions of the field had I glossed over the inconsistencies and limitations of research on fundamental issues by providing over-simplified summary pronouncements backed up by isolated examples. More importantly, I would have short-circuited my portrayal of the data-based mode of inquiry with which most scholars in this field identify.

Indeed, one of the pronounced strengths of the peer relations field is the close link between research and applied practice. I am well aware that many students approach the field with a thirst for solutions to the difficulties faced by children who do not enjoy satisfactory relations with their peers. I also know very well that some scientists are sceptical of the applied interventions that have been developed. I have attempted herein to describe in sufficient detail the many ways in which peer relations research has been translated into practice. I have also attempted to be authoritative and clear about the extent to which these interventions have been successful.

Of necessity, the majority of the scholarly works I discuss are from the United States, where the lion's share of the work in this field has been accomplished. Nevertheless, in writing this book, I have kept in mind the world-wide interest in children's peer relations that has burgeoned over the past few decades. The problems tackled by peer relations scholars have always been matters of international concern, though their cross-cultural relevance is not always evident in the most influential books or articles.

I would like to acknowledge the invaluable assistance of the students who assisted with the background research and with the preparation of the tables: Ian Broom, Keren Fyman, Maya Fowlie, Paul Greenman, Natalie Manocchi, Dante Picchioni and Jacques Richard. I am grateful for the support of my colleagues at the University of Ottawa and for the gracious secretarial support of Jeanine Cameron and Kibeza Kasubi.

Barry H. Schneider
Ottawa, January 2000

Acknowledgements

Figure 2.1 appeared originally in the November 1987 issue of *Psychological Bulletin*, Vol. 102, number 3, p. 389, in an article by Jeffrey Parker and Steven Asher entitled 'Peer relations and later personal adjustment: Are low accepted children at risk?'. Reprinted by permission of the American Psychological Association.

Figure 4.1 is from *Interaction in Cooperative Groups: The theoretical anatomy of group learning* (1992) by Rachel Hertz-Lazarowitz and Norman Miller. Reprinted by permission of Cambridge University Press.

Figure 6.1 appeared originally in a chapter by Steven Asher in B. H. Schneider, J. Rubin, and J. E. Ledingham (eds), *Children's peer relations: Issues in Assessment and Intervention* (1985). Reprinted with permission of Springer–Verlag Publishers.

Figure 6.2 is a photograph by Andrew German.

Figure 11.1 originally appeared in Volume 18 (M. Perlmutter (ed.) 1986) of the *Minnesota Symposium on Child Psychology* in a chapter by Ken Rubin and Linda Rose-Krasnor entitled 'Social cognitive and social behavioral perspectives on problem solving'. Reprinted by permission of Lawrence Erlbaum Associates.

1 Theoretical and historical roots of peer relations research

This chapter is a sketch of the intellectual contexts of research on children's peer relations from its inception to the present day. Pioneer theorists explored peer relations as part of their search for an alternative to psychoanalysis. The political climate of the 1930s and 1940s resulted in sustained interest in the childhood roots of leadership and intolerance. During the post-war years, the community mental health movement provided strong impetus for the development of social-competence interventions in schools and communities and for research to help shape these efforts and document their success.

Far more than any other species, humans seem programmed to form relationships with others, to rely on their relationship partners for support and assistance in times of trouble and to derive a sense of well-being from the relationships they create and cultivate. On the most fundamental level, human beings are driven to engage in sexual cooperation. The needs of children also reveal a biological preparedness to cooperate. In all human societies, there is a long period of child rearing, which requires a cooperative relationship between child and caregiver long before the child is capable of being taught how to form relationships with others. Infants are ready to feed, interact and relate to their mothers from very soon after birth (Argyle, 1991). Babies' actions are coordinated both actively with the caregivers from birth onward (Hartup, 1996). Research suggests that cooperation between children begins to emerge at approximately two years of age, at the latest. Some of the cooperative behaviours that emerge include general abilities aimed at coordinating interaction around a set goal, behaving reciprocally and communicating effectively (Brownell and Brown, 1992). In addition, cooperative problem-solving, evidenced by children coordinating their actions with those of other children in order to achieve an otherwise unattainable goal, occurs quite frequently among 24-month-olds (Brownell and Carriger, 1990).

In many societies, children spend a great deal of time in each other's company. This has been the standard way of growing up in many agricultural societies for centuries: while adults work together, children play together; older siblings have responsibility for the care of their younger brothers and sisters (Whiting and Edwards, 1988). In contrast, children in the United Kingdom, the United States and Western Europe are depicted as having spent most of their time with their families until the late nineteenth century and early twentieth century. The Industrial Revolution and the resulting rapid societal change led to the decline of the family as the fundamental economic unit, as people of all ages began to work in factories together with co-workers outside their families. As a result, children began to congregate in play groups in the streets of large cities, without any substantial supervision by adults. If children are so intensively involved in interaction with their peers, it is logical to expect that children would have a major influence on the development and personalities of other children. The desire to understand that influence – and put it to good use – is the reason sometimes given for the earliest interest by scholars of many disciplines, such as psychology, sociology and education, in the scientific study of peer relations, i.e. of children's relations with other children (Renshaw and Parke, 1992). The debate as to how much of children's behaviour and personality are determined by peers and how much by family rages until the present day. Such comparison of the weights of parent and peer influences has perhaps never received as much public attention until after Judith Rich Harris (1998) published a controversial best seller entitled *The Nurture Assumption: Why Children Turn Out the Way They Do* (see Chapter 3).

The first major theories of personality and child development also emerged at the end of the nineteenth century and the start of the twentieth. The theorists of the time speculated extensively about the importance of peer relations in child development (see Renshaw and Parke, 1992, for a more detailed review). G. Stanley Hall, the pre-eminent psychological theorist of that time, believed that children's association with other children was part of the process wherein ontogeny recapitulates psychology – in going through the stages of development, children repeat the process of evolution from more primitive species to more sophisticated ones. Hall saw herd-like association with other children as an important expression of an inborn 'social instinct'. He maintained that following the social instinct by associating with other children during the primary years enabled children, especially boys, to achieve independence from their parents and prepare themselves for the trials of adult life. Most of the other major theorists of the late 1800s and early 1900s offered theories that were not as bold as Hall's, but they too emphasized children's peer relations as an important element in child development. Another major psychological theorist, James Mark Baldwin, was interested in the ways children change as they grow from independent, separate individuals into cooperative members of society. He believed that being a member of a team in childhood play was an important part of that process. In a similar vein, the influential educational theorist John Dewey emphasized the value of children's informal learning though play, with social experience a major source of the benefit. He believed that playgrounds should be run as miniature, democratically governed towns, with mayors, policemen and other civil servants, so that children prepare for their roles as adults in a democratic society.

The importance of interpersonal relationships seems so obvious that one would expect relationships to be core elements of any and all theories of personality and human development. Therefore, it is surprising that many of the early scholars interested in the peer relations of children and adults felt that they were regarded as heretics in a psychology that was dominated in the 1920s by a fascination with events occurring inside single individuals – their feelings, instincts, drives and complexes. In the writings of peer relations researchers in the 1920s, Freudian psychoanalysis is depicted as a tyrannical force that suppressed not only interest in interpersonal relationships, but in systematic research about human behaviour in general. Nowhere is this clearer than in the provocative writings of Jacob Moreno (1889–1974), the flamboyant founder of sociometry and psychodrama, two techniques that will be described later. Moreno was a physician of Romanian origin, who trained in Vienna and who was interested in social relations and in intergroup and international problems. He dubbed psychoanalysis 'the vengeance of mediocrity' (1953, p. xxxiv), because of its passivity, its stifling of creativity and its insistence that healthy, creative, everyday events were the source of sickness. If God had been no more active or creative than a psychoanalyst, taunted Moreno, the world never would have been created. However, God could well have been a psychodramatist, analysing from on high the relationships between the things he had created and endowing them with new ways of relating to each other (1953, p. xvi). It is thought that Moreno met Freud only once, at a lecture given by Freud in 1912. After the lecture, Moreno spoke briefly with the founder of psychoanalysis:

> Well, Dr. Freud, I start where you leave off. You meet people in the artificial setting of your office, I meet them on the street and in their homes, in their natural surroundings. You analyze their dreams, I try to give them the courage to dream again.
>
> (Moreno, 1972 cited in Hare and Hare, 1996, p. 7)

Mary Northway, the Canadian pioneer of peer relations research with children, echoed the call for a counter-revolution against the psychoanalytic revolution and for a theory based on interpersonal relationships:

> Consciously known living relationships are of major importance to the individual . . . The early relationship to his mother in infancy or to his

father at his Oedipal stage has historical rather than dynamic meaning
. . . The early psychoanalytic doctrine which considers society as an
oppressing and stultifying prison is replaced by a view of society as a
potentially rich soil out of which the individual derives nutriment for
his growth and the sustenance necessary for an enriched life.

(1952, p. 49)

Obviously, such ideas were unwelcome in the community of mental-health
professionals that was still in a state of euphoria because of the recent major
contributions of Freudian theory: the acceptance of psychiatric problems as
natural, human phenomena that were to be understood rather than as manifestations of evil forces that had to be defeated (Goodwin, 1990).
Moreno's assault against what he saw as the uselessness of psychoanalysis
('stillborn to start with', 1953, p. liv) reached a climax when he belittled a
psychoanalytic description of the personality of Abraham Lincoln that
appeared in an American newspaper in 1932 (Hare and Hare, 1996).
Moreno felt that more could be learned by analysing the reasons why mod-
ern psychoanalysts chose the particular historical personalities they chose
to dissect than by analysing the personalities of dead people whose social
relationships could not be studied meaningfully from historical documents
('neither transference [the direction of positive feelings and desires towards
a new object or person] nor resistance [the often unconscious refusal to
admit to one's awareness potentially useful insights] can be expected from
a dead person' (1953, p. xlvi). From that point on, Moreno and his followers became outcasts in the community of mental-health professionals, outcasts who themselves studied people who were outcasts. Instead of studying
people's feelings, instincts and drives, as psychoanalysts do, Moreno and
his followers focused on the roles people play in groups. Relationships and
roles in them were to become the major unit of analysis; by no means were
relationships to be considered a surface by-product of primitive sexual drives, as they are in Freudian theory as it was interpreted by Moreno and his
followers. Moreno used the term 'role' as it is often used in social psychology, to refer to the privileges and responsibilities that accompany a given
position in society. One can have the role of teacher, leader, scapegoat, sup-
porter, etc. In Moreno's 'spontaneity theory', an individual's personality is
a reflection of the roles he or she plays in life. A psychologically healthy person is one who, in relating to others, can assume healthy roles in a flexible
and spontaneous way (Hare and Hare, 1996; Moreno, 1953).

The nature of the child: normal and abnormal patterns of development

Inattention to the social world was not the only flaw in Freud's approach to
which Moreno and his followers objected. Early peer relations researchers

also objected vociferously to the Freudian preoccupation with the exclusive study of abnormal behaviour without learning, if only for comparison purposes, how the 'normal' individual thinks, feels and relates. The study of both normal and abnormal development is another feature of early peer relations research that has survived to the present day. As in the past, many contemporary peer relations researchers believe that, in order to understand and help children who cannot get along with others, it is important to understand the social behaviour of children who have no problem with their relationships with others. Northway maintained that:

> From the days of Freud on, investigations of the neurotic and the psychotic, of emotionally disturbed or retarded children, of criminals and delinquents, of deprived infants, have been made. On the basis of these discoveries, theories of mental health have been established, but these have not told us the whole and may have told us a distorted story. Mental health is not simply a lack of mental illness and a theory of mental healthiness can hardly be completed by saying that mental health is what these patients do not have. Mental health can only become understood by observing mental healthiness as it exists.
>
> (1956, p. 3)

In the years since this criticism was voiced, much more research has been conducted on the development of normal children, though, according to many influential contemporary social scientists, still not enough. For example, Martin Seligman, in his 1999 presidential address to the American Psychological Association, called for:

> a reoriented science that emphasizes the understanding and building of the most positive qualities of the individual: optimism, courage, work ethic, future mindedness, interpersonal skill, the capacity for pleasure and insight and social responsibility . . . Psychology has moved too far away from its original roots, which were to make the lives of all people more fulfilling and productive and too much toward the important, but not all-important, area of curing mental illness.
>
> (1999, p. 559)

The early behavioural scientists' infatuation with psychoanalysis was seen at the time as a suppressor not only of interest in interpersonal relationships, but also as an inhibitor of objective, scientific research about human development. The peer relations research community felt that the psychoanalytically inspired researchers of that period refused to design studies and discuss the results in a scientific way that was free of jargon and unproven theoretical explanation. It would be unfashionable to observe and describe exactly what children did in specific situations – for example, whether they cried, laughed, hit, approached others — and how they did these things. Such unfounded pronouncements as 'Jeffrey exhibited attention-seeking behaviour demonstrating regression to an early stage' would have been much more respectable. In a perhaps over-zealous reaction to the ubiquity of such unscientific thinking, many members of the first generation of peer relations scholars set out deliberately to describe exactly what children did in the company of other children, in plain, everyday language. They felt it premature to offer elaborate theories to explain the relationship-building behaviours they observed. In particular, they wanted to use precise, direct observations to corroborate their impression that children were not as selfish, insensitive and even cruel as Anna Freud depicted them in her famous theories about children's psychological defence mechanisms (Renshaw, 1981).

Just as Sigmund Freud's teachings were based on the psychoanalysis of distressed adults, Anna Freud and her colleagues based many of their more pronounced observations about the nature of the child on their study of children who had been evacuated from the blitz bombings in London. Contemporary scholars who were more sceptical about Freudian teachings took exception to Anna Freud's conclusion that 'children are born as little savages' (Burlingham and A. Freud, 1942). Blatz (1944), for example, maintained that, even if the child is born as a 'non-social being' (which most present-day researchers of the infancy period would dispute), that does not necessarily mean that the child is born 'savage'. To resolve this issue, more intensive and more systematic study of children under normal conditions was needed. It is important to note that Freudian theories were also seen by some as less harsh and harmful than they were seen by many peer relations scholars in the early and middle 1900s. For example, Littledale (1946, cited in Renshaw and Parke, 1992) observed that psychoanalytic theories about childhood were of help to parents trying to understand children's instincts, drives and moments of animal-like rage. Instead of trying to stamp out these inevitable aspects of human development by force, parents could learn to accept them as natural and try to channel them.

Because of its emphasis on the precision of observation and on scientific rigour rather than creativity in explaining behaviour, the field of children's peer relations was widely tainted as being atheoretical – not designed to prove any particular theory. This disrepute continues somewhat to the present day. However, there are some important theoretical roots of contemporary peer relations research. For example, one of the important functions of contemporary research on children's peer relations is to prove or disprove attachment theory or Sullivan's interpersonal theory of psychiatry, which will be discussed in Chapters 2 and 3. Even though peer relations researchers of all periods have shown little regard for theories that are not supported by evidence, the scientific methods of peer relations research –

such as sociometrics and direct observation (see Chapter 6) were used as early as the 1930s by scholars such as Isaacs (1933) who wanted to demonstrate the validity of the theories by Freud and others.

Putting peer relations research to work: helping individuals in distress

However, proving or disproving theories has never been the only reason for studying peer relationships. The field of peer relations has always attracted scientists and practitioners with particular interest in the practical applications of their work. This has been evident since the 1920s. Although Moreno developed highly technical methods for finding out what roles people play in groups, his main purpose was to help people understand their roles in groups and try out new roles. Within his theory, this enactment of roles is seen as enabling reduction of stress.

One of the first 'real-world' problems that inspired peer relations research was the observation that groups of children and adolescents were united in their alienation from schools (Renshaw, 1981). The writings of peer relations researchers who worked during the interval between the two world wars indicate their desire to take up the challenge posed by predominant theorists of the time, including Piaget (1932), who criticized the emphasis on rote learning in the school curriculum (Renshaw, 1981). Piaget saw rote memorization as stunting children's social development along with their academic achievement. This early concern by researchers for the social relations of children in schools was one of the reasons for the creation of systematic methods for observing children at school, such as Parten's (1932) well-known categories for children's interaction (see Chapter 6 for discussion of observational methods), which, with very few changes, remains in use until now. Concern about the massive problem of unemployment among adolescents and young adults led to research on interactions between members of street gangs. This started in Chicago with the advent of Thrasher's (1927) methods for scientific observation from the vantage point of membership of the group being studied.

Moreno was deeply concerned about the social and political problems of the years between World Wars I and II, especially the conflicts between nations and between racial, religious and ethnic groups. He believed that the world could be fixed from the ground up – by fixing one interpersonal relationship at a time and, especially, by helping individuals such as chronic outcasts to obtain different positions and roles in their peer groups. He proposed psychodrama, also known as sociodrama, a therapeutic technique that is the very antithesis of Freudian psychoanalysis, as a way of doing this. In his work on psychodrama, Moreno went so far as to design special theatres in Vienna for psychodrama. In psychodrama, people experiencing distress could achieve insight about the roles they played in their interpersonal relationships and practise the enactment of new roles. The trusting, empathic relationship (called 'tele') between the person whose roles were being played out and the other participants in the psychodrama, enabled the enactment of new roles in an atmosphere of flexibility and spontaneity. In a typical psychodrama, the protagonist is the person whose roles and relationships are being analysed. Other actors play the various persons involved in the relationships. Other players act as auxiliaries, who follow the main players about the stage, expressing the inner feelings and perceptions of the main players. There might be several sequences in which a critical conversation is first enacted exactly as the protagonist remembered it, followed by repeat enactments in which the actors change roles. The session might end with a soliloquy during which the protagonist reflects on what has happened during the session. Psychodrama is still practised today, although it has declined in importance among the major therapeutic techniques. Elements of psychodrama live on in many of the social-skills training techniques that will be discussed in Chapter 11.

Moreno defended with great vigour the emphasis on action in his psychodramatic movement. Psychodramas were to be staged with spontaneity and creativity. However, Moreno also wanted the therapeutic techniques of psychodrama to be informed by the scientific study of peer relationships. Therefore, he devoted much energy not only to the development of his psychodramatic technique, but also to the refinement of precise sociometric techniques for measuring individuals' reputations in their peer groups. He also devoted some attention to 'living sociometrics', i.e. studying relationships by observing them directly, as in his studies of children's interactions in a state primary school in New York.

Putting peer relations research to work in the service of society

Moreno emigrated to the United States before World War II to avoid the Nazi persecution of Jews. By the time of his arrival, the pioneers of peer relations research in the United States had already established laboratory schools on the grounds of several universities in order to study human development in great detail. They managed this despite the fact that by then Freudian psychoanalysis was deeply entrenched in the United States as the main theory of human behaviour. Psychodrama had attracted a loyal following among therapists working with adults in both institutions and in the community. Nevertheless, peer relations researchers felt the need to venture beyond the niche they had carved for themselves in the research community and in the helping professions and to use what they had learned to construct a less troubled world.

It is not difficult to understand this concern with real-world social and political problems when one considers the turbulence of the times. Leadership is a frequent theme in the articles published in the 1930s on relationships between children, reflecting the widespread alarm in the United States, Canada and the United Kingdom about the appeal of the charismatic leaders of Germany and Italy at that time (Jack, 1934). Discovering the childhood precursors of effective leadership became a pressing scientific concern. Of course, when one studies leadership, one studies not only the leaders, but also the followers and the relationships between the leaders and the followers. These researchers were well aware that similar research was being conducted in Germany at the time, for many of the same reasons. Blatz (1944), who was the leading Canadian scholar of child development at the time, offered the observation that one can become a leader of a group by either direct or indirect means. 'Direct' means include becoming proficient at activities that are central to the purpose of the group and relating to others in a friendly, persuasive and sensitive manner. Indirect means include securing leadership by force and bullying, as was done by the Nazis. The problem of bullying continues to preoccupy scholars interested in children's peer relations, as will be discussed in Chapter 5.

One can also trace to the writings of the World War II years some of the principles that are used to this day in teaching children how to get along with other children (see Chapter 11), although the reasons for wanting to help children in this way have changed dramatically. For example, Blatz (1944) attributed Hitler's leadership to the fact that Hitler's teaching contained no ambiguities: there was only one way of behaving. In a democracy, children and adults have many choices in their relationships with others; that is what makes it a democracy. Blatz noted that it is more difficult to be effective socially in such a climate of choice and that individuals need help in understanding their choices and deciding which of their options to select in managing their interpersonal relationships. This is, essentially, the basis for social problem-solving lessons, which are often used to prevent children from suffering social failure (see Chapter 11).

Many theorists and researchers around the time of World War II attempted to determine the type of parenting that might lead to children becoming cooperative citizens of democratic societies. Running a home democratically was often seen as the way to do this. Arnold Gesell, one of the foremost child-development theorists of the mid-1900s, was influenced by the work of Kurt Lewin, the social psychologist, on the effectiveness of democratic leadership of social and work groups. Gesell advocated democracy in child-rearing (Gesell and Ilg, 1943; Renshaw and Parke, 1992). This theme was to be continued many years later in Baumrind's research into the type of parenting that is associated with children being socially successful and cooperative. Her work will be discussed in Chapter 3.

Determining the long-term importance of peer relations in childhood

In contrast to Moreno's lofty ambition of changing the world, his work with psychiatric patients and troubled adolescents was aimed at alleviating their psychological symptoms, which is of course a major responsibility of mental-health professionals. In their therapeutic work, the pioneer scholars in the peer relations field insisted on finding out exactly which problems of children would lead to psychological problems in later life and which might disappear as children mature. They felt that this information was needed in order to decide which children require treatment and how to treat them. Therefore, in the 1930s, a number of longitudinal studies – studies in which the same individuals were followed from childhood into their adult years – began (e.g. Walcott, 1932). Undertaking expensive, long-range studies of this type required some scepticism about yet another assumption made by Freud, namely that it was impossible to predict psychological health over the long term:

> So long as we trace development from its final outcome backwards . . . we feel we have gained an insight which is completely satisfactory or even exhaustive. But if we proceed the reverse way, if we start from the premises inferred from the analysis and try to follow these up to the final result, then we no longer get the impression of an inevitable sequence. Hence the chain of causation can always be recognized with certainty if we follow the line of analysis [i.e. backwards], whereas to predict it . . . is impossible.
>
> (Freud, 1920; cited by Kohlberg, Lacrosse and Ricks, 1972)

If, as Freud maintained, it is impossible to predict adult mental health from aspects of children's life, it becomes difficult to understand when and how to provide help to troubled children (Kohlberg, LaCrosse and Ricks, 1972). However, the results of many longitudinal studies, as summarized in Chapter 2, have shown that some degree of prediction is indeed possible and, as will be detailed in that chapter, that success in early relationships with other children is a reasonably good predictor of doing well as an adult. This has become the reason most scholars of peer relations cite nowadays in explaining why they conduct their research. It has also inspired the development of techniques to assist young children to improve their relationships with other children.

Practical techniques for helping children improve their relationships with others achieved enhanced respectability as mental-health practitioners wanted to work more extensively in communities, homes and schools rather than confine their activities to hospitals, clinics and professional offices. The peer relations researchers of the 1930s went so far as to publish books of advice for parents on how to raise their children to be self-reliant but effective in establishing relations with others. A classic example is Isaacs' (1933) concise interpretation of child development research, which was a best-seller in Britain. In order to place such value on the dissemination of psychological information to the general public, yet one more Freudian precept had to be debunked: the idea that transference (the transfer of previous relationship attachments by the patient in psychoanalysis to the analyst) was the only serious mechanism for achieving therapeutic change and, furthermore, that transference could only occur in the relationship with the analyst. In classical Freudian terms, helpers in the community, as well as supportive friends, parents and teachers, can serve, at best, as secondary outside adjuncts to treatment, if they do not sabotage the therapeutic process entirely (Nietzel, Guthrie and Susman, 1991). Interestingly, some contemporary psychoanalysts have discovered the value of 'transfer of the transference' to important people in their clients' lives (Wallerstein, 1989). But how can one conduct psychoanalysis in a working-class neighbourhood or inner-city school? It is not surprising that most of the techniques that have been developed to assist children in relating to their peers do not involve analysis of deep, repressed feelings, but, typically, the practical teaching and learning of the ways that lead to being accepted by potential relationship partners. This was attempted, with some success, as early as the 1930s, when Jack (1934), a scholar at the University of Iowa, found that children who were disliked by other children could be helped by simply teaching them to follow the basic rules of a game. Contemporary techniques for improving the peer relations of children and adolescents are considered in Chapter 3.

Thus, by the end of World War II, the gap between peer relations scholars and psychoanalysts was clear and wide. There were acute differences in terms of the basic understanding of the nature of child, the methods used to learn about child development and the techniques used to assist individuals in difficulty. Between then and now, the traumatic breach with psychoanalysis has healed only somewhat. Perhaps the best example of recent interest in psychoanalytic ideas in relation to children's peer relations is the growing acceptance of attachment theory in explaining the origins of individual differences in children's ways of relating to other children. Attachment theory, which has been called an 'ethological adaptation of psychoanalytic models' (Rubin, Stewart and Chen, 1995, p. 259), is considered more fully in Chapter 3. In their landmark handbook chapter on children's peer relations, Rubin, Bukowski and Parker (1998) cite only one psychoanalytic theory, that of Peter Blos and note that the impact of Blos' work has been minor. Blos (1967) described adolescence as a period in which individuals restructure their childhood relationships with their parents in an attempt to achieve qualitatively different relationships with peers. Sexual drives during adolescence, among other forces, lead to efforts at resolving dependencies upon parents.

Peer relations research and the community mental health movement

Although their rupture with the psychoanalytic community resulted in many peer relations scholars becoming outcasts in the mental-health community in the 1930s, their popularity surged in the post-war years. Their emphasis on rigorous research techniques and real-world applications was a good match for many of the ideas about child development and mental health that emerged after World War II. Psychological examinations of men reporting for wartime military service in the United States indicated that mental illness was far more widespread than had ever been thought. Over a million men had been rejected from the armed services because of mental-health disturbances. Furthermore, 40 per cent of those who were discharged from service were discharged because of mental or neurological disorders (Brand, 1966). It became apparent that such traditional modes of treatment as psychoanalysis would never minister to more than a tiny fraction of those in need (Albee, 1959).

As early as the 1930s, psychiatrists in Western Europe began to experiment quietly with alternatives to institutional care of psychiatric patients, including family care (Brand, 1966). However, large-scale de-institutionalization did not become a matter of public policy in many Western countries until the 1960s (ibid.). In the United Kingdom, the population of psychiatric hospitals fell from 151,400 in 1954 to approximately 60,000 in 1993, as community service provision became a tenet of national policy (Weller, 1993). More sweeping policy changes occurred in Italy, leading to the almost total abolition of psychiatric hospitals and schools for children with special learning needs (Donnelly, 1992; Dosen, 1994); similar reforms took place in the Scandinavian countries.

Some sources assign part of the credit for the de-emphasis on institutions to the emergence of psychoanalysis, which sensitized both professionals and the general public to the possibility that institutional care was not the only viable mode of treatment for individuals with psychiatric disorders (Brand, 1966). However, it soon became clear that the most viable and useful treatments that could probably be offered to the individuals being released from institutions would be oriented to the 'common problems of common existence' (Galdston, 1965), despite the fact that the psychoanalytic emphasis on in-depth personality change and growth had received widespread acceptance, especially in America. One of the most important of these common problems is, in the words of the prominent community psychologists Albee and Gullotta, how to obtain 'simple sustained human friendship' (1997, p. 18). Unfortunately, many of the psychiatric patients released from institutions, or not admitted to institutions, could not form the interpersonal relationships in the community that were envisaged by proponents of the de-institutionalization movement. Therefore, the need arose for research on the social skills required for community living and the ways of teaching them.

Inclusiveness in schools and the social interaction of pupils

The de-institutionalization movement was extended to school systems in most Western countries. Until the 1960s, it was commonly held that the best way to provide a sound education for children with learning and behaviour problems was to establish special classes or special schools for them. In those self-contained settings, special education techniques could be used to maximize learning. It was a common belief that after a few years of such intensive, needs-specific learning, children would return to regular classes and schools near their homes. This assumption was challenged vociferously by ardent critics in the 1960s and the 1970s. Wolfensberger (1972; Wolfensberger and Tullman, 1982), for example, attacked separate special-education classes and schools as a vehicle for the oppression of children with handicaps and for ensuring that their conditions would be perpetuated. In response to such criticisms, legislation in the United States, Italy, Sweden and many Canadian provinces regulated the placement of children with learning and behaviour problems. Attempts at educating those children in regular classes and schools increased even where they were not required by law.

Critics such as Wolfensberger emphasized the advantage to children without handicaps of being educated together with peers who have special learning needs. They hoped that children without disabilities would become familiar with children who have disabilities. Proponents of mainstreaming – educating pupils with handicaps in regular schools and classes, rather than in separate, self-contained facilities – expected that, once children with and without disabilities came into regular contact with each other, they would form relationships with other. The stigma attached to having a disability was also supposed to decrease. These expectations were based on the contact hypothesis, which was formulated by the personality theorist Gordon Allport (1954) in the 1940s and 1950s. Simply stated, the contact hypothesis holds that contact between majority and minority groups should lead, in general, to reductions in prejudice. However, it is often forgotten that Allport specified that only certain types of contact with a minority group would lead to diminished prejudice. The contact must be regarded by the members of the majority as pleasurable; they must feel a sense of common goals with the members of the minority and regard the individual with whom they interact as a positive exemplar of the minority group.

Sadly, despite many successes, it was quickly determined that many of the mainstreamed children with special learning needs were rejected socially by the peers who were supposed to benefit from their presence (Gresham, 1982). Many peer relations researchers took up the task of studying and helping to promote acceptance of children with disabilities as companions in work and play and as friends by children without disabilities.

Cultural diversity in schools and relations among pupils

The contact hypothesis also applies to relationships between children in schools and neighbourhoods composed of persons from different cultural heritages. Much attention was paid world-wide to the racial desegregation of US schools in the 1960s. Massive immigration resulted in many families from Asia, Africa, Eastern Europe and Latin America coming to the United States, Canada, most countries of Western Europe, Australia and Israel. Daily contact between children with such diverse backgrounds has never been more possible.

As attention throughout the world centred on the civil rights movement in the United States, which insisted that the separation of the races in schools, public transport and universities be brought to an end, Northway (1967) urged peer relations scholars to increase their attention to relationships between members of different racial and cultural groups:

> In this era of the 1960s, when violence has erupted in the North American continent in race riots, senseless murders, tragic assassinations and the like, has sociometry no more to say than it has on this point? . . . Has it neglected its potential contribution to the understanding of groups precipitated into violent action? . . . Would it not be profitable for sociometry to investigate the structure of the huge apartment block, the sprawling vast industry, the suburban neighbourhood, the ghettos, the separatists and indeed the Eskimos and Indians of Canada and the Negro-White relationships of the United States? As social chaos has increased, have sociometric relationships broken down? What, for instance, would a sociogram of the hippies look like? . . . The [socio-metric] technique is now ready to be used to gain insight into a society . . . living under the threats of extinction by a nuclear bomb . . . and by the pollution of its interpersonal relationships from within.
>
> (1967, pp. 51–2)

Thus, thirty years after Moreno first called on peer relations scholars to address problems of the world in the throes of world wars, Northway implored the post-war generation of researchers to address real-world social phenomena. Her call was not unheeded. Although some peer relations studies seem to focus on matters of theoretical interest only, others have examined directly such issues as the social relations of children living in poverty and the friendships between children of different races and cultural backgrounds, which will be considered in detail in Chapter 10.

Interpersonal relationships and the search for happiness in life

Although not mentioned as frequently as the other reasons reviewed in this chapter for studying peer relationships, there is some interest in studying and promoting peer relationships for the simple reason that relationships make people happy. Perhaps the quest for happiness is universal or perhaps it is a form of indulgence that can only be afforded by individuals who have no need to be preoccupied with their survival in spite of adverse economic, social and political conditions. The second half of the twentieth century saw massive economic progress in North America, Western Europe and many other countries, though, even in those privileged places and especially elsewhere, a great many individuals still need to be concerned with their own survival. Some authors maintain a major shift in people's priorities occurred in North America and Western Europe during the 1960s (e.g. Hewitt, 1998). Striving for economic or educational advancement was no longer as strong or ubiquitous a goal as it was in the years after World War II. Happiness and personal fulfilment became important objectives for many. Many parents became concerned with their children's happiness and self-concepts. Helping improve children's social relationships is an excellent way to achieve these goals.

Where to from here?

The social and political conditions of the third millennium will certainly shape the reasons why scholars continue to study children's relations with other children. In the final years of the twentieth century, Hareven (1989) summarized the demographic changes that result in children in most Western countries spending more and more time in the company of other children of approximately the same age. In contrast with the street life of children after the first years of the Industrial Revolution, children spend less and less time with older and younger siblings and peers, for several reasons. Perhaps the most important of these reasons is that the birth rate has declined in many Western countries and, consequently, there are fewer and fewer younger or older siblings to spend time with. In addition, an increasing proportion of mothers are participating in the workforce. This constitutes a shift from a pattern of childrearing involving a mother staying at home with her children, which was more typical of the middle of the twentieth century than either the beginning or end of that century. Indeed, improved medical care is making it more possible than ever for children to know their grandparents. However, grandparents are far less likely than a century ago to live in the same community and home and, hence, to be part of children's daily networks of social contacts. Furthermore, despite some innovative educational practices such as having older pupils tutor younger ones (see Chapter 4), schooling occurs more than ever in groups segregated by age, as do organized sport and other leisure time activities in the community.

Therefore, children today may typically have fewer opportunities than previously to assume the roles of older sibling, younger sibling, senior pupil, junior pupil, or grandchild. Perhaps it will become useful to resurrect Moreno's concepts of social roles and to make more use of techniques derived from the classic principles of Morenian psychodrama in order to provide children with the opportunities to try new social roles that they rarely play in their natural lives.

2 The importance of peer relations

Coping with the stresses of life

The dynamics by which peer relations are thought to affect adjustment and maladjustment across the lifespan are outlined, with particular attention to the role of social competence in fostering resilience in the face of adverse early experience. Longitudinal research documenting the links between childhood social competence and subsequent psychological adjustment is critically reviewed, as is research addressing the importance of social competence as a protective factor for children at risk for maladjustment.

The reasons for studying children's relations with their peers mirror the reasons for studying child development in general. Adler and Adler (1998) classify the reasons for studying childhood into two main categories. The first category is the study of children because they are considered 'incomplete adults' (Adler and Adler, 1998, p. 6, see also Qvotrop, 1990). From that perspective, one studies children's lives in order to understand how childhood experiences contribute to the understanding of the same individuals as adults. According to Adler and Adler, this involves the assumption that adulthood is the most important period of life. Childhood is just a transitional period from which one graduates into real life. Adherents of this point of view typically devote considerable attention to how adults prepare children for their future roles in adulthood. They often view children as passive recipients of the teachings of adults.

The alternative is to study childhood because it is an important period worthy of attention in its own right. Proponents of this position offer the image of childhood as a permanent feature in society: Although individuals grow out of childhood, childhood remains an ever-present feature of human existence. Therefore, children's peer relations should be studied as an important aspect of life itself, not as a part of preparation for life (Sutton-Smith, 1982). Those who advocate direct attention to the study of children for its own sake are influenced by the fact that children are quite active in developing independent ways of thinking and functioning quite independently of adults. Having introduced the distinction between these two categories of reasons for studying child development, Adler and Adler point out that the distinction can only be carried so far, because it is not really possible to study children without studying the adults in their social worlds at the same time.

The history summarized in Chapter 1 suggests many reasons for studying children's relationships with their peers specifically. However, even the most cursory scan of articles and books in the field will confirm that one of these reasons is widely seen as the most important, namely, the fact that successful peer relations during childhood is linked with general psychological well-being throughout life. It is perhaps human nature that causes parents and teachers to contemplate the behaviours of young children and use what they see as the basis for predicting the children's futures. When it becomes apparent that an adult has not turned out to be the well-adjusted individual that was hoped for, it is also human to look backwards at that person's childhood years in an attempt to find out what went wrong. In the peer relations field, forward and backward predictions of these kinds serve very crucial purposes. First and most fundamentally, they confirm that it is important to study children's peer relations. Second, they indicate which childhood social behaviours are of greatest importance because they are most likely to lead to problems later on. For example, there have been many efforts to compare aggressive behaviour with shyness/withdrawal during childhood years in order to determine whether either or both remain stable and whether they are equally connected with problems during the adolescent and adult years; studies on that issue will be considered shortly. Such efforts at predicting adult mental health are particularly useful in determining the content of special programmes aimed at preventing and treating mental illness. They also help to identify children who are showing early signs of maladjustment, so that early assistance can be provided to minimize the negative outcome.

As noted in Chapter 1, Freud was quite pessimistic about the possibility of predicting the future adjustment of an individual from his or her current behaviour. However, considerable knowledge has accrued since Freud's time as result of the work of scholars who have taken up the challenge of prediction despite Freud's admonitions. Nevertheless, it turns out that Freud was quite perceptive in sensing the pitfalls in making long-term predictions of adjustment.

It is a slow and costly enterprise to collect data about the functioning of large groups of children and follow them into adolescence and adulthood. One of the problems in making predictions from longitudinal studies is that some of the children who participate may move to other schools or cities. Of course, this is more of a problem in places where there is high population mobility. However, it is conceivable that, in any location, persons with psychological problems relocate more frequently, perhaps because of difficulties in finding work and keeping jobs or because of strained interpersonal relationships in other settings. In some studies, individuals who revealed to the researchers that they had personal problems may refuse to participate in subsequent phases of the same study, which they could experience as uncomfortable. The possibility that dropout from longitudinal studies is not a random phenomenon was confirmed by Spiel, Weixelbaum and Spiel's (1999) comparison of the data from participants who agreed and refused to continue in a longitudinal study in Vienna: Those who refused to continue were far more maladjusted than those who remained in the study. Thus, the possibility of losing the most maladjusted individuals before the intended follow-up study is a real one, which may be more acute a problem in places such as the United States where adults tend to change homes and communities more often than in most other places.

Another major challenge is selecting the child behaviours that one thinks will be associated with adjustment and maladjustment later on. It is impossible to change the measures of a longitudinal study retroactively to accommodate improvements in measurement or new thinking about the sources of problems that may emerge as the participating children are growing up. Rubin, Bukowski and Parker (1998) provide some notable examples of longitudinal studies that have been influential and valuable, but that do not provide all of the important information one would now want about the early peer relations of the participants. One of them is a longitudinal study by Roff, Sells and Golden (1972), an influential study in which 38,000 children, aged 8 to 11 at the start of the study, were followed for several years. They assessed peer acceptance by asking the participants to indicate the schoolmates whom they would choose as companions (see more detailed discussion of sociometric methods in Chapter 6). In the Roff study, children who tended not to be chosen as companions displayed a significantly greater chance of becoming juvenile delinquents by age 14. However, as did many (but not all) researchers at the time, the researchers did not ask for 'last choices' – children who would not be chosen. The 'last choices' are likely to be actively disliked, not just ignored. More recent research has confirmed that being actively disliked presents a far greater risk for later maladjustment than simply not being chosen or liked. Furthermore, the combination of being actively disliked (rejected) by peers and displaying aggressive behaviour has been found to increase the risk even further (e.g. Coie *et al.*, 1995; Kupersmidt and Coie, 1990).

Follow-back studies are an alternative to the costly and difficult strategy of collecting data about children and following them into adulthood and adolescence. In follow-back studies, adults or adolescents who are known to have such difficulties as juvenile delinquency or psychiatric disturbance are the participants. The researchers study their backgrounds based on recollections or on information about their childhoods that can be retrieved from archives such as school records. For the most part, this alternative is decidedly an inferior one (see Parker and Asher, 1987), for several reasons. The vagaries of the human memory make recollections a very unsatisfactory source of information. People experiencing current problems may try to read the origins of their problems into their recollections of the past, or, like anyone else, they may fail to have recognized or fail to remember important information about their social relations during their childhoods. Very often, school or clinic records do not contain the information the researcher is looking for about childhood peer relations, because they were not designed to include such information systematically. Finally and most importantly, follow-back studies may be biased because they usually fail to include children who may have had problems during childhood, but managed to overcome them. It is not surprising, then, that follow-back studies generally indicate that adolescents and adults experiencing maladjustment are more likely than others to have had problems getting along with their peers during their childhood years (Parker and Asher, 1987; Rubin, Bukowski and Parker, 1998).

Despite the problems with follow-back studies, probably the most influential existing longitudinal study of children's peer relations used something of a follow-back strategy. Cowen, Pedersen, Bagigian, Izzo and Trost (1973) gained access to a registry of persons receiving psychiatric services in their county in New York State. They were able to compare the names with those of participants in a study they had conducted in the schools 11 to 13 years earlier. The names of children who had been identified by their classroom peers during the earlier study as being either aggressive or withdrawn were much more likely to appear in the psychiatric register. In fact, of all the information available, it was only peer relations problems that predicted the later use of psychiatric services.

Gender differences in the correspondence between childhood social competence and adult adjustment have often been neglected in the interpretation of longitudinal data. Such gender differences are often considerable. For example, the results of the Jyvaskyla Longitudinal Study of Personality and Social Development, in which 160 males and 151 females in Finland were followed from age 8 to 36, indicate substantial differences in both the childhood behaviours that are forerunners of later difficulty and in the specific difficulties they predict. Overt behavioural problems during childhood predicted later maladjustment for males, whereas more internal emotional problems were the risk factor for females. Having many social problems during childhood predicted 'outer strand' problems, such as career failure, for both males and females, but the overall accumulation of social problems also predicted an inner sense of failure for females only (Pulkinnen, 1999).

In summary, the many longitudinal studies have documented that problems in early peer relationships do predict adjustment difficulties in later life. It is important to remember that the prediction is not perfect and, therefore, that there are many individuals who experience problems in relating to others during childhood but who none the less overcome these problems during later stages of development. The longitudinal evidence of the predictive power of early peer relations has inspired many programmes for the prevention and early correction of social-skills deficits in schools, as will be discussed in Chapter 11.

Tables 2.1 and Table 2.2 provide the reader with an opportunity to peruse the results of these longitudinal studies. (Readers unfamiliar with literature reviews in the behavioural sciences may wish to refer to Box 1 on pp. 34–5 before examining the tables.) The studies reviewed in Table 2.1 leave little doubt that aggression during the childhood years is a 'risk factor' – in other words, aggressive children are more likely than others to become adults with adjustment problems of various kinds. Table 2.2 indicates much the same for shyness/social withdrawal during the childhood years. The cultural difference in the social acceptability of shyness, documented in China, is discussed further in Chapter 9.

Children's friendships as the foundation for intimate relationships in later life

By far, most of the attention in longitudinal studies of peer relations has been devoted to the long-term consequences of being disliked, aggressive, or withdrawn in large groups, such as classrooms or schools. However, it has been argued that this emphasis on rejection by the peer group as a whole obscures a potentially vital link between early peer relations and later adjustment that occurs because of the benefits of having even a single close friend (e.g. Furman and Robbins, 1985). Nowhere are the advantages of friendship assigned as much weight as in the influential theories of the American psychiatrist Harry Stack Sullivan (1953). Sullivan was born in the small agricultural town of Norwich, New York in 1892. Appalled by the 'waste of human abilities' (Perry, 1982, p. 5) that he observed in his work as a psychiatrist, a researcher and a consultant for Selective (conscription) Service during World War II, Sullivan became determined to increase the available base of knowledge about raising children. He developed an interpersonal theory of development in which friendships play a key role. Sullivan posited that friendships are necessary because they satisfy the human need for interpersonal intimacy and they help develop vital social skills and competencies (Newcomb and Bagwell, 1996). More specifically, Sullivan proposed that the formation of close, one-on-one relationships during pre-adolescence is crucial to the acquisition of these social competencies (Kerns, 1996). These relationships, called chumships, prevent loneliness and enhance children's sense of self-worth. Their relationships to their chums provide children with a means to develop sensitivity to others' problems and perspectives of mutuality in their interpersonal relations (ibid.). This relational base is reflected in intimate heterosexual relationships later on.

Table 2.1 Longitudinal studies linking aggression during childhood with long-term adjustment

Author	Population description		Sources of Information		Long-term outcomes associated with childhood aggression
	N	age (T1*)	age (T2**)	Aggression	Adjustment	

Studies conducted within North America

Author	N	age (T1*)	age (T2**)	Aggression	Adjustment	Long-term outcomes associated with childhood aggression
Ledingham and Schwartzman (1984)	753	6 10 13	10 13 16	Peers	School placement information	Academic difficulty (repeating year on transfer to special class)
Roff and Wirt (1984)	2453	8–11	Young adult	Teachers	Juvenile records, welfare records	Delinquency Adult criminality Female: welfare status
Huesmann, Eron and Warnick-Yarmel (1987)	427	8	19 30	Peers	School records Achievement measure	Poor intellectual achievement
Moskowitz and Schwartzman (1989)	408	7 10 13	14 17 20	Peers	Intelligence test Self-report Medical records	Low intelligence test Problem in school More likely to receive psychiatric treatment High rates of health problems More gynaecological problems
Hymel, Rubin, Rowden and Le Mare (1990)	87	8	11	Peers Observation Teachers	Self-report Teachers	Externalizing behaviour[1]

Study	N	Age	Informant	Age	Source	Outcome
Kupersmidt and Coie (1990)	112	11	Peers	18	School records; Juvenile police and court files	Delinquency; Early school withdrawal; Police contacts
Kupersmidt and Patterson (1991)	613	8 9 10	Teachers; Peers		Self-report	Delinquency
Serbin, Peters, McAffer and Schwartzman (1991)	853	6 9 12	Peers	11–17 14–20 17–23	Medical records	Problematic patterns of sexual activity; high prescription of birth control, gynaecological problems, sexually transmitted disease, elevated rates of adolescent pregnancy
Brook, Whiteman and Finch (1992)	412	5–10	Mothers	13–18 15–20	Self-report; Parents	Drug use; Delinquency
Roff (1992)	711	8–11	Teachers	Young adult	Juvenile records	Delinquency
Brook, Whiteman, Finch and Cohen (1995)	397	5–10	Mother	13–18 16–21	Self-report; Parents	Intrapsychic distress; Unconventionality; Illegal drug use
Coie, Terry, Lenox, Lochman and Hyman (1995)	1147	8	Peers	11 13 15	Self-report; Parents	Externalizing behaviour[1]

Table 2.1 Continued

| Author | Population description | | | Sources of Information | | Long-term outcomes associated with childhood aggression |
	N	age (T1*)	age (T2**)	Aggression	Adjustment	
Loeber, Green, Keenan and Lahey (1995)	177	7–12	12–17	Participants Parents	Diagnosis of condict disorder	Conduct disorder
Rubin, Chen, McDougall, Bowker and McKinnon (1995)	60	7	14	Peers Teachers Direct observation	Self-report	Externalizing difficulties
Brook, Whiteman, Finch and Cohen (1996)	358	5–10	13–18 16–21 22–27	Mothers	Participants Parents Self-report	Delinquency in adolescence Drug use in adulthood
Vitaro, Gendreau, Tremblay and Oligny (1998)	742	12	15–16	Teachers	Self-report Parents	Delinquency and disruptive behaviour Oppositional defiant disorder Conduct disorder
Studies conducted outside North America						
Stattin and Magnusson (1989) Sweden	1027	10, 13	26	Teachers	Police and child welfare records	Criminal activity
Chen, Rubin and Li (1995) People's Republic of China	290	8 10	10 12	Peers	School records	Peer rejection Lower school competence Lower academic achievement

| Chen, Rubin, Li and Li (1999) People's Republic of China | 162 | 8 10 | 12 14 | Peers | Peers Parents Self-report School records | Externalizing problems[1] Rejection by peers |

Notes: * Age of participants when data was first recorded, rounded to the nearest year.
** Age of participants at follow-up, rounded to the nearest year.
[1] Externalizing problems include aggression, defiance, delinquency and attention deficit.

Table 2.2 Longitudinal studies linking shyness or withdrawal during childhood with long-term adjustment

| Author | Population description | | Sources of information | | Long-term outcome associated with childhood withdrawal |
	N	age (T1*)	age (T2**)	Shyness/withdrawal	Adjustment	
Studies conducted within North America						
Frazee (1953)	46	12	21	Institution records	Hospitalization for schizophrenia	Schizophrenia
Caspi, Elder and Bem (1988)	182	8–10	30 40	Mothers Teachers	Interviews with participant	Male: Delay in marriage Delay in parenthood Delay in establishing stable careers Female: Homemaker rather than out-of-home career
Rubin and Mills (1988)	55	7	9, 10	Direct observation Peers	Teachers Self-report	Internalizing difficulties[1]
Moskowitz and Schwartzman (1989)	408	7 10 13	14 17 20	Peers	Self-report Medical records	Problems in school Female: Higher proportion of terminated pregnancies Twice as likely to abort an unwanted pregnancy
Rubin, Hymel and Mills (1989)	77	5–7	9–10	Direct observation of free-play	Self-report Teachers	Internalizing difficulties[1]
Hirshfeld, Rosenbaum, Biederman, Bolduc, Faraone, Snidman, Reznick and Kagan (1992)	120	1	8		Mothers	Anxiety disorder Multiple anxiety disorders Phobic disorder

Study	N	Age	Source	Age	Source	Outcome
Rubin, Chen, McDougall, Bowker and McKinnon (1995)	60	7	Peers Teachers Direct observation	14	Self-report	Internalizing difficulties[1] negative self-regard, loneliness, feels insecure among peers and family
Schwartz, Snidman and Kagan (1996)	79	1–2	Direct observation	12–13	Mothers Self-report	High internalizing behaviours[1] Low externalizing behaviours[2]
Gest (1997)	205	8–12	Self-report Peers	17–24	Self-report	Rejection by peers in early adulthood Negatively associated with moving out of the home by early adulthood
Studies conducted outside North America						
Asendorpf and van Aken (1994) Germany	99	4	Direct observation Teachers	12	Self-report	Low self-esteem
Chen, Rubin and Li (1995) People's Republic of China	290	8 10	Peers	10 12	School records	At 8–10 years: Leadership Academic achievement School competence Accepted by peers At 12 years: Peer rejection

Table 2.2 Continued

Author	Population description			Sources of information			Outcome
	N	age (T1*)	age (T2**)	Shyness/withdrawal	Adjustment		
Kerr, Lambert and Bem (1996) Sweden	212	8 10	25 35	Mothers Teachers	Self-report		Male: Delay in marriage Delay in parenthood Female: Low education level
Chen, Rubin, Li and Li (1999) People's Republic of China	162	8 10	11 14	Peers	Teachers School records		Academically successful Honour or leadership positions in school
Hagekull and Bohlin (1998) Sweden	93	2	9	Parents	Parents Teachers		Introverted

Notes: *   Age of participants when data was first collected.
      ** Age of participants at follow-up.
      1   Internalizing problems include depression, anxiety and psychosomatic symptoms.
      2   Externalizing problems include aggression, defiance, delinquency and attention deficit.

Popularity and friendship may contribute in different ways to children's well-being, although children who are generally popular with peers also have a greater likelihood than others of cultivating close friendships. There are convincing reasons why close friendships might have particular implications for coping with life's challenges. As will be detailed in Chapter 7, a relationship with a close friend is characterized by intimacy, unlike children's more superficial relations with the classmates who might regard one as popular. Learning how to form and manage close, intimate relationships may lead to having a close friend to serve as confidant during moments of stress and to having someone who would provide considerable time and practical help when needed the most. Participation in a close friendship is also thought to foster flexible thinking in many ways; flexible thinking is known to relate to successful coping with stress (Cantor and Harlow, 1994). One of the modes of flexible thinking that is associated with adaptation in the face of adversity is the ability to understand how other people think about things and appreciate that they may have views about a specific situation that are quite different from one's own (see Selman, Levitt and Schultz, 1997, for a detailed exposition of how this might occur). It has been emphasized that friends not only gain more knowledge about interpersonal relationships from their friendships than from their contacts with acquaintances, but that one gains in friendship qualitatively different knowledge about relationships, knowledge and skills that are particular to close, supportive bonds (Barr, 1997).

Despite the widespread interest in Sullivan's theory, there is much less longitudinal research documenting the long-term implications of friendship during the childhood years specifically than there is with regard to acceptance or rejection by peers in large groups; this limited literature is summarized by Hartup and Stevens (1997) and by Berndt (1996). Indeed, Sullivan emphasized 'chumship' at the very beginning of adolescence; perhaps for that reason, more longitudinal research documenting the benefits of friendship has followed individuals from adolescence into early adulthood. Most of the longitudinal studies conducted with children involve follow-ups for relatively short periods of time, typically less than two years. The range of outcome measures of adjustment is also limited, with more data available about the implications of friendship for adjustment to school than with regard to any other aspect of well-being. Several excellent studies have been conducted to gauge the importance of friendship in the transition to a new school, either at the beginning of primary school at age 5 or 6 years (e.g. Ladd, Kochenderfer and Coleman, 1996), or between primary and middle school, at about age 12 years (e.g. Berndt and Keefe, 1992). In general, the supportiveness or closeness of friends seems to facilitate successful adaptation to the new school, whereas 'head counts' of the number of friends one has, regardless of how close they are as friends or how positive they are as models of behaviour, seem to be unrelated to adjustment

(Hartup and Stevens, 1997). Much more will be said about ways of assessing friendship in Chapter 7 and about friendship and school adjustment in Chapter 4. Table 2.3 summarizes research documenting the link between various aspects of friendship (see Chapter 7) and indices of well-being. The studies depicted in Table 2.3 generally indicate that friendship is associated with adjustment, although there are not as many studies on that topic as there are, for example, on the long-term risk associated with aggression.

Some research has confirmed that friendship serves as a protective factor contributing to the resilience of youngsters considered at risk because they were raised in adverse environments. Typically, these studies have used short-term longitudinal designs in studying children who are known to be at risk for maladjustment because they are undergoing stressful family circumstances such as divorce or parental unemployment, or because one of their parents has a psychiatric disorder. Children who have experienced the same risk factor, but who differ in the support they receive from friends, are compared. Conrad and Hammen (1993) found that friendship served as a protective factor for the children of medically ill mothers, though not depressed mothers. Similarly, Pryor-Brown and Cowen (1989) found that social support from both friends and family mediated the relation between stressful life events and adjustment in a large sample of American children in the late elementary-school years. In an important study with particular implications for intervention, Schwartz, McFayden-Ketchem, Dodge, Pettit and Bates (1999) found that friendship helped break the cycle of victimization by bullies: children with good friendships at ages 5 or 6 years were less victimized by bullies three years later. Wasserstein and LaGreca (1996) reported that the quality of support from friends mediated the relationship between child-reported parental marital conflict and teacher reports of behavioural problems. Thus, although there are many inconsistencies, limitations and problems with the data available and far more longitudinal studies in particular are needed, there is some basis for accepting the contention that friendship is associated with adjustment, particularly among children at risk for maladjustment.

Successful peer relations and children's happiness

As summarized until this point, exhaustive efforts have been made to prove that peer relations in childhood are linked with maladjustment in general, with psychiatric conditions and with such blatant indications of maladjustment as criminality. This investment of research resources has brought very satisfactory returns although much still remains to be learned about the long-term course of children's peer relations and their psychosocial adjustment. However, it is important to remember that interpersonal relationships are a major source of satisfaction in their own right.

There has been very little research on what makes children happy, but

Table 2.3 Selected studies showing that friendship is linked with children's well-being

Author	Age (Years)	n	Measure of friendship	Measure of well-being	Results
Mannarino (1978) (USA)	12	60	Friendship stability Chumship Checklist (communication and honesty between friends)	Self-concept	Preadolescent males involved in chumships had higher self-concepts than those not involved in a chumships.
Feldman, Rubenstein and Rubin (1988) (USA)	11–12	103	The Friendship Support Scale (questions relating to emotional support provided by friends).	Depression	Participants who reported more depressive affect experienced their friendships as less supportive, less loyal and more stressful. Positive features in friendship contributed to protection against depressive affect.
Parker and Asher (1993b) (USA)	9–11	881	Peer nominations and ratings of friendship quality	Loneliness and social dissatisfaction	Friendship qualities (validation and caring, companionship and recreation, help and guidance, and intimate exchange) were associated with higher satisfaction with the relationship. Friendship offered a buffer against loneliness.

Table 2.3 continued

Author	Age (Years)	n	Measure of friendship	Measure of well-being	Results
Vandell and Hembree (1994) (USA)	Mean: 9	326	Peer nominations	Self-concept, academic adjustment and socio-emotional adjustment	Self-concepts, academic adjustment, and teacher-reported socio-emotional adjustment were each found to be positively correlated with mutual friendships.
Ladd, Kochenderfer and Coleman (1996) (USA)	Mean: 6	82	Interview aimed at discovering features of children's friendships Peer nominations	School adjustment: perceived affect in school, loneliness, perceived peer support, school liking and avoidance, classroom engagement, and academic readiness and progress	Children who perceived their friendships as conflictual were less likely to see themselves as having positive affect in school. Perceived exclusivity in friendships was associated with lower levels of achievement.
Oldenburg and Kerns (1997) (USA)	10–12	322	Sociometric ratings Friendship quality with a questionnaire	Self-reported	Friendship quality was associated with fewer depressive symptoms.
Erdley, Nangle, Carpenter, Newman, and Grover (1999) (USA)	9–12	192	Sociometric ratings, peer nominations and measure of friendship quality	Loneliness and social dissatisfaction questionnaire Self-reported depression	Peer acceptance, number of friendships, and quality of those friendships significantly predicted loneliness. Depression was predicted by group acceptance only for boys

there are a few relevant studies. Westman (1990) asked young adults to recall what made them happy when they were children. She was interested particularly in determining whether it was contact with people or the receipt of toys or other gifts that would remain more salient in their memories. Interpersonal contact was cited as the main source of childhood happiness. Contrary to folk wisdom, 89 per cent of the participants in the study mentioned specific persons in their responses, compared with only 39 per cent who mentioned gifts they had received, most frequently a bicycle. Although many of the interpersonal contacts that were recalled as sources of happiness involved family members (parents 60 per cent, brothers and sisters 17 per cent, other relatives 24 per cent), friends were involved in as many of the happy recollections as parents were: 60 per cent (totals exceed 100 per cent because many of the university students recalled more than one happy childhood experience). Several Canadian studies conducted with early adolescents have demonstrated that pupils who consider themselves socially withdrawn or introverted also indicate that they are unhappier than other pupils in the same classes (e.g. Young and Bradley, 1998).

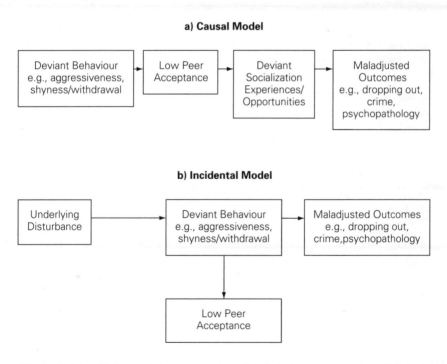

Figure 2.1 Implicit models concerning the link between peer relationship problems and later maladjustment (Source: Parker and Asher, 1987)

Children's peer relations: cause or effect of life-long adjustment or maladjustment?

It is very important to remember that the longitudinal evidence reviewed in this chapter provides no proof that positive peer relations in childhood are the cause of mental health or mental illness. This issue is discussed in detail by Parker and Asher (1987) in their very influential review article. The difference between causal and incidental models is depicted in Figure 2.1, reproduced from Parker and Asher's paper. As suggested by the title of their figure, these models represent implicit assumptions made by the authors of the original research, who often skirt the issue of causation. According to the causal model, poor peer relations result directly in maladjustment. As depicted in Figure 2.1, this may occur because children who do not relate well with peers may be excluded from social interactions where important new skills are learned and practised. In contrast, the incidental model maintains that the maladjustment is already there at the time of the child's difficulties with other children. The peer relations deficit is but one of many manifestations of the disorder.

Of course, most peer relations scholars and most teachers and parents who advocate the promotion of social competence in schools and communities, probably ascribe, if only implicitly, to the causal model. Recent sophisticated statistical techniques, called structural equations modelling, can be applied to longitudinal data in order to determine how likely it is that patterns of peer relations cause psychological well-being or distress. However, even that technological advance cannot provide conclusive proof of causation. Therefore, it is important not to over-interpret the very convincing longitudinal evidence.

Box 1 The little book with many tables

As discussed in Chapter 1, scholars in the area of children's peer relations are characterized by their insistence on proving their ideas by well-designed research. This is one of the strong points of the field. New, unproven theories and the opinions of individuals do have their place – as sources of ideas for new studies, for example. However, it is expected that statements about the nature of peer relations be backed up by scientific evidence, and that procedures for improving children's peer relations be subjected to research to prove their effectiveness.

The tables in this book offer the reader the opportunity to review the evidence for many of the main points without being burdened by extensive detail on each. The tables have been designed to be understandable by readers without extensive background either in the peer relations area or in general research methodology. However, although they contain less technical information, most of the tables are quite similar to those found in articles devoted to summarizing research on any given topic. Articles of this type can be found occasionally in the major child development journals. There are also journals whose main purpose it is to disseminate reviews of research: *Psychological Bulletin* and *Development Review* are among the best known of these.

Although they are not completely exhaustive, the tables do contain the major studies on each topic. Therefore, the first step in using the tables is to look at how many studies have been done. If only a few studies have been completed, the conclusions may be specific to the samples and methods used. Other sampling considerations are important: have studies been conducted with children of different ages and with both genders? Given the enormous investment of resources on child development research in the United States, it is inevitable that most studies will have been conducted there. Nevertheless, the findings may not apply to other societies. Many of the tables contain a separate section for studies conducted outside North America in order to highlight them. If only a few studies have been conducted outside the United States, the results may not be applicable to other societies.

It is also important to consider the range of methods that have been used to answer each research question. The tools for assessing children's peer relations are discussed in Chapter 6. In scanning the tables, it is important to look for links between the results and the methods used. For example, of the studies on a given topic, those in which ratings by teachers were used might seem to prove the researcher's hypotheses, whereas studies using ratings by children's schoolmates might not.

In the social sciences, it is unrealistic to expect that every study will confirm the hypothesis, for several reasons. First of all, almost every phenomenon being studied has multiple causes, not just the cause expressed in the researchers' hypothesis. Furthermore, even the best measures available are far from perfect. Therefore, the tables should be perused for the predominant patterns of findings. It is worth remembering, though, that the published findings, which are summarized in the tables, may be biased in favour of the authors' hypotheses. That is because professional journals are more likely to accept for publication the reports of studies that bring significant findings and, thus, timely 'news'.

3 Where does social competence come from?

This chapter provides a capsule sketch of the antecedents of children's social competence. Genetic factors appear to explain individual differences in social behaviour to a substantial degree. However, attachment bonds between parents and children are also linked to children's peer relations, as are parents' styles of childrearing. Relatively little is known about the potentially important influences of siblings, schoolmates and neighbours in influencing the social interactions of children. The chapter closes with a challenge to popular thinking about the causes of social behaviour by insisting that variations in social behaviour probably have multiple roots rather than single causes that can be pinpointed.

For a species that is supposed to be programmed for cooperation in order to survive, humans show remarkable variation in their cooperativeness and in many other aspects of their social behaviour. As detailed in the previous chapter, individual differences in social behaviour have been traced longitudinally from early childhood through adulthood. The differences are often stable and are related to some extent to individual differences in well-being. Hence, determining the origins of individual differences in patterns of relating to others is not only important because it satisfies our curiosity, but, to the extent that the differences stem from causes that can be controlled or modified, such research can lead to meaningful measures aimed at preventing maladaptive social behaviour. This book would be incomplete without some discussion of the origins of children's peer relations. However, space permits only a cursory treatment of these issues.

Children's temperaments: the joint gift of nature and nurture?

Figure 3.1 depicts the major theories offered in the developmental literature to explain individual differences in social behaviour. The central issue in the debate about which theory is the most valid is how much of children's social behaviour is caused by heredity versus how much can be

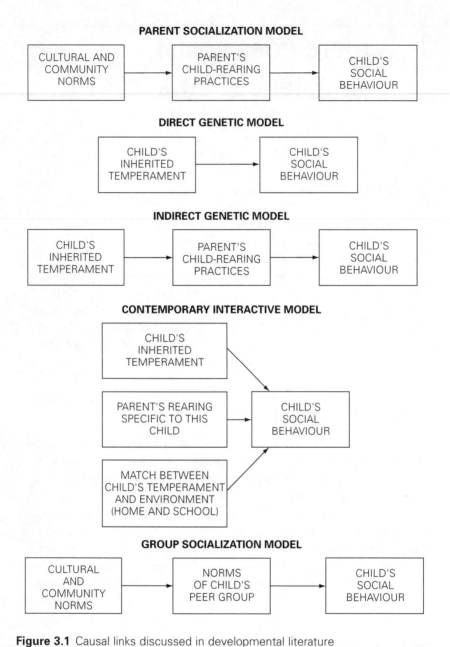

Figure 3.1 Causal links discussed in developmental literature

explained by the environment, especially the environment provided by parents. The concept of temperament has been useful in research designed to determine whether patterns of social behaviour are inherited or acquired from the environment. Temperaments are stable modes of responding in social situations; temperament can be considered the childhood equivalent of the notion of personality, which is used more frequently in reference to adults. There are wide differences in temperaments among children, ranging from approachable and sanguine to colicky and distant. These wide differences in sociability and temperament and their relative stability have led some authorities to suspect that children are, at least to a certain extent, pre-wired to behave a certain way. The field of behavioural genetics aims at teasing out the relationship between inborn, predispositional influences and the effects of the human environment on children's temperament and social behaviour. In order to do this, behavioural geneticists focus their study on genetic influences and environmental influences that are and are not shared by family members. Much of that research must, of necessity, be conducted with atypical family situations, such as twins who were separated at birth and reared apart, or adopted children. This is because, in studying children who are not twins and who come from intact families, it is difficult to separate the genetic and environmental influences, precluding any quantitative estimate of hereditability. Nevertheless, studying these exceptional populations is not without its problems, for example, if the innate temperament of the adopted child determines in some way the family environment into which he or she is adopted.

Buss and Plomin (1984), leaders in research on children's temperament, have mainly focused on the hereditability of aspects of young children's temperament that may be precursors of withdrawal, aggression and social competence in middle childhood: emotionality, activity and sociability, together referred to as 'EAS traits'. EAS traits of parents are often measured through self-reports, whereas the temperaments of children are typically assessed by both parental and teacher ratings, occasionally complemented by direct observation. However, the overwhelming majority of studies on the origins of temperament, conducted with literally tens of thousands of twin pairs (Loehlin, 1989), have featured questionnaires as the major tool, usually questionnaires by parents. Emotionality refers to the individual's level of emotional arousal and manifests itself in high or low levels of love, pride, contempt, fear and anger, among other emotions. Activity refers to the child's energy level and tendency to explore new situations. Sociability refers to the infant's preference for contact with other people. Shyness is viewed by Buss and Plomin (1984) as a derivative of sociability and emotionality.

Twin studies using parental ratings to study the EAS traits of twins have for the most part supported the hypothesis that there is a substantial inherited component in the genesis of EAS traits (e.g. Buss and Plomin, 1975). This applies even to studies where the twins are followed for as long as 59 years, as in one project conducted in Sweden (Plomin *et al.*, 1988). Had identical twins, who share the same genetic make-up, been found to be no more similar in EAS than fraternal twins, the possibility of an inherited component could have been discounted. However, the differences between the correlations representing the similarities of identical and fraternal twins are very similar across studies and quite substantial, supplying evidence of a certain degree of hereditability. In fact, the correlations between the EAS traits of fraternal twins are often not significantly greater than zero; this is particularly applicable to the Activity trait and suggests no influence of the shared environment. It should be noted that one important study is an exception to the general rule that genetic causation is evident in twin studies based on parent ratings: Schmitz, Cherny, Fulker and Mrazek (1994) found very little indication of genetic influence on either the externalizing (e.g. aggression, attention problems) or internalizing (e.g. melancholy) dimensions of the parent ratings of the mothers of 229 2-year-old and 3-year-old twins, but did find evidence of environmental influence.

An alternative explanation for the findings of twin studies is that they are attributable to parental contrast and not to heredity at all. In rating their children's temperament, parents may be comparing fraternal twins, labelling one as active and the other as inactive. This may not be a problem in ratings of identical twins because they may be so similar as to preclude parental contrast (Buss and Plomin, 1984). This is an example of the problem inherent in using measures with shared method variance, in other words, relying on the same source of information for data on several processes that are thought to be connected. For example, it is less than ideal to ask mothers if they themselves are shy and also ask them if their children are shy. It would be far better to measure either the parents' personalities or the children's temperaments in another way, perhaps through direct observation.

The parents' ratings of their own temperaments or personalities were probably valid, because the ratings of spouses have been shown to correlate with each other. However, there are still problems in using parents' ratings of both their own and their children's temperaments as the only source of information on the temperaments of both. Some respondents are prone to see negative features in both themselves and in others, other respondents tend to overlook negative features. It is difficult to be objective about one's own personality and about the personality of one's offspring. This is a very substantial problem and not a nicety to be discussed by methodologists only. In the few behaviour-genetic studies where children's social behaviours have been observed directly, the evidence of hereditability is far less convincing than in studies relying exclusively on parents' ratings (Plomin, 1990). For example, in an observational study by Plomin and Rowe (1979), there was inconsistent evidence for an inherited component in children's shyness. It depended on the nature of the social interaction: the results suggested a genetic component for infants' social responsiveness to a stranger in their homes, but not for responsiveness to their mothers. Plomin, Foch and Rowe (1981) conducted an observational study of school-age children's aggressiveness and found no evidence of hereditability.

Before accepting the results based on observation as inherently superior to those based on rating scales, it must be remembered that observations can usually be conducted only for relatively short periods of time and in only a few of the social settings in which children interact with others. Several more recent and more comprehensive studies using multiple sources of information about children's social behaviour suggest both a genetic component and some degree of environmental influence. Such studies include a comprehensive study by Leve *et al.* (1998) of 154 twin pairs, using both reports by parents and direct observations of the children's behaviour. Again, the observational data provided only weak evidence of genetic influence, in contrast with the parent ratings.

As will be discussed in Chapter 6, it is also possible to measure children's social behaviour using reports from teachers as well as parents. Although parents know their children's behaviour very well, teachers may be more objective and have more experience with larger numbers of children to use as a reference in making their ratings. Zahn-Waxler *et al.* (1996) used both teacher ratings and direct observation in their study of the externalizing and internalizing behaviour problems of 5-year-old twins. They found consistent evidence for genetic influence on the externalizing behaviours. Evidence for genetic causation was also evident in the teacher ratings used by Schmitz *et al.* (1996) to study the EAS traits of 7-year-olds.

Adoption studies, such as the Colorado Adoption Project (DeFries, Plomin and Fulker, 1994), provide less consistent proof of the genetic origin of children's social behaviour than do twin studies featuring parent ratings. The Colorado Adoption Project is noteworthy because it involves multiple measures of children's social competence, as well as longitudinal measurement of social competence during several stages of development, ranging by now from infancy into adolescence. The results so far provide varying indications of hereditability depending on the outcome measure. There is little suggestion of genetic influence on EAS traits in middle childhood (Schmitz, 1994), but some suggestion of genetic origin in ratings obtained from the participants' teachers of the children's popularity and leadership (Neiderheiser and McGuire, 1994). The reasons for the discrepancies between the measures and, more globally, for the discrepancies between twin and adoption studies, are not understood very well at this point.

In any case, it is important to bear in mind that, whatever they indicate about hereditability, adoption studies rarely provide evidence that the shared family environment is the cause of children's adaptive or maladaptive patterns of social behaviour (Rowe, 1994). The fact that the evidence for genetic causation stops short of indicating that children's social competence is almost entirely inherited does not mean that the general atmosphere of a family home or parents' general ways of rearing children are a major factor in determining individual differences in temperament and personality. In fact, it is quite rare in the literature, though not totally unheard of, for shared family environment to emerge as a substantial causal factor. However, non-shared environmental influences do account for some portion of the origins of children's temperament according to most studies and often appear to be a very substantial cause. Non-shared environmental influences include, for example, child-rearing by the parents that is specific to each child and not common to all children of the family. Siblings may receive different parenting from the same mothers and fathers because of differences in the children's temperaments, because the parents are of different ages and different stages in their marital and work lives, or because the surrounding societies have changed as each sibling reaches the same stage of development. Non-shared environmental influences also include those of children's neighbourhood peer groups, because siblings within the same family may gravitate towards different groups of peers. There is by now considerable evidence that parents treat each of their children in a far more individual manner than is often thought. It is also possible that different children within the same family are affected differently by certain aspects of their parents' behaviour. In any case, relatively little is known about the non-shared environmental influences that repeatedly emerge in behaviour-genetic studies as a very substantial cause of children's temperament. Much more research is needed to learn about what these non-shared environmental influences are and how they work (Caspi, 1998).

In summary, recent research has not contradicted the results of a host of early twin studies, which indicated that children's social competence was largely of genetic origin. However, this sweeping conclusion in favour of genetic determination is tempered by several well-designed twin studies in which multiple sources of information were used in studying children's peer relations. The results of adoption studies also provide less clear-cut evidence of hereditability. Thus, although results are not entirely consistent, it is reasonable to conclude at present that genetics tell an important part of the story, but not all of it.

Attachment

Attachment theorists profess that an attentive caregiver provides a 'secure base' to support the child in its exploration of its objective and interpersonal environment. Bowlby (1969, 1978, 1990) suggested that infants create 'internal working models' of themselves, their world and social contacts within their world. This follows from Craik's assertion that 'the organism carries a small-scale model of external reality and its own possible actions within its head' (1943, p. 61). 'Internal working models' are essentially mental pictures of relationships that the child uses to understand and predict others' behaviour. As the child matures, his or her models broaden and evolve to incorporate the growing social world.

Internal working models are adaptable to environmental change, but their modification is not an easy task. This is because such models are centred on conservative expectancies which can govern behaviour so as to confirm these expectations. An example of this would be an individual who expects repudiation and consequently invites such an attack, thereby confirming prior, ingrained expectations. Because models of others' behaviour are influenced and sculpted by a child's particular environment, they may be resistant to change regardless of their incompatibility with and inaccurate reflection of the reality of the child's peers.

The basic assumption that security of attachment influences a child's adjustment has been challenged by several investigators. For example, Grusec and Lytton (1988) questioned the causal nature of attachment, proposing that attachment reflects the child's overall adaptation and adjustment; these forms of resilience may have other sources. Arguing that the 'internal working model' has been used as a catch-all, Hinde (1988) contended that it is used in attachment theory to explain stability too generally. Hinde maintained that the existence and role of internal working models have not been determined convincingly and that temperament and other non-attachment models may explain stability just as effectively. Lewis and Feiring (1989) also maintained that there is weak empirical evidence for the major suppositions of attachment theory. They asserted that there exist non-parental figures who may be crucial to a child's socialization, but that theorists often fail to acknowledge this. Belsky and Cassidy suggest that theorists should be cautious when applying internal working models to developmental processes: 'the notion of internal working models as the causal process explaining the associations between attachment security and the developmental sequelae remains a useful interpretive heuristic in need of empirical evaluation (1995, p. 383). Parent–child attachment bonds are sometimes thought to be the result of the parent's sensitivity and responsivity (Spieker and Booth, 1988). In addition, the child's temperament, the parent's personality and the stress under which the parent lives may also influence the attachment bond. Together with the infant's emotionality, the infant's sociability is assumed to influence the security of the attachment between children and parents.

Attachment is usually measured with either the Strange Situation technique or the Q-sort method, with the Strange Situation technique the better known of the two. That procedure involves studying the interactions of mothers and children in an unfamiliar situation, the laboratory, that can produce some stress. At the beginning, the mother and the child become familiar with the laboratory room, which contains several chairs and some toys so that the infant is free to explore his or her new surroundings; the baby's initial willingness to explore is carefully noted by the researchers from behind a one-way mirror. A stranger then enters the room and, a minute later, begins a conversation with the mother. Next, the mother leaves the child alone with the stranger. Then, the stranger leaves and the mother returns. At the end of the procedure, the baby is alone for a short time, then the stranger returns and finally the mother returns for a reunion with her child (Ainsworth and Whittig, 1969). The situation is probably no more stressful than separations and reunions that occur in a typical infant's life, but, of course, the more stressful sessions are shortened if the baby shows a very strong reaction to the procedure, which can be aborted totally in the rare case of an extreme reaction. The children's behaviour in the Strange Situation is used to classify their attachment bonds. If they are secure enough to explore the new surroundings before their mothers leave, become distressed when Mom leaves and welcome her cheerfully upon her return, the infant is securely attached, which characterizes about two-thirds of the child population. Secure attachment is believed to serve as a healthy foundation for exploring the world and the vagaries of close personal relationships later on (Bowlby, 1980). More than 20 per cent of children are typically classified as anxious-avoidant in their attachment bonds because they are not anxious when their mothers leave and avoid her when she returns. About one child in ten is classified as anxious-ambivalent; they show signs of distress during the whole procedure, but especially when separated from their mothers (Ainsworth *et al.*, 1978). Cross-cultural studies indicate substantial similarity in the proportions of children assigned to the various groups, although the proportions of babies in the two categories of insecure attachment does vary somewhat in non-Western cultures (e.g. van IJzendoorn and Kroonenberg, 1988).

Although the Strange Situation technique has been the predominant tool in attachment research, there has been some call for alternatives that would allow for the measurement of attachment in more natural situations and without stress induction. Of course, this is more than a matter of measurement: instruments designed for use outside the laboratory and under different conditions may not be measuring attachment in the same sense as the Strange Situation. The Attachment Q-set (Waters and Deane, 1985) is a scale of 90 items, each pertaining to attachment, that can be used by observers of the interaction between parents and their children. There is some evidence that observers' scores correlate with Strange Situation data, although mothers' own ratings using the Q-set items appear not to (Tarabulsy *et al.*, 1997).

Inspired by this intriguing theory, a number of researchers have conducted studies comparing children's parental attachment histories with their peer relationships. Some of these studies measure attachment and peer relationships at the same point in time. Others are longitudinal studies, in which the researchers try to predict the nature of children's peer relationships from earlier attachment data. Of course, the latter provides the better test of the theory, but even longitudinal studies documenting the link between early parent-child attachment and children's peer relations at later stages cannot rule out the possibility that some other cause is responsible for the children's successes or failures in their relationships with other children. Schneider, Atkinson and Tardif (manuscript submitted for publication) conducted a meta-analysis (a statistical summary of the results of research conducted to date) of the studies on attachment and children's peer relations. Their data base consists of 63 studies, about half of which are longitudinal studies. The average correlation between mother-child attachment scores and data pertaining to children's peer relations is .20, which is significant but by no means large. This statistic supports the validity of attachment theory only to some extent and seems somewhat incongruous with the sweeping causal statements made by attachment theorists. Importantly, the average correlations seem not to differ substantially between studies in which Strange Situation and Q-sort methods were used. However, Schneider, Atkinson and Tardif noted that the correlations were somewhat higher in studies where the indicators of peer relations pertained to close friendships rather than to relationships in large groups; the correlations between parent-child attachment and indicators of friendship were substantially higher than the overall average, in the .30 range. The authors maintained that because a primary intimate relationship is more likely to be mirrored best in subsequent intimate relationships, the data on friendship may be the more relevant indices of the predictive strength of attachment theory. In contrast with the 63 studies on mother-child attachment, there were very few studies of attachment to fathers, providing as yet little clear-cut evidence of its importance.

Child-rearing

It was established earlier in this chapter that shared environmental influences, such as parents' child-rearing styles, explain very little of the origins of children's social competence, to the disappointment of many, including the hundreds of researchers who have conducted studies on the topic. Judith Rich Harris (1998), the outspoken American writer mentioned in Chapter 1, has mounted a vociferous challenge to the time-honoured 'nurture assumption' – the belief that children's behaviour is caused by the way their parents raised them. She insists that many people – university researchers, religious leaders and psychologists who give advice to parents – possess a passionate need to believe in the nurture assumption. Their fervour blinds them to scientific fact that, although many children do resemble their parents, it is not necessarily the parents' child-rearing that accounts for the similarities. (In rejoinder, several critics, such as the Harvard University professor Jerome Kagan [1998] have lambasted Harris for attending selectively to evidence that supports her position and ignoring other data.)

Nevertheless, there remain many important reasons for studying child-rearing practices. Perhaps the most important reason is that, of the various causes of children's social competence, parents' child-rearing is one of the most amenable to change. Science may yet develop methods for altering genetic material on a large scale. Attachment theorists recognize that exceptional positive life experiences can mitigate the negative effects of insecure attachment bonds between parents and children, but maintain that such effects tend to be relatively stable (Ainsworth and Marvin, 1995). In contrast, parents' ways of raising their children are, at least in theory, under their own control. Although changing those ways is not easy, it can be accomplished, as evidenced by the success of many systematic parent-training programmes, such as those of Gerald Patterson, whose structured parent training intervention has proven successful in managing the anti-social behaviours of predelinquent youth (Forgatch and Patterson, 1998). Even if a trait is genetically determined to a considerable extent, an appropriate environment may mitigate the effects of the genetic pre-programming on the observable behaviour of the individual child. This is the core of Thomas and Chess' concept of goodness of fit (Chess and Thomas, 1996), which emphasizes that children's overt behaviour and adjustment depend on the abilities of families and schools to provide them with an environment that 'fits' their temperaments - that is, an environment that offers the degree of structure, predictability and support needed by individuals of one's particular temperament. It is also very important to remember that much of the heated nature-versus-nurture debate about the origins of children's social behaviour centres on individual differences – deciding, for example, whether parents' child-rearing practices explain why some children are more aggressive than others, some children more shy, etc.

Emphasizing individual differences obscures to some extent the very important responsibility that parents have in the upbringing of all children: teaching the general values of the culture and the way its institutions and interpersonal relationships work. It is sometimes said that the influence of the family is weakening in contemporary Western societies. However, the Norwegian sociologist Ivar Frones (1995) maintains that the family is more necessary than ever in teaching children about the cultures of adults because institutions outside the family are becoming less guided by tradition and therefore less active and less consistent in promoting its maintenance.

It is also possible that some important effects of child-rearing have been overlooked in research to date. Scarr (1992) proposed that, within the range of family atmospheres and child-rearing methods that characterize most of the population, differences in family environments may not be very consequential. However, extreme environments may indeed exert a heavy toll on children growing up in them. Such extreme conditions are not represented very adequately in behviour-genetic studies. Although extreme negative conditions come first to mind when this concept is discussed, it is also possible that extreme positive environmental conditions may be very important to the child who is prone to maladaptive behaviour by virtue of his or her genetic predisposition.

Because parents and children share some of their genetic predisposition, research results showing correlations between parents' child-rearing and children's social behaviour cannot prove that child-rearing is the cause of the children's social-interaction styles (Scarr, 1992). However, as mentioned previously, research of this type is important in providing guidance for parent-education programmes and for the treatment of children displaying atypical patterns of social behaviour.

Although parenting practices can be described in a myriad of ways, Baumrind's classification system has served as the basis for the most comprehensive and influential research on parenting styles. Baumrind (1989) distinguished between authoritarian, permissive and authoritative parenting styles. The authoritarian style involves strict limits, enforced by punishment, whereas permissive parents place very few restrictions on their children. The authoritative style involves parental warmth and clear limits backed up by reasoning rather than punishment (or, as clarified and emphasized in her more recent writings, reasoning plus the occasional, judicious use of non-abusive forms of punishment within the context of a positive parent-child relationship [Baumrind, 1996]). The child-rearing practices linked to children's social competence are hard to synthesize. As summarized by Rubin, Bukowski and Parker (1998), parents of socially competent children have been found to be more child-centred, feelings-oriented and warmer than parents of other children; they also tend to use reasoning very frequently in disciplining their children. Table 3.1 provides a summary of the findings of the major studies of parents' child-rearing practices as they relate to children's aggression. As shown, the most frequent findings implicate parents' coldness, harshness, lack of consistency and lack of supervision. Table 3.2, page 55, provides a synthesis of the limited literature on parenting in relation to children's shyness and social withdrawal. Parents who are distant, cold, protective and domineering tend to have shy, withdrawn children. Finally, Table 3.3, page 59, summarized studies that indicate that parents who are involved with their children, who explain their thinking to them and who provide democratic households tend to have children who are competent socially. Thus, most research is consistent with Baumrind's (1989) well-known longitudinal studies that indicated the superiority of authoritative parenting over permissive or authoritarian styles, by showing that the children of authoritative parents grew up to have more positive peer relations.

In addition to their roles as disciplinarians, parents act as managers of their children's access to social contacts with peers. Parents may actively initiate peer contacts for their children either on an *ad hoc* basis, such as inviting neighbours' children to their homes or by enrolling the children in organized extracurricular activities. They may also provide direct guidance and informal 'coaching' to their children regarding ways of making friends. These modes of parental facilitation have been linked to the peer participation of young children (e.g. Ladd and Hart, 1992). This aspect of parenting is characteristic of parents of middle and upper

Table 3.1 Studies linking parenting with childhood aggression

Author	Sample description		Aspects of parenting measured	Parenting measure	Aggression measure	Results
	N	Age (years)				
			Studies conducted within North America			
Symonds (1939)	56	5–23	Dominating or submissive parenting style	Structural parental interview	Direct observation	Children of submissive parents are more aggressive than children of dominating parents
Baldwin (1948)	67	4	Control, democracy and level of parent–child interaction	Structured home interviews	Home and free-play observation	Democracy is related to higher levels of aggression, especially in homes where there is a lot of parent–child interaction.
Sears, Whiting, Nowlis and Sears (1953)	40	3–5	Mothers' child-rearing practices	Interview with mother	Direct observation Teacher rating Standardized doll play procedure	The more severely boys are punished for aggression by their mothers, the more aggressive they are.
Sears Maccoby, and Levin (1957)	379	5	Discipline, tolerance, warmth, severity of punishments, level of demand and values	Interview with mother	Interview with mother	The more disagreement with the husband about child-rearing practices, the more permissiveness by the mother, the more severe punishments and the less demand placed on the child, the more aggressive the child.

Study	N	Age	Variable measured	Method	Method	Findings
Lesser (1957)	44	10–13	Permissiveness for aggression	Parental questionnaire	Peer report Stimulus cards shown to children	Aggression is positively correlated with mother's permissiveness.
Becker, Peterson Hellmer, Shoemaker and Quay (1959)	57	8–9	Justification of punishments and amount of emotional expression towards the child	Self-reports	Parental report Interviews with mothers	Parents of aggressive children are arbitrary. Mothers of aggressive children tend to be dictatorial, thwarting and suggestive, whereas fathers tend to be permissive.
McCord, McCord and Howard (1961)	174	9	Parental methods of discipline and control	Home observation	Reports of psychiatrists, physicians, ppsychologists, school officials, ministers, police officials, YMCA officials and employers	Direct parental attacks (frequent use of threats, constant unfavourable comments or physically punitive discipline) and inconsistent parenting styles are strongly associated with a high rate of delinquency.
Sears (1961)	160	12	Mothers' permissiveness and punitiveness	Interview with mother	Self-administered aggression scale	High permissiveness and low punitiveness are correlated with anti-social aggression.

Table 3.1 Continued

Author	Sample description		Aspects of parenting measured	Parenting measure	Aggression measure	Results
	N	Age (years)				
Becker, Peterson, Luria, Shoemaker and Hellmer (1962)	64	6	Warmth, permissiveness, anxiety, physical punishment and use of reasoning	Self-reports	Parental interview Parental report Teacher report	Aggressive children have parents who use physical punishment and do not use reasoning. Their fathers are strict.
Eron, Walder, Toigo and Lefkowitz (1963)	800	8	Intensity of punishment used	Parental questionnaire	Peer report	Children who are exposed to high-intensity punishments are more aggressive.
Gordon and Smith (1965)	48	3–4 6–7	Strictness by mother	Structured parental interviews	Children's response to hypothetical situations	If mothers use physical punishment, aggression for girls is related to higher levels of strictness.
Levy (1966)	20	4–16	Mothers' overprotectiveness, rejection and overindulgence	Case histories	Case histories	Mothers of aggressive children tend to be overindulgent.
Patterson and Cobb (1971)	24	6–13	Types of punishment used	Home observation	Teacher report Peer report Home observation	Physical punishment to reprimand the aggressive act of an already aggressive child is related to subsequent aggression. Physical punishment to reprimand an aggressive act of a typically non-aggressive child is related to a decrease in subsequent aggression.

Study	N	Age	Variables measured	Method	Method	Findings
Larzelere (1986)	1136	3–17	Frequency of spanking and the use of reasoning	Parental questionnaire	Peer report	Aggression is related to the frequency of spanking. However, this effect is negated for the pre-adolescent children of moderate spankers if they incorporate reasoning into the punishment.
Felson and Russo (1988)	292	9–12	Whether parents punish siblings after a fight	Parents reported which sibling was punished after a 'big fight'	Self and parental reports of physical and verbal punishment	The probability of aggression is greater when some punishment is used, particularly when it is directed at an older sibling
Pettit, Dodge and Brown (1988)	46	5	Mothers' values, discipline styles and levels, and teaching styles	Semi-structured parental interviews	Peer report Teacher report	Children with mothers who use restrictive discipline are more aggressive.
Pettit, Harrist, Bates and Dodge (1991)	30	3–7	Mothers' responsiveness, coerciveness, intrusiveness and reflection	Home observation	Teacher report	Aggression with peers is related to coercive and intrusive interactions with the child's mother.
Harralson and Lawler (1992)	50	6–12	Achievement pressure and degree of control	Parental questionnaire	Self-reports	Parenting styles of achievement pressure and high control are related to impatience and aggressive behaviours in children.

Table 3.1 Continued

| Author | Sample description | | Aspects of parenting measured | Parenting measure | Aggression measure | Results |
	N	Age (years)				
Harrist (1992)	30	3–5	Parent–child synchrony (extent to which the dyad is able to engage in shared rituals, songs, activities)	Home observations	Teacher report Peer report Home observation	Negative synchrony (synchrony is present but affective balance is negative) and non-synchrony (synchrony is not present) are related to high levels of aggression.
Strassberg, Dodge, Bates and Pettit (1992)	219	5	Strategies for dealing with conflict	Parental responses to hypothetical situations	Peer rating	The more the parents use aggressive strategies to deal with conflicts, the more aggressive the child.
Strassberg, Dodge, Pettit and Bates (1994)	273	5	Occurrence and severity of of spanking	Parental questionnaires	Playground and classroom observation	Children whose parents do not spank them are the least aggressive, children whose parents use light spanking are moderately aggressive, and children whose parents use heavy spanking or hitting are the most aggressive.
Weiss, Dodge, Bates and Pettit (1992)	584	4	Severity of punishment	Parental interview	Teacher rating Peer rating	As severity of punishment increases, ratings of aggressiveness increase.

Study	N	Age	Construct	Method	Outcome measure	Findings
Dumas and LaFrenière (1993)	120	4	Interaction styles	Laboratory observation	Teacher rating	Mothers of aggressive children fail to reciprocate positive behaviour; they respond positively to aversive behaviours and do not disapprove actively of non-compliance.
Boyum and Parke (1995)	50	5–7	Affect directed at the child	Taped dinner interaction	Teacher rating	Verbally aggressive girls receive more neutral affect from mothers and fathers. All aggressive children receive more questioning from mothers.
Mize and Pettit (1997) Study 1	43	3–6	Mothers' social coaching and interaction style	Observation of interaction during a puzzle task	Teacher rating	The lower the mother–child synchrony score (extent to which mother and child engage in mutually focused, reciprocal and responsive exchanges), the more aggressive the child. Children whose mothers suggest less positive strategies and do not encourage the child to take an optimistic approach to the task are more aggressive.
Mize and Pettit (1997) Study 2	62	3–7	Mothers' social coaching and interaction style	Observation of mother-child play and child play with another child	Teacher rating	For girls, the less the mothers elaborate during the interaction, the more aggressive the child.

Table 3.1 Continued

Author	Sample description		Aspects of parenting measured	Parenting measure	Aggression measure	Results
	N	Age (years)				
Studies conducted outside North America						
Olweus (1980) Sweden	127	12–14	Mothers' permissiveness for aggression and parents' use of power-assertive discipline techniques	Parental interview	Peer rating	Mothers' permissiveness for aggression and use of power-assertive discipline are associated with higher ratings of aggressiveness in children.
Schneider, Attili, Vermigli and Younger (1997) Italy	156	7.5	Mothers' emotional responses to problematic social behaviours and beliefs about parenting	Mothers' responses to hypothetical situations	Peer rating	Mothers of aggressive and non-aggressive children reported similar beliefs and practices.
Hart, Nelson, Robinson, Olsen and McNeilly-Choque (1998) Russia	207	4–7	Parenting style	Parenting behaviour questionnaire	Teacher rating	Parents who report using more coercion have more aggressive children. Coercion by mothers is significantly related to higher ratings of relational aggression for girls.
Pakaslahti, Spoof, Asplund-Peltola and Keltikangas-Jäevinen (1998) Finland	58	12–13	Parents' social-problem solving	Semi-structured parental interview strategies	Peer rating Teacher rating	The parents of aggressive girls are more likely to reprimand them or show indifference, whereas parents of non-aggressive girls are more likely to discuss problems with their children.

Table 3.2 Studies linking parenting with childhood shyness

Author	Sample description		Aspects of parenting measured	Parenting measure	Aggression measure	Results
	N	Age (years)				
Studies conducted outside North America						
Symonds (1939)	120	4	Dominating or submissive parenting styles	Structured parental interview	Direct observations	Children of dominating parents are shyer than children of permissive parents.
Watson (1957)	68	5–12	Strictness	Parental questionnaire	Psychological testing Teacher report	Children from homes with less freedom are more shy.
Eisenberg (1958)	26	4–16	Overprotection and anxiousness	Parental interview Case histories	Parental interview Case histories	Children of mothers who are overprotective are shy and do not want to go to school.
Becker, Peterson, Hellmer, Shoemaker and Quay (1959)	57	9	Justification of punishments and amount of emotional expression towards the child	Self-report	Parental reports	Fathers of shy children tend to offer fewer explanations for their punishments.
Becker, Peterson, Luria, Shoemaker and Hellmer (1962)	64	6	Warmth, permissiveness, anxiety and use of physical punishment	Self-report	Parental interview Parental report Teacher report	Fathers of shy children tend to be hostile, punitive and strict.
Rosenthal, Ni, Finkelstein and Berkowitz (1962)	406	5–14	Numerous aspects of the father–child relationship	Case histories	Case histories	Shy children have cold, distant, and neglectful fathers.

Table 3.2 Continued

| Author | Sample description | | Aspects of parenting measured | Parenting measure | Aggression measure | Results |
	N	Age (years)				
Siegelman (1966)	106	9–11	Love, punitiveness and demand	Child questionnaires	Peer report	Boys who perceive their parents as punishing are rated as withdrawn.
Baumrind and Black (1967)	95	9	Authoritative, authoritarian, indulgent and neglectful parenting styles	Self-report Home interview	School observation	Children of authoritarian parents are socially withdrawn.
Lorion, Cowen, Kraus and Milling (1977)	267	6–11	Parental pressure for academic success Homes lacking educational stimulation Overprotection Rejection	Case histories	Teacher report	Children who are under family pressure to succeed are more shy than children experiencing a lack of educational stimulation. Children of overprotective parents are more shy than children of rejecting parents.
MacDonald and Parke (1984)	27	3–4	Amount of parent–child physical play, engagement, verbal behaviour and directiveness	Home observation	Teacher report Peer report	Children whose mothers use low amounts of verbal inter-change are socially withdrawn.

Study	N	Age	Factor	Measurement 1	Measurement 2	Findings
Harrist (1992)	30	4–5	Parent–child synchrony (extent to which the dyad is able to engage in shared rituals, songs, and activities)	Home observation	Teacher rating Peer rating Direct observation	Negative synchrony (synchrony is present but affective balance is negative) and non-synchrony (no synchrony is present) are related to high levels of social withdrawal.
Dumas and LaFrenière (1993)	120	4	Interaction style	Laboratory observation	Teacher rating	Mothers of anxious or withdrawn or isolated children are aversive and return their children's negative affect.
Hart, DeWolf and Burts (1993)	106	5	Discipline techniques	Home parental interview	School observation	Older boys of power-assertive fathers engage in more withdrawn behaviours than older boys of inductive (similar to authoritative) fathers. The same is true of girls of any age with their mothers.
Mills and Rubin (1993)	122	5–9	Belief in the importance of various methods for learning social skills Strategies for teaching social skills to their children	Parental questionnaire	Direct observation Teacher rating	Parents who place emphasis on directive teaching and who believe in using direct and immediate strategies in facilitating children's social relations have the shyest children.

Studies conducted outside North America

Study	N	Age	Factor	Measurement 1	Measurement 2	Findings
Engfer (1993) Germany	39	Birth to 6	Numerous factors from rigidity to overprotection	Parental interview Parental questionnaire	Direct observation Parental rating	Overprotective mothers, impatience and punitiveness are positively correlated with shyness.

Table 3.2 Continued

| Author | Sample description | | Aspects of parenting measured | Parenting measure | Aggression measure | Results |
	N	Age (years)				
Schneider, Attili, Vermigli and Younger (1997) Italy and Canada	156	8	Mothers' emotional responses to children's problematic social behaviour Mothers' belief about preventing	Mothers' responses to hypothetical situations	Peer rating	Mothers of withdrawn and non-withdrawn children reported similar beliefs and responses.
Chen, Hastings, Rubin, Chen, Cen and Stewart (1998) People's Republic of China	258	2	Mothers' child rearing attitudes and beliefs	Questionnaire completed by mother	Observation of free-play session	Among Chinese participants, childhood inhibition is associated with mother's positive attitudes acceptance, lack of punitiveness and encouragement of achievement.

Table 3.3 Studies linking parenting with children's popularity, peer acceptance, friendship, social competence, or sociability leadershp

Author	Sample description		Aspects of parenting measured	Parenting measure	Acceptance or popularity measure	Results
	N	Age (years)				
Studies conducted within North America						
Ayer and Bernreuter (1936)	40	3–4	Discipline style	Parental interview	Teacher rating Peer report	Children who are rewarded by their parents for doing things they are supposed to do, are more sociable with other children.
Baldwin (1948)	67	4	Control, democracy and levels of parent–child interaction	Structured home interview (Parent Behaviour Ratings)	Direct home observation Free-play observation	Children of democratic parents are more likely to be leaders in nursery school.
Levy (1966)	20	4–16	Overprotection by mother Rejection Overindulgence	Case histories	Case histories	Overprotected children have difficulty forming friends and maintaining normal friendly relationships.
MacDonald and Parke (1984)	27	3–4	Physical play involving parent and child	Home observation	Teacher rating Peer report	Physical play with the father, engagement of the child in play with parents, and mothers' verbal exchange with child during play were associated with child's popularity among peers. Many gender differences in the findings.

Table 3.3 Continued

| Author | Sample description | | Aspects of parenting measured | Parenting measure | Acceptance or popularity measure | Results |
	N	Age (years)				
Peery, Jensen and Adams (1985)	120	4–5	Attitudes towards child-rearing practices	Self-report		Less popular children have parents whose attitudes reflect the following: belief in a patriarchal family structure, infrequent use of praise, lack of promotion of independence, low use of discipline by mother coupled with the belief that child-rearing is a mother's duty, low child orientation, infrequent use of threats and negative reactions by father to child's intrusive behaviour.
MacDonald (1987)	48	3–5	Amount of physical play the parent and child engage in Level of affective arousal during play Amount of direction provided by the parent during the interaction	Video taped home observation	Teacher rating	The more physical play the parents engage in, the more affectively stimulating they are during the interaction and the less they try to direct the session, the more popular the child.

Study	N	Age	Variables	Method	Source	Findings
Putallaz (1987)	55	6	Behavioural measures including agreeableness and clarity of communication	Parent–child interaction observation through one-way mirror	Peer report	Mothers of higher status children interact in a more positive and agreeable manner with their children and are more concerned with feelings during the interaction (both their own and their children's).
Roberts and Strayer (1987)	30	6	Parental responsiveness to emotional distress	Home observation Parental self-report Child interview	Teacher report	Parental encouragement of emotional expressiveness is positively correlated with children's social competence in school.
Roopnarine and Adams (1987)	37	3–5	Teaching style	Structured interaction involving a puzzle task	Peer report	Parents of popular children use more explanations in aiding their children to complete the task.
Ladd and Golter (1988)	58	4–5	Frequency of initiating peer contacts for their child and the way parents monitor close contacts	Parental interview	Peer report Teacher report	High initiators have children who are more accepted by their peers. Children of parents who use indirect monitoring strategies (oversee what their child is doing but are not present at all times) have more popular children.

Table 3.3 Continued

Author	Sample description		Aspects of parenting measured	Parenting measure	Acceptance or popularity measure	Results
	N	Age (years)				
Pettit, Dodge and Brown (1988)	46	5	Mothers' values Discipline style Harshness of discipline Teaching style	Semi-structured home interview	Peer report Teacher report	The less mothers endorse aggression and the less restrictive their discipline, the more popular the child.
Heflin (1989)	179	3–4	Nurturance and control	Self-report	Child interview Child questionnaire Peer report Teacher report	Parental nurturance is positively related to social status.
Austin and Lindauer (1990)	8	4–5	Cognitive involvement, support, guidance, discipline and problem solving	Taped interactions	Peer report	Parents of better-liked boys are less controlling, directive and less intrusive.
Dishion (1990)	206	9–10	Quality of monitoring and discipline practices	Home observation Observer impressions Parental interview Child interview Child report	Peer report	Children of parents who use effective, fair, consistent or even-handed discipline techniques, or who establish clear guidelines of conduct, or who properly monitor the child's daily activities, receive high scores for peer acceptance.

Study	N	Age	Construct	Assessment 1	Assessment 2	Findings
Feldman and Wentzel (1990)	159	11	Child-centredness (the extent to which parents act in a way that promotes the psychological welfare of the child) Harshness of discipline	Self-report (Weinberger Parenting Inventory)	Peer report	Child-centredness is related to being liked by the child's peers.
Hart, Ladd and Burleson (1990)	144	5–7 9–10	Discipline style	Home interview	Peer report	The less mothers use power-assertive discipline, the more popular the child.
Henggeler, Edwards, Cohen and Summerville (1991)	24	8	Parental receptivity to their children's statements	Observed interaction during a cooperative task	Peer report	Father's receptivity to their children's proposed solutions is positively correlated with popularity.
Kennedy (1992)	52	3–5	Mothers' beliefs and strategies regarding teaching her child social competence	Structured interview	Free-play behavioural observation Peer report	Mothers of popular children are more likely to teach their children about social skills, spend more time in child-centred activities, use less punishment and use more reasoning or explanation in discipline.
Pettit, Harrist, Bates and Dodge (1991)	30	5	Mothers' responsiveness Coerciveness Intrusiveness Reflection	Home observation	Teacher rating	Social competence with peers is related to responsive mother interactions.
Burleson, Delia and Applegate (1992)	51	6–9	Reflection-enhancing mother communication	Parental questionnaire	Peer report	As communication with mother increases, peer acceptance increases.

Table 3.3 Continued

| Author | Sample description | | Aspects of parenting measured | Parenting measure | Acceptance or popularity measure | Results |
	N	Age (years)				
Harrist (1992)	30	3–5	Parent–child synchrony (extent to which the dyad is able to engage in shared rituals, songs and activities)	Home observation	Teacher rating Peer report Direct observation	Positive synchrony (shared activity that is positive in affective tone) is related to high levels of social competence.
Hart, DeWolf, Wozniak and Burts (1992)	106	3–5	Discipline technique	Home interview	Peer report	Preschoolers of inductive mothers (similar to authoritative) are more accepted by their peers than preschoolers of power-assertive mothers.
Ladd and Hart (1992)	83	4–6	Parent initiation of informal play opportunities	Parental interview Parental questionnaire	Parental rating School observation	Frequent parent initiation is associated with greater peer acceptance.
Strassberg, Dodge, Bates and Pettit (1992)	219	5	Strategies for dealing with conflicts	Parental responses to hypothetical conflict situations (Conflict Tactics Scale)	Peer report	The less aggression the parent uses to resolve conflict, the more popular the child.

Study	N	Age	Construct	Method	Outcome measure	Findings
Dumas and LaFrenière (1993)	120	4	Interaction style	Laboratory observation	Teacher rating	Mothers of socially competent children display more positive affect often return their children's positive affect.
Laird, Pettit, Mize, Brown and Lindsey (1994)	39	5	Conversations by mother and child regarding peers (frequency, references to emotion and advice giving)	Parental interview	Peer report, Teacher rating	Acceptance by peers is higher for children whose mother's conversation includes more emotion and more advice. Overall frequency of such conversations is related to peer acceptance.
Black and Logan (1995)	43	2–5	Communication patterns	Observed interactions	Teacher rating, Peer report	Parents of rejected children make more requests but fail to allow their children time to respond.
Boyum and Parke (1995)	50	5–7	Affect directed at the child	Taped dinner interactions	Teacher rating	Popular children receive less angry affect from their fathers. Popular boys receive less angry affect from their mothers and more expressions of disgust. Popular girls receive less neutral affect from their mothers and more happy affect from their father.

Table 3.3 Continued

Author	Sample description		Aspects of parenting measured	Parenting measure	Acceptance or popularity measure	Results
	N	Age (years)				
Eisenberg, Fabes and Murphy (1996)	148	8–12	Parents' reaction to their child's negative emotion	Self-report	Teacher rating	Dismissing and punitive reactions are negatively related to popularity, whereas mothers' problem-focused reactions are positively related to popularity in girls.
Franz and Gross (1996)	82	9	Parental responsivity to children's behaviour	Direct observation during a co-operative task	Peer report Teacher rating	The more commands, suggestions, explanations and praise the parents use, the more popular the child.
Auerbach-Major (1997)	96	3–4	Discipline style	Parental reports Direct observation	Peer report Teacher rating	Boys with negative affect who have parents who practise power-assertive styles have lower scores for social competence.
Lindsey, Mize and Pettit (1997)	35	3–6	Parent–child interaction, initiations, compliance, and sychrony	Observed interactions	Teacher rating	Children whose fathers respond more often to their child's play initiations, and children who are in a synchronous mother–child relationship are better liked by their peers.

Study	N	Age	Variables	Measure	Outcome measure	Findings
Mize and Pettit (1997) Study 1	43	3–6	Social coaching by mothers Interaction style	Observed inter-actions during a puzzle task	Peer report	Children in mother–child dyads that receive high synchrony ratings, whose mothers suggest more positive strategies, whose mothers encourage the child to take an optimistic approach to the task and whose mothers take a problem-solving approach to the task, are better accepted.
Mize and Pettit (1997) Study 2	62	3–7	Social coaching by mothers Interaction style	Observed inter-actions during play with each other and another child	Peer report	Coaching of prosocial strate-gies is related to popularity for girls.
Pettit, Brown, Mize and Lindsey (1998)	36	3–6	Parents' level of involvement, pro-social coaching and elaborative coaching (hints, clues or descriptions)	Observed inter-action in a co-operative environment and in a peer-child context	Peer report Teacher rating	The following are associated with high peer acceptance: high levels of parent-child play for boys, coaching by mother for girls, low levels of mother involvement in the child-peer segment and high levels of father involve-ment in the child-peer segment.

Table 3.3 Continued

| Author | Sample description | | Aspects of parenting measured | Parenting measure | Acceptance or popularity measure | Results |
	N	Age (years)				
Studies conducted outside North America						
Finnie and Russell (1988) Australia	40	4–5	Encouragement of children to engage in social interaction Methods suggested by mothers to interact	Situational observation	Teacher rating	Mothers of more social children encourage them to initiate social interactions and model appropriate methods for doing so.
Dekovic and Janssens (1992) The Netherlands	112	6–11	Warmth, responsiveness, power assertion, reasoning demandingness and restrictiveness	Home observation	Peer report	Authoritarian or restrictive parents have children who are less popular, whereas authoritative or democratic parents have children who are more popular.

socioeconomic status. Socioeconomic status (SES) and the related concept of social class refer to the prestige of a person's occupation, the education needed to prepare for it and the salary one earns. Within a given country or society, differences between the beliefs and behaviours of members of different SES levels have often been found to be greater than the differences between countries. One of the reasons why lower SES is associated with social withdrawal among younger children is that parents from lower-SES backgrounds are less active than others in facilitating peer contacts for their children, at least in the United States (Ladd, Hart, Wadsworth and Golter, 1988).

Older children may be less dependent than younger children are on parental structuring of their social lives (Rubin and Sloman, 1984). As issues of autonomy become more important to the maturing child and adolescent (Krappmann, 1989), parental structuring of peer contacts may become less acceptable than to younger children. Thus, there are several reasons for believing that the managerial role of parents is pivotal only for young children and may be more important in Western countries and not in societies where child-rearing is guided more extensively by tradition and where raising children is considered much more the collective responsibility of the community and society. Some support for this comes from an intriguing cross-cultural study by Hart and his colleagues (Hart *et al.*, 1999), conducted with 5-year-olds from Utah, China and Russia and their parents. The Chinese mothers were more active in facilitating peer contacts for their children, perhaps because there were relatively few children in the immediate neighbourhood for the children to play with. However, only in Russia did such facilitation relate in any way to children's social competence (the lack of findings in Utah represents a failure to replicate the results of the US studies mentioned earlier in this paragraph). Two studies, one conducted in Germany (Krappmann, 1989) and one in Canada (Schneider, Richard, Younger and Freeman, in press) indicated that direct facilitation by parents is no longer important in fostering the peer contacts of children once they reach the middle years of primary school.

In summary, very extensive research demonstrates that children who display competent and incompetent social behaviour receive very different treatment from their parents. Since the children's own temperaments could affect the parents' behaviour as much as the parents' child-rearing affects the children, it is impossible to corroborate the common belief that the parents' child-rearing *causes* the children positive or negative social behaviour with peers. Nevertheless, interventions aimed at improving the child-rearing practices of parents whose children display maladaptive patterns of relating to other children may be a promising avenue of intervention for those children.

Socialization research in the third millennium

The lingering doubts left by twentieth-century research provide ample material for more intensive study of the origins of children's ways of relating to each other. New advances in behaviour-genetics methodology may permit improvements on the methods used in existing twin and adoption studies. Hopefully, more behaviour geneticists will make fuller use of the range of methods for studying children's behaviour that have been developed by scholars specializing in children's social development (see Chapter 6). As well, there may be many advantages in targeting specifically the influences of families who provide unusually positive and negative environments for children already at risk for social maladjustment. Much more needs to be known about the influences of community and school peers on children's social competence. In that specific regard, much has been learned about the influences of aggressive peers on aggression, in studies starting with Thrasher's classic work on street gangs at the beginning of the twentieth century (see Chapter 1), but little is known about neighbourhood peers' influence on sociability or on leadership behaviours. It is unlikely that the massive evidence indicating a genetic component in the origin of children's styles of relating to peers will be refuted. Nevertheless, more intensive intervention studies (see Chapter 11) will hopefully determine how amenable to change problematic patterns of social behaviour really are, despite the fact that those patterns derive in part from genetic preparation.

Socialization by peers

As discussed in Chapter 1, the amount of time children spend in the company of other children has fluctuated through history and depends heavily on the organization of adults' work activities. In agricultural societies, boys often work together with adult men, whereas girls often work with adult women, resulting in relatively little contact between children (Frones, 1995). Most other economic activities result in children spending large amounts of time in each other's company, with older children taking responsibility for supervising younger ones and in doing so, participating very extensively in child-rearing (Whiting and Edwards, 1988). The great potential of peer socialization was recognized historically by several peoples, who went as far as having children live separately from adults so that the older children could inculcate the values of the society unfettered by the distracting influences of parents (this occurred more frequently among warrior peoples such as the Aztecs and ancient Spartans; Frones, 1995). In contemporary Western societies, organized child-care and recreational activities account for many children being together for much of their free time (ibid. 1995).

Just as parents are often blamed when their children go wrong, the influences of peers have been studied most extensively when scientists try to explain why some children become aggressive. Some of this literature will be discussed in Chapter 7, in the section pertaining to the sometimes negative influences of friends.

In Judith Rich Harris' (1998) group socialization theory, peers and not parents are seen as the major socializing agents that determine the ways in which children relate to others, in counterpoint with a definite but not unlimited degree of genetic causation. Harris correctly points out that children are innately programmed to imitate other children and that children also seem to seek out the company of other children even in cultures where children spend much of their time with parents. According to the theory, children acquire their styles of social interaction by attempting to conform to the norms of their peer group, or the norms of children slightly older than themselves. Harris cites a variety of extreme situations in support of group socialization theory. The situations include the children of deaf parents, who learn both language and culture and the children of immigrants, who learn the languages and cultures of their host countries, even though their parents could not have taught them. Harris' strong advocacy of group socialization theory and her outspoken attacks on the 'nurture assumption' are certain to stimulate more and better research on the influences of peers.

Siblings as coaches in peer relations

There are many literary accounts of older siblings serving as coaches of their younger brothers and sisters of the social skills needed to get along in the world of peers. If one compares interaction with siblings to interaction with parents, learning to relate to siblings is more similar in many ways to the skills needed to relate to peers. Sibling influences *per se* have been somewhat overlooked in literature on the origin of children's social competence, although, of course, siblings have been studied extensively in order to establish the heritability of temperament from parents to children. There have been, however, a few very careful studies in which the social interactions of the same children with their siblings and peers were compared. This research has been conducted with young children and has featured observational methods that provide rich detail on social interaction. There is some evidence children display similar styles in interacting with siblings and with peers, although the results of the few studies available are not entirely consistent (Abramovich, Corter, Pepler and Stanhope, 1986; Mendelson, Aboud and Lanthier, 1994; Volling, Youngblade and Belsky, 1997). However, the fact that the interaction styles are similar does not necessarily mean that the children learned the patterns of relating from their siblings, then applied them to peers. The reverse could have occurred, or they could have acquired the relationship styles from their parents.

Results of a longitudinal study by Abramovich, Corter, Pepler and Stanhope (1986) suggest that one's birth position in the family could affect the way one relates to peers. Older siblings were more outgoing, initiating both more aggressive and more helpful interactions than were initiated by younger siblings. In contrast, Stoneman, Brody and MacKinnon (1984) found that older brothers and sisters who were dominant with their younger siblings showed few signs of dominance in interactions with their own friends. In any case, more research is needed not only on the similarity of children's social behaviours with their siblings and friends, but also on the processed by which children learn from their siblings.

So, what is the cause?

Most people have their own theories about what causes children and adults to relate to others in their individual ways. Probably few of these personal theories implicate genetics to the extent that it is featured in child-development research on the origins of children's social competence. Folk wisdom assigns parents most of the credit for their children's achievements and most of the blame for their weak points. As noted above, that may not be justified, but improving parenting practice may still be a very fruitful way of helping children who display atypical patterns of peer relations such as problematic aggression and social withdrawal.

Changing the habitual thinking pattern of searching for the supposed single cause of any problem is no easy matter. However, there is good reason to believe that, for the most part, individual differences in children's social competence have several causes, as has been recognized, in principle, by the mental health professions (American Psychiatric Association, 1994). It may be difficult or impossible to identify 'the cause' of any single case of maladaptive social behaviour.

4 Peer relations and success at school

This chapter begins with a review of research on the links between social and cognitive development. Emphasis is placed on work by Piaget, Vygotsky and Doise. The second half of the chapter is devoted to research on the links between peer relations and academic success, both in terms of achievement and personal adjustment to the school setting.

There has been heated debate as to whether the main priority of the school should be to teach children social skills or to foster their academic achievement. Proponents of the latter goal maintain that the role of the school is to educate its students in various disciplines and to maximize academic achievement. This 'back to basics' position gained some prominence in the 1980s, which brought a general conservatism to the field of education in many Western countries, resulting in an emphasis on the acquisition of facts and academic skills (called 'Thatcherism in education' by Johnson, 1989). Social development was seen as the family's domain. Indeed, Klindová (1985), an Eastern European researcher, postulated that the home and school tend to play different roles in children's development. Whereas kindergartens may teach children practical skills, it is the family life which may account for their social development.

However important academic achievement may be, proponents of the social role of education argue that the school should be responsible for teaching children social skills and encouraging social and emotional learning. Elias *et al.* (1997), who are the developers of one of the best-known social-skills curricula for schools, maintain that the goal of the school is to produce knowledgeable, responsible and caring individuals; promotion of social development, they assert, is unfortunately absent from agendas of school reform. The influential pioneer educationalist John Dewey (1900) claimed that the child was a product of the social world, and that the school should reflect the goals of the home and community. Early humanists such as Dewey hoped that the school might buffer the effects of a stressful family environment. To do so, the school had to be sensitive to the child's needs.

There have been some attempts to translate Dewey's ideas about schooling into practice and to study the effects. Peres and Pasternack (1991) compared the adjustment of Israeli primary-school children of divorced parents in six structured, traditional schools and one experimental school. Results indicated that the children from the traditional schools were less accepting of other children than control-group participants from the experimental school. Relations among children were better in the experimental school, which was characterized by more student participation, and by a longer, more diverse school day.

Elias *et al.* assert that there may also be academic gains to fostering social and emotional learning in children: 'when schools attend systematically to students' social and emotional skills, the academic achievement of children increases, the incidence of problem behaviors decreases, and the quality of the relationships surrounding each child improves' (1997, p. 1). The Canadian educationalists Isherwood and Ahola (1981) maintain that instrumental and expressive socialization can coexist peacefully within the classroom setting. They, like Bloom (1977), the prominent US educator, refer to two modes of school influence and socialization. *Instrumental objectives* emphasize adherence to school rules and learning of the academic curriculum. *Expressive socialization* places importance on less formal learning that is facilitated by peer group and peer culture. Perhaps it is possible to combine these two priorities to encourage both social and academic competence. Can a compromise be reached? To begin with, the debate between social and academic priorities may have less substance than is apparent at first. Research has suggested that academic success and social competence are interdependent, that achievement may facilitate social development and vice versa (e.g. Chen, Rubin and Li, 1997).

Social competence and its effects on cognitive development

The social world of the child has a monumental influence on his or her development. Traditionally, research has addressed the role this social context plays in the development of the child's social competence. However, there is a growing field of research that explores the links between social interaction and academic competence. Indeed, there have been numerous findings that illustrate the positive effects of social interaction on cognitive development. It has even been suggested that social competence is a more accurate indicator of achievement than measured intellectual capacity (Wentzel, 1991). Such findings imply that social forces within the classroom are integral to children's academic achievement.

Chen, Rubin and Li (1997) studied the correlation between academic achievement and social functioning in 10- to 12-year-old children from four Shanghai schools. They identified three different models useful in explaining the relationship between academic and social competence. The first model maintains that children's prosocial behaviour fosters a positive attitude towards the school experience, which, in turn, compels them to succeed academically. Children who display positive social behaviour may be more likely to receive requested teacher help, and this may affect their academic results. The second model is essentially the converse of the first: children's academic success is seen as causing their social adjustment. Finally, the third, 'bidirectional' model combines the first two, and asserts that academic achievement and social competence are interactive and mutually influential. Findings from Chen, Rubin and Li's (1997) study indicated that academic achievement was influenced by social competence and peer acceptance, which were in turn affected by levels of academic success; this supports the bidirectional model. Results also showed that aggression and externalizing behaviour were negatively correlated with later academic achievement. Chen, Rubin and Li found that popular children surpassed unpopular children in Chinese language and mathematics. They suggest that the peer group could have a positive effect on academic performance by acting as a social resource. Similarly, in a landmark study of student culture in ten heterogeneous US secondary schools, Coleman (1961) found that students' bonds with their peer group were crucial to the entire school experience. Students without friends were disengaged and alienated, which could, in turn, lead to premature school leaving.

What aspects of social development mediate learning?

There is speculation as to specifically what must occur during interaction between children in order for cognitive gain to occur. Piaget (1932) asserted that cognitive growth could only occur between peers of more or less equal status. Although he emphasized the child's interactions with the physical world and did not focus on the social world as a developmental force, he did maintain that, through interaction and conflict, children encounter disequilibrium which causes a restructuring of their logic and cognitive growth. Smith (1996) likened Piaget's line of reasoning to Aristotle's analysis of economic transactions: 'Two partners to an economic exchange may have different products and so a decision about their equality, or lack of equality, requires the construction of a common scale so that either product can be compared with the other' (ibid., p. 119). In her study of peer interaction and problem solving, Margarita Azmitia (1988) first paired children into novice, expert and novice/expert (mixed) dyads and determined which children were subsequently able to generalize the skills learned while working on a task. She found that generalization depended on the quality of the discussion between the children, the amount of observation and imitation, and the provision of instruction by experts.

The eminent Soviet psychologist Lev Vygotsky also maintained that the ability of expert peers (or adults) to provide guidance was a key factor in cognitive development, for, within the 'zone of proximal development,' the expert provides the scaffolding needed to support the novice's attempt to perform new and higher-level skills. The child is then able to internalize new knowledge and apply it independently: 'What the child can do in cooperation today, he can do alone tomorrow' (Vygotsky, 1962, cf. Bearison, Magzamen and Filardo, 1986). Rogoff (1991) found that children learned more from an adult than a peer, whether the peer was skilled or unskilled at the task to be mastered, confirming the importance of experts who represent the adult culture.

Socio-cognitive conflict is an important component of social interaction that may modify the extent of cognitive growth. Bearison, Magzamen and Filardo (1986) examined the effects of socio-cognitive conflict on cognitive change and hypothesized that dyadic interactions characterized by salient disagreements and opposing solutions would foster more cognitive growth than those characterized by compliance. Bearison, Magzamen and Filardo found that there was a curvilinear relationship: small and large amounts of conflict did not promote significant cognitive growth, whereas intermediate amounts did. They stressed the importance of 'interindividual reequilibration', wherein disagreement between children is followed by some sort of consensus. Mugny, Giroud and Doise (1979) also maintained that socio-cognitive conflict is a major spur for cognitive growth. They showed that pairs of children engaged in conflict were able to solve cognitive tasks at a more advanced level than singletons. Cooper, Marquis and Edward (1986) suggested that the importance of socio-cognitive conflict emerges in middle childhood, when children possess the skills necessary for maintaining effective, task-related conflict. Peers act as 'attentional anchors' for younger children, helping to focus on the task at hand.

Table 4.1 is a summary of selected studies documenting the link between children's social interactions and their cognitive or academic prowess. The research evidence leaves little doubt that social interaction facilitates cognitive development and academic achievement. This applies to both general social interaction with peers and the interactions of close friends, which are discussed next.

Friendship and cognitive growth

Nelson and Aboud (1985) suggest that close relationships between children offer unique benefits to their cognitive development. In their study of 8-year-olds and 9-year-olds, they found that friends explained their opinions and criticized their partners more often than did non-friends. Higher levels of disagreement led to more cognitive change than did compliance. Nelson and Aboud concluded that friends who experience conflict undergo more social development than non-friends do in conflict. Their work supports other findings that friends who work together are more prosocial and share

Table 4.1 Selected studies showing that social interaction with peers is associated with higher cognitive abilities or better academic performance

Author	n	Age of participants	Measure of peer relations or social interaction	Measure of academic achievement or cognitive development	Results
Doise, Mugny and Perret-Clermont (1975) Switzerland	60	6 years	Reconstruction of a Lego village in pairs or in an individual situation (contrived)*	Ability to reconstruct Lego villages (simple and complex variations)	Children working together were capable of completing a spatial coordination task that children working alone were not capable of completing.
Doise and Mugny (1984) Switzerland	72	7–10 years	Group performance on 3-pulley game in either a communication or no communication condition. (contrived)*	Participants were asked to move a marker through the course of a circuit only using 3 pulleys (one for each participant). In the no communication condition, participants were asked not to talk to each other. In the communication condition, participants were permitted to talk to each other.	For the younger children, an inability to communicate with peers was linked to a much poorer performance than that of children allowed to communicate.
Doise and Mugny (1984) Switzerland	48	7–10 years	Individual and group performances on a 2-pulley game (contrived)*	Participants were asked to move a marker through the course of a circuit only using 2 pulleys. In the individual condition, children used both pulleys themselves; and in the group condition, each person in a pair would use a pulley.	Performance by 7–8 year-olds in the group condition was significantly better than performance in the individual condition.

Table 4.1 Continued

Author	n	Age of participants	Measure of peer relations or social interaction	Measure of academic achievement or cognitive development	Results
Light and Glachan (1985) UK	30 / 34	7–8 years and 12–13 years	Initial individual session and then either a paired or individual training session (contrived)*	Computerized version of logic-based game 'Mastermind'.	Working together in pairs on problems significantly facilitated subsequent individual problem-solving performance.
Berndt, Perry, and Miller (1988) USA	130	9 and 13 year-olds	Participants working either with classmate or with close friend. (contrived)*	Engaging in conversations related to task or study topics that were later quizzed.	In a post-task questionnaire, the pairs of friends said they engaged in more academic and nonacademic activities outside the experimental setting than did other pairs of classmates.
Azmitia (1988) USA	132	5 year-olds	Participants working alone in a pre-test to gauge their ability, then expert or novice participants working alone and in 3 types of pairs: novice, expert, and mixed-ability. (contrived)*	Copying of a complex Lego model requiring children to both represent spatial relations and break down a complex problem.	Collaboration was more conducive to learning than independent work. Children in mixed-ability pairs built more accurately than either children working alone or in matched ability pairs.
Taylor and Machida (1994) USA	63	2–5 years	Peer social preference and mutual friendships. (natural)	Learning skills, perceived self-competence, and observation of peer play skills.	Children involved in mutual friendships at the beginning of the school year showed better classroom behaviour, and greater involvement in social play and cooperative pretend play at the end of the year.

Study	N	Age	Condition	Measure	Findings
Roazzi and Bryant (1998) Brazil	90	4–5 years	Participants working together with confederates to complete inferential balance-scale task. (contrived)*	Performance on balance-scale task.	Interaction with other children with higher inferential capacities had a positive effect on the development of logical inferential skills.
Goldbeck (1998) USA	85	10 and 12 years	Peers working in a matched skill or unmatched skill dyad. (contrived)*	Correctly identifying water levels in a Piagetian water-level task.	Children working with peers showed greater improvement on spatial knowledge task. Children in the matched and in the less-competent unmatched pairs showed significant improvement from pre-test to post-test.
Diehl, Lemerise, Caverly, Ramsay and Roberts (1998) USA	323	7 and 8 years	Sociometric choice measures. (natural)	Measure of attitudes towards school.	School adjustment was positively correlated with peer acceptance and whether or not children had friends.

Note: * Contrived means a work situation set up expressly for the study.

more information than do non-friends (Berndt, 1981; Newcomb and Brady, 1982; Newcomb, Brady and Hartup, 1979).

Evidence of the link between the intimacy of children's relationships and their cognitive growth also suggests that interaction between siblings may offer important benefits to development. Azmitia and Hesser (1993) compared peer influence to sibling influence. During an unstructured building session, children, their older siblings, and older acquaintances each built a construction. This was followed by a teaching session, in which an older child (sibling or peer) taught a younger child how to build a windmill. A subsequent post-test required the younger child to build the windmill on his or her own. Results from Azmitia's study revealed that young children relied on their siblings for consultation, observation and imitation more than on their peers. Also, during teaching sessions, siblings provided more explanations and allowed the younger children more control than did the peers. The younger children attempted to gain more control from their siblings than from peers. Children who had been paired with a sibling achieved higher post-test scores than did the children who had been taught by a peer. Hartup (1989) suggests that relationships between siblings allow children to develop negotiation skills, as well as to practise socio-cognitive conflict. These are also important roles for friends and classmates. Hence, more research is needed to help clarify how differences in the quality of relationships with peers or siblings affect children's learning from other children.

Montessori schooling: planned social interaction in learning

The findings discussed above indicate that the structure and organization of the classroom, independent of the actual classroom curriculum, may influence children's development. In their case study of interactive learning, Cooper, Marquis and Edward (1986) conducted naturalistic observations on children aged 5 to 12 in a Montessori elementary school. This form of schooling encourages collaboration and recognizes its impact on cognitive growth. Whereas imitation might be negatively labelled as 'copying' or 'cheating' in a more traditional school environment, children taught in Montessori schools are urged to learn skills and techniques directly from observation of their peers. This offered Cooper, Marquis and Edward a unique opportunity to study the effects of peer interaction on cognitive development. They identified several different types of peer learning that occurred in the classroom environment. *Onlooker learning* consisted of a child observing another rather than engaging in work of his or her own. Onlookers tended to be younger children or children who did not work *effectively* in collaboration with other students. In *parallel-coordinate learning*, a group of two or more children work independently but refer to each other for help or information. *Guidance* involves one child actively teaching and guiding another child to help accomplish a task. *Executive guidance* is a more elaborate form of guidance, in which one child helps a peer by instructing a third child. *Collaboration* consists of equal sharing of power, whereby children share teaching roles or do not adopt a defined leader-follower formation. This taxonomy should be useful in future research studying the implications of patterns of social interaction among children in learning environments.

The contribution of friendship to adjustment following school transitions

Research into the relationship between children's friendships and school adjustment has indicated that social relations may positively influence adaptation after stressful school transitions, in which children are thrust into new and often daunting environments. Howes (1983, 1988) maintained that children may influence each other and thus facilitate school transitions by substituting for the parental/caretaker attachment that is lost at least temporarily when children leave home. Her work also indicates the importance of attachment to the teacher or caregiver, who were not mentioned at all in Bowlby's or Ainsworth's classic attachment theories (see Chapter 3). Schwartz (1972) explored the effect of close attachment between children on their reaction to novel situations. In Schwartz's experiment, children were paired with either a close friend or an unfamiliar peer, or they were left alone, to explore an unfamiliar environment; one may infer that this setting mimics the new world of a child's first kindergarten or junior high school class. Schwartz found that those children who were paired with a close friend were more willing to explore the environment and exhibited more positive affect than their counterparts in the other experimental conditions. Furthermore, such an effect was more evident among children paired with an unfamiliar peer than among solitary children. This suggests that even the presence of an unknown peer may lower a child's stress level and facilitate adjustment to a new environment.

In their case study of four African-American students who underwent the transition from a regular programme to a special programme for gifted students, Slanina (1996) highlighted certain factors that may facilitate adjustment. Prominent among these factors were positive peer influences. Three of the students continued to associate with their neighbourhood peer group after they had transferred from their home schools to the gifted programme. After these students took time to adjust to their new situation, there did not appear to be negative effects of the transition. However, the student who did not maintain contact with his neighbourhood friends found it difficult to adjust to the new gifted programme. This suggests that having a stable peer group outside the classroom may facilitate adjustment after a transition.

Classroom structure may also affect adjustment to school transition, for children who remain together throughout the day may find that a stable classroom composition facilitates their adjustment. In a study by Berndt, Hawkins and Jiao (1999), self-esteem declined for students who were organized into traditional junior high school classrooms, in which the composition of the classroom varied throughout the day according to subject. However, in 'teacher-student-teams,' in which the classroom rotated as a whole from teacher to teacher according to subject, permitting the peer group to remain together, there was little change in general self-esteem. McDougall and Hymel (1998) examined the transition to middle school, which occurs in Canadian schools at age 12 or 13. The participants were 160 students from Ontario who were entering a single middle school from a number of different primary schools. McDougall and Hymel postulated that, in schools where students remain with the same classmates throughout the day and change location from subject to subject, the transition to middle school should be relatively smooth due to the formation of a stable peer group. Findings from this study supported that hypothesis, and indicated that those participants who reported a difficult transition reported poor social adjustment and self-concept.

There is also evidence that the nature of the friendship itself may influence school adjustment. Berndt, Hawkins and Jiao (1999) studied the influences of friendship on adjustment to school transition. Using peer nominations, self-reports, teacher ratings, and school records, they assessed adjustment levels of students entering junior high school, which also occurs in the United States at about age 12 or 13. These students were interviewed in the spring of the year before the transition and again in their new schools the fall and spring of their subsequent school year. Berndt, Hawkins and Jiao (1999) postulated that the quality and stability of friendships would relate to school adjustment and that students' adjustment would relate to, and be influenced by, their friends' adjustment (Berndt, 1996; Hartup, 1996). Results indicated that those students who had high-quality friendships increased their social and leadership skills across the transition period. Also, students with friends who perceived themselves as competent socially in the fall of the year following the school transition reported that they consolidated their social competence even further during the school year.

In their study of peer relations and adjustment to kindergarten, Ladd, Kochenderfer and Coleman (1996) also hypothesized that the nature of friendship influences children's adaptation to school transition. They postulated that positive friendships that included validation and self-disclosure would bolster children and facilitate their adjustment; conflictual friendships were expected to have a negative effect on children's adjustment. The findings indicated that boys who perceived their friendships as characterized by conflict were more lonely and avoidant than others, and less liking of school. Ladd, Kochenderfer and Coleman suggest that this gender difference may be attributable to the fact that boys tend to be more negatively affected by conflict, and/or tend to be slower at resolving conflicts than girls. Boys and girls who perceived validation and aid in their friendships also perceived support from classmates; aid was predictive of improvement in attitudes regarding school.

There have been some attempts to determine whether it is the number of friends or frequency of contact with them that best explains the facilitative effects of friendship on schooling. In their longitudinal study of 410 students, Fenzel and Blyth (1986) examined the benefits of supportive peers on adjustment to junior high school (age 12–15 years, approximately). There was a gender difference in the nature of the link between friendship and adjustment. Boys whose self-esteem levels increased after the transition to junior high school had more frequent peer contact and were somewhat more intimate with their friends than boys whose self-esteem diminished after the transition. However, girls who attained higher levels of self-esteem had equal or lower intimacy levels with peers than those who declined in self-esteem. Fenzel and Blyth speculated that females who gain in self-esteem may receive family rather than peer support. Alternatively, it may be the case that girls who face new roles and changes may be more involved with their peers, but these peers may not offer them adequate emotional support (ibid.). Results from this study indicated that facilitation of school adjustment is not affected by the number of important peer relationships. However, significant findings suggested that the frequency of contact with peers did affect the adjustment of boys , because boys who gained in their perception of their social integration in the school had associated more frequent contact with same-sex peers than did boys who declined in their perception of school integration; there were no such benefits of contact for girls.

In contrast, Ladd and Price (1987) found that kindergarten children's initial school adjustment at about age five was positively correlated with the number of their classroom friends. Moreover, children with classroom friends who had been their friends prior to the start of kindergarten displayed more positive attitudes towards school and less avoidance of school. In a subsequent study, Ladd (1990) found that children who maintained their friendships with their prior friends acquired more positive attitudes towards school than those who did not.

More research on the possible benefits of friendship for school adjustment is needed. Little is known at present about the benefits of friendships among pupils outside North America. The findings could be very different, for example, in societies where parents expect a greater say in their children's choice of friendships, or in societies where school plays a less central role in children's social lives.

Applying the findings: cooperative learning

The cooperative learning movement represents a major effort at organizing education in order to capitalize on the facilitative effects of positive peer interaction. Many studies have indicated that there are numerous positive effects of cooperative learning, compared with the traditional competitive learning method that exists in many classrooms. Stevahn, Johnson, Johnson, and Real (1996) define competitive behaviour as working against a person to achieve an individual goal. As they define it, competition is motivated by self-interest and is short term in nature. Individualistic learning involves working individually towards personal goals. Cooperation, however, is defined as individuals collaborating for mutual gain. Compared with competition, cooperation is more long-term in nature. It is important to note that other conceptualizations of competition do exist. For example, Tassi and Schneider (1997) differentiated between task-oriented competition, in which a person competes with others with the goal of measuring his or her own achievements, and other-referenced competition, which is aimed at proving that one is better than other individuals in one's social context. Their concept of task-oriented competition is different from the individualistic learning defined by Johnson and his colleagues, because it still involves competition, albeit good-natured competition: the person is in a competitive situation and is not working individually. Of course, Tassi and Schneider believe, and provide some data to demonstrate, that it is other-referenced competition, not task-oriented competition, that damages harmonious social relationships.

There are many different forms of cooperative learning, but they do have common elements. Cooperative learning not only means that students sometimes were together in groups, which happens in most schools. It means that students must have an active stake in each other's learning. In some cases, this extends to not competing with each other for individual marks in their subjects. This requires a total overhaul of traditional styles of teaching and of classroom instructional materials, to achieve the optimal combination of 'group goals and individual accountability' (Slavin, 1991). Hertz-Lazarovitz (1995) provides a rich, multidimensional model consisting of six inter-related 'mirrors', depicted in Figure 4.1, to illustrate the aspects of classroom life that can reflect competition or cooperation. Only by focusing on the first four mirrors - physical organization, learning and task structure, teacher's instructional style, and patterns of communication - can one predict what the images in the fifth and sixth mirrors - student academic achievement and social behaviour - will look like.

Cooperative learning has been linked with academic gains (Slavin, 1987), improvement in self-esteem (Johnson and Johnson, 1989), and prosocial behaviour (Lloyd, Crowley, Kohler and Strain, 1988), among others; the research on cooperative learning is summarized by Slavin

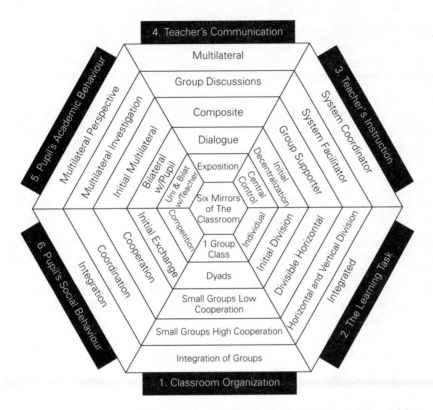

Figure 4.1 Six mirrors of the classroom (Source: Hertz-Lazarowitz and Miller, 1995)

(1991). Many studies have focused on the academic gains offered by cooperative learning, comparing planned group collaboration to the traditional, competitive learning that exists in many classrooms. Such research is essential in order to confirm that the cooperative, non-competitive context does not stunt learning, and may, in fact, facilitate it. For example, Klinger, Vaughn and Schumm (1998) examined whether collaborative learning has an effect on reading comprehension. In the cooperative condition, students were taught Collaborative Strategic Reading (Klinger and Vaughn, 1996; Palinscar and Brown, 1984), which provides instruction in reading comprehension strategies in a cooperative-learning context. Students in the competitive condition learned from their social studies texts, but the instruction was teacher-led and did not incorporate Collaborative Strategic Reading. Findings indicated that the students in the collaborative condition improved in reading comprehension more than their non-collaborative counterparts; both groups improved equally in understanding of content. Klinger, Vaughn and Schumm (1998) asserted that this form of learning is especially appropriate for classrooms that are heterogeneous in terms of the cultural origins or ability levels of the students.

Research into cooperative versus competitive learning has also addressed the influence of cooperation on children's peer relations and social skills. In one such study, Ashman and Gillies (1997) examined the effect of cooperative learning on peer interactions. Results indicated that students trained in cooperative learning skills exhibited more prosocial behaviour than their untrained counterparts. For instance, students trained in cooperative learning were more helpful and cooperative, and strove to include group members by using inclusive words such as 'we'. They actively helped each other by providing explanations and assistance. The cooperative-learning students also performed better than untrained students on a questionnaire assessing learning. Ashman and Gillies suggest that learning groups must be properly structured and monitored to foster effective cooperation.

Providing descriptive details of the interpersonal benefits of cooperative learning that have been documented in many empirical studies, Jordan and Le Métais (1997) observed a qualitative improvement in social skills after implementation of a 10-week cooperative learning programme. For instance, children agreed to work with students they disliked previously, and displayed more desire to interact with children outside their immediate peer group. Students who were identified as isolated at the start of the study showed improved relations with their teacher and peers. In learning groups, children welcomed the responsibility of group roles and focused on the task. In some instances, the group exerted a positive influence on disagreeable students.

There are indications that cooperative learning may facilitate the inclusion of children with learning, developmental, and behavioural exceptionalities who are integrated into a regular-education classroom. Putnam, Markovchick, Johnson and Johnson (1996) examined the effects of co-operative learning on peer acceptance in a study conducted with regular-education students and special-education students enrolled in the same classroom. The regular-education students rated their classmates' desirability as work partners at the beginning and end of the study. Results indicated that the regular-education students' peer ratings of their regular- and special-education classmates were more likely to improve if these students had been taught in the cooperative learning environment. The students in non-cooperative classes, however, tended to perceive their special-education classmates as undesirable, and this perception remained stable throughout the year.

Cooperation may facilitate the learning of conflict resolution skills, which may prove invaluable in the classroom and school playground. In Stevahn, Johnson, Johnson, and Real's (1996) study, children learned conflict-resolution skills in a cooperative setting. Results from this study suggested that students in the cooperative condition learned the conflict-resolution skills more effectively than their counterparts taught in more individualistic contexts. These students were also more constructive and positive, and retained more of the information learned.

Peer tutoring

Another major way of harnessing the effects of peer interaction on academic achievement is to enlist the help of competent peers in tutoring other children who need help. Greenwood, Carta and Kamps (1990) highlight some important requirements of peer tutoring in order for it to be effective: it must be highly structured, tutors must be trained, teachers must monitor and provide feedback, and students must know who their partner is, what material is to be taught, and how to correct their partner, prior to the tutoring session.

Accounts of children teaching other children can be traced back as early as the first century AD; the formal designation of peer tutoring as an educational technique dates back to the late eighteenth century (Goodlad and Hirst, 1990). Several theories have been used to explain the possible benefits of peer tutoring to the tutors (see Kennedy, 1990). According to role theory, children who assume the role of the teacher may develop empathy for their teachers; this could help improve classroom behaviour, unless, of course, they develop the belief that teachers are not really necessary. Cognitive-dissonance theory would lead to the expectation that the role of teacher is incompatible with the belief that one is incompetent in the subject matter to be taught; therefore, peer tutoring should modify the feeling that one is ineffective as a learner (Kennedy, 1990).

The benefits of peer tutoring have been confirmed in some recent research. For example, Gumpel and Frank (1999) examined the effects of peer tutoring on social interactions using a case-study method. Two 12-year-olds tutored socially rejected/isolated 5-year-old boys in social skills. The investigators postulated that, even though the tutoring focused on the younger children, there would be reciprocal positive effects. Results supported this hypothesis: there was a maintained increase in prosocial behaviour among all four boys. Indeed, benefits to the tutor as well as the tutee are emphasized throughout the literature.

Recognizing the potential benefit to the tutors, there have been many studies of peer tutoring by children with immature social skills, behaviour disorders, and learning problems. Most studies demonstrate positive effects, but sometimes the results are mixed or even negative (Kennedy, 1990). Hogan and Prater (1998) paired tutors with behaviour disorders and tutees with learning disabilities tutees and found that, during peer tutoring, there was improvement in the tutees' academic achievement and on-task behaviour. Disappointingly, there were no improvements in disruptive behaviour. Summarizing the extensive research on peer tutoring using children with special learning and emotional needs as tutors, Osguthope and Scruggs (1990) conclude that there is usually academic gain, but the evidence for social and emotional growth is inconsistent.

Putting learning first

The Committee for Economic Development is an influential research and policy organization of 250 business leaders and educators in the United States. As summarized in its mission statement, entitled *Putting Learning First: Governing and Managing Schools for High Achievement* (Committee for Economic Development, 1994), the committee's mission is to promote schools that will foster learning and achievement, that will provide a sound grounding in language arts and mathematics, and that will re-align their priorities away from social service and 'the social agenda' (ibid., p. 4). I hope that the research discussed in this chapter is ample evidence that one of the best ways of putting learning first is arranging for cooperative social interaction among children.

5 Defining social competence

Divergent concepts of social competence are introduced here. These derive from a wide range of theoretical roots ranging from behaviourism to the psychology of motivation to moral education. Consideration is given to the criteria for determining that a given behaviour of ability pertains to social competence. In addition to conceptual issues in measuring the peer relations of individuals, I also discuss techniques such as those developed by Cairns for identifying cliques and groups of peer associates within schools and classrooms, and their use in studying mechanisms of peer influence on the behaviours and attitudes of individuals.

In musing about the problems that plague researchers in defining friendship, Contarello and Volpata (1991) remembered Louis Armstrong's comments about the difficulty of defining jazz: 'If you have to define it, you cannot possibly understand it'. Indeed, the greatest jazz musicians have not been deterred from their work by the lack of a common definition of jazz. Neither has the absence of a clear definition of social competence stopped researchers from studying the phenomenon. However, it is often believed that much of the research lacks focus because there is no clear, common understanding of where social competence begins and ends. Deciding how to define 'social skill' and 'social competence' has consumed vast amounts of energy. Nevertheless, a commonly accepted definition has failed to emerge, which has been a source of agony for many scholars. Because there are so many different reasons for studying peer relations, which were reviewed in Chapter 2, it is not surprising that there are so many diverse concepts of what it means to be socially skilled or socially competent. A few extreme examples will illustrate the diversity in common usage of these terms. In reading the following examples, the reader is invited to think about whether each example is consistent with the way he or she would use the terms 'social skill' or 'social competence' in his or her own conversation or writing.

A feature story of the front page of the *Toronto Globe and Mail*, the leading Canadian newspaper, on 3 July 1999, bore the headline: 'Minding one's manners a matter of course: social skills'. The article was about a summer camp in Vancouver for primary-school children from 5 to 12 years old where children are taught in five days such aspects of etiquette as basic table manners, how to shake hands, how to answer the telephone politely, and holding doors for older people. The article concludes with a debate as to whether parents who send there children to this social-skills camp are admitting failure and abrogating their responsibilities as parents to teach social skills. The last paragraph in the newspaper story contains an admonition from a professional consultant that these skills have to be taught as part of everyday life, not as a special set one-week summer course.

Another example of a concept of social skills is provided by Stephens' work. Stephens (1992) derived his model of social skills by asking teachers what skills are needed by pupils in order to achieve social success in their classrooms. The resulting list included some skills that most people would consider 'social', such as greeting others in an appropriate way. However, not everyone would consider some of the other skills as social skills: bringing appropriate supplies such as pencils, respecting school property, etc. Nevertheless, Stephens' model does not lack internal consistency to the degree that functioning well as a pupil leads to successful social relationships, which include, in this case, relationships with adults as well as peers.

In a classic essay published in the *American Psychologist*, Zigler (1978) lambasted the community of researchers and theoreticians for their inability to agree on a definition of social competence. He saw this problem as a major impediment to both research and practice. There may be as many conceptual modes of social competence as there are theorists in the field (Dodge, 1985). Various definitions of social competence encompass a very wide range of behaviours and traits. The delineation of what should be considered socially competent is dictated by the theoretical model one chooses. The model might indicate, for example, that whatever leads to acceptance by peers should be considered competent, or whatever is effective (as defined by the theory) in social situations, or even whatever leads to successful functioning in the classroom (Anderson and Messick, 1974; Greenspan, 1981; Stephens, 1976; Zigler and Trickett, 1978). Despite the diversity of these proposed definitions, however, it is possible to isolate several main themes.

Trait vs situationally specific approaches

Definitions of social competence may be seen as adhering to either a trait or a situationally specific perspective. Trait approaches assume, at least implicitly, that a socially competent person (as defined by inherent personality characteristics) will be equally competent in all social situations. This mirrors a classic debate in psychology as to whether enough human behaviour is similar across situations to warrant the use of such concepts as 'personality' (Mischel, 1983). Greenspan (1981) outlines two major trait approaches, the *bag of virtues strategy*, and the *factorial strategy*. In the bag of virtues strategy, all possible behaviours that the theorist considers as desirable are included, making it difficult to make any distinction between social and other forms of competence (such as physical or intellectual competence). The factorial strategy delimits a number of behavioural dimensions that relate more strictly to interpersonal behaviour.

Theorists who emphasize the situational specificity of social competence suggest the need to take into account the extent to which children's ability to function in socially appropriate ways is contingent on specific contexts. Greenspan (1981), in discussing the necessity for a more situation-specific model of social competence, suggests that the anxiety experienced in a situation may inhibit appropriate social behaviour more than the general lack of knowing what to do. An example of this is the fact that many children who are shy and isolated at school seem to have a surprisingly sound network of interpersonal relationships at home (Daniels-Beirness and Leshono, 1988). Articulating a situationally specific definition of social competence, Hargie defines social skills as 'a set of goal-directed, situationally-appropriate social behaviours' (1986, p. 12). According to both trait and situationally specific perspectives, children must develop a heightened sensitivity to subtle verbal expressions and non-verbal behaviour in order to learn the rules that govern a wide range of social settings.

A related distinction is whether individuals or behaviours should be considered competent and incompetent. Children's behaviours, such as approaching a group of peers at play, or personal characteristics, such as their temperament or knowledge of social situations, are seen by some as prime determinants of social competence. In contrast, *molecular models*, which stress behavioural components of social competence, primarily view social skills as discrete observable behavioural units. *Trait models* define social skills as response predispositions that remain stable across situations and underlie behaviour. Both, however, have their limitations. Trait models are sometimes seen as poorly defined and fail to take into account a great deal of research indicating that human behaviour varies enormously from situation to situation. Molecular models, in contrast, are often not complete enough to enable one to determine which discrete units of behaviour and which situations to observe when studying social competence.

Social competence vs conformity

Many definitions of social competence have emphasized personal needs and goals. From this perspective, social competence hinges on fulfilling one's own needs for affiliation or social support. Parks (1985), incorporating personal goals into his model, defines social competence as 'the degree to which individuals have satisfied their goals in a given social situation without jeopardizing their ... opportunity to pursue other subjectively more important goals'. Another definition of social competence that stresses an individual's goals is that stated by Ford (1982). According to Ford, social competence may be defined as 'the attainment of relevant social goals in specified social contexts, using appropriate means and resulting in positive developmental outcomes'.

Contrary to these theorists' conceptions of social competence, many researchers base their concepts of social competence on the opinions or reactions of peers. For example, Libet and Lewinsohn (1973) defined social skills as the ability to emit behaviours that are reinforced by others and to refrain from emitting behaviours that are punished by the group. Bellack and Hersen (1979) also define social skills as being normative or socially sanctioned. This definition is limited in that it cannot accommodate the increasing emphasis on individual differences in children's social goals (Parkhurst and Asher, 1992). Basing one's notion of social competence entirely on the reactions of groups may also be seen as empowering deviant sub-groups to define behaviours or persons as socially competent that the majority would consider anti-social.

Social vs general competence

At first glance it seems odd that many scholars include physical ability, motor coordination, and abstract reasoning skills in their models, because these features seem so disconnected from interpersonal relationships. However, as will be illustrated in the tables to appear later in this chapter, these seemingly far-flung characteristics often have a great deal to do with adjustment to society and acceptance by peers. Some theorists attempt to solve this problem by outlining a specific relationship between social competence and general (or personal) competence; usually social competence is considered a subset of general competence. In particular, scholars studying competence as a protective factor in overcoming the effects of stress emphasize the social and non-social aspects of competence in achieving psychological well-being (e.g. Garmezy, 1989; Rutter, 1979).

Sometimes, the distinction between general and social competence is accomplished by using the terms 'competence' and 'competency' in different ways, or by differentiating between 'competence' and 'skill'. Waters and Sroufe (1983) propose that competence refers to 'a general ability to generate and coordinate flexible adaptive responses to demands and to generate and capitalize on opportunities', whereas competency would refer to specific skills. Many theorists consider social competence as larger than, and encompassing, social skills (Gresham 1986). In Gresham's model, social competence has two elements: social skills and adaptive behaviour. Social skills include appropriate play behaviour and cooperativeness, expression of feelings, positive self-concept, and conversational skills. Adaptive behaviour includes language development, academic functioning, physical development, and self-care skills such as grooming.

McFall (1982) refers to social skills as specific behaviours performed well, whereas social competence is an evaluative term based on judgements by others of the adequacy of task performance. Similar to McFall's model, Hops and Finch (1985) use the higher-order concept of social competence to refer to both social and non-social competence. As a reminder of the importance of non-social skills in achieving peer acceptance, they cite research showing that motor skills, such as the ability to throw a ball well, are among the leading predictors of acceptance in boys' groups.

Social competence as outcome or process

In some models, social competence is inferred from the outcome of specific behaviours, in terms of whether they lead to peer acceptance or successful interpersonal relationships. In other models, behaviours as well as perceptual or cognitive processes are considered competent in their own right.

Many theorists treat overt behaviours as but the tip of a large iceberg. Theorists in the cognitive domain view social behaviour as driven and guided by crucial perceptual and cognitive processes (e.g. Trower, Bryant and Argyle, 1978). Motivational or affective 'structures' are seen as underlying both overt behaviours and cognitive processes. Strayer states that social competence must be viewed as 'a dynamic system of knowledge and value that both emerges from and structures the child's perceptions, representations and actions in the social world' (1989. p. 151).

Social competence as capacity or as demonstrated knowledge

Definitions and models of social competence differ with regard to whether social competence should be seen as the theoretical capacity or ability of an individual to behave in a socially competent manner, or the individual's actual performance in a social situation. One solution is to propose that social competence or social skills refer to abstract ability in social situations, or in handling social situations adequately, whether or not one actually uses these abilities. In most cases this distinction is not very important because, if an individual possesses this capacity, he or she will likely proceed to behave in a competent manner. Nevertheless, it is important to make a distinction between individuals who are capable of initiating social contact but choose not to do so and those who experience distress because of their social isolation and inability to remedy it. Despite the inherent value of social contact in human society, being isolated may constitute no problem if that is a person's choice, made on the basis of personal preference rather than the inability to form relationships, and if the isolation does not cause distress to the individual.

Social competence as dependent on development stage

The seminal work of Jean Piaget illustrated that children's ideas about their social worlds change radically as they proceed through different stages of development. From that standpoint, it becomes difficult to accept a notion of competence that is composed of discrete skills, few of which would be relevant across developmental levels. Some 'skills' that may be assets at certain levels of development can become liabilities at other stages. For example, rote imitation of peers' play behaviour, though important in achieving interpersonal contact in early childhood (Nadel and Butterworth, 1999), may become a liability in achieving social relations at later stages, as in early adolescence when that 'skill' could lead to imitating the risky or anti-social behaviours at school. Nevertheless, there are examples of skills that have potential for application across developmental levels. Going over and joining in a game in an appropriate way may be competent both for very young children and adults, even if its importance is not equal across ages.

Social competence as relational competence

Schneider proposed an emphasis on relationships in his definition of social competence as 'the ability to implement developmentally-appropriate social behaviours that enhance one's interpersonal relationships without causing harm to anyone' (1993, p. 19). The difference between this definition and those based on peer acceptance and reinforcement by peers is little more than a difference in nuance. Some social behaviours, such as the ability to greet others in an appropriate, friendly way, are common to both close and superficial relationships. Other behaviours, such as disclosing one's private experiences in an appropriate way, at the right time, and in relationships where self-disclosure is accepted and wanted, could be overlooked in applying definitions of social competence built on the unelaborated contingencies of peer acceptance or reinforcement.

The social competence of groups

It is an undeniable fact that social competence, or lack of it, is treated as a characteristic of individuals in the overwhelming preponderance of studies in the recent literature. Nevertheless, the original purpose of the technique was first and foremost to study the structure of groups, and, then, to repair the structure if it leads to contact. Groups can be considered socially competent or incompetent depending on the values that cement them and the behaviours they hold in high esteem.

The best-known contemporary technique for studying patterns of associations within groups was developed by Robert Cairns and his colleagues

(Cairns and Cairns, 1994). They construct a 'social map' of the group by asking children to indicate which peers they associate with most frequently, and then determining in interviews with children the reputations each group has in its school or community. This research has revealed that the distinct groups are very easy to identify; the children often refer to them by names such as 'jocks', 'nerds' and 'preppies' (for readers unfamiliar with North American slang, those terms refer to, more or less, athletically inclined people, bookish people, and young followers of fashion, respectively); Hargreave's (1967) classic studies of social relations in Lumley, an urban, industrial area identified as overcrowded and prone to social problems, revealed that very similar groupings occur in schools in the United Kingdom. Some of the groups may have core values that emphasize defiance of authority through the use of aggression or that deprecate educational aspirations. Hargreave provided considerable detail of the norms and functions of the 'delinquent group' at Lumley Secondary School in the 1960s. Some anti-social behaviours were encouraged by the group, such as stealing expensive articles. However, other infractions were frowned on, especially malicious damage to property. As might be expected, the members of the delinquent group had very strained relations with the school authorities. However, their group membership served to insulate them against attacks by other pupils.

The person-group similarity model (Stormshak et al., 1999) considers the interface between the characteristics of individuals and those of the peers in their immediate groups. In a study conducted with an enormous sample (2,895) of 6-year-olds in the United States, Stormshak et al. tested the predictive strength of the person-group similarity model. They found some support for the model, because the acceptability of aggressive and shy, withdrawn behaviours increased with the number of behaviour problems found in the children's school classrooms.

What social competence looks like: behaviours associated with social competence and incompetence

All of the conceptualizations of social competence are of interest from a theoretical standpoint and in clarifying the values of scholars. However, the theoretical models of social competence reviewed in this chapter have not been applied equally to research. Of all the elements of all the definitions, by far the most research has been conducted to find out exactly which behaviours or features lead to acceptance and rejection by the peer group, assuming that peer acceptance is what determines social competence.

Table 5.1 depicts the results of the major studies of the characteristics of popular children. It is obvious that a wide array of behaviours and personal characteristics can lead to being accepted or rejected in children's peer groups. Some of these features are not aspects of social behaviour, such as

Table 5.1 Personal and behavioural characteristics of popular children

Author(s)	Characteristic	Sample Gender	Sample Age (years)
Studies conducted within North America			
Tuddenham (1951)	Athletic ability Physically attractive Friendly	M/F	6, 8, 10
Dion and Berscheid (1974)	Physically attractive	M/F	4–6
Buchanan, Blankenbaker and Cotton (1976)	Academically outstanding Athletic ability	M/F	9–11
Lerner and Lerner (1977)	Physically attractive	M/F	9–12
Vosk, Forehand, Parker and Rickard (1982)	Spends time on-task Academically successful	M/F	8–9
Coie and Kupersmidt (1983)	Engages in active social interaction Non-aggressive	M	9
Dodge (1983)	Good leader Cooperative play Physically attractive Engages in social conversation	M/F	7–8
Dodge, Schlundt, Schocken and Delugach (1983)	Competent entry behaviours into peer group	M/F	5, 7–8
Ladd (1983)	Cooperative play Engages in social conversation Less onlooking behaviours Spends time in social interaction with peers	M/F	6–11
Putallaz (1983)	Able to perceive the group's ongoing activity Attempts to fit in	M	6
Vaughn and Langlois (1983)	Physically attractive	M/F	4–5
Hops and Finch (1985)	Proficient motor skills	M/F	3–6
Wright, Giammarino and Parad (1986)	Prosocial behaviours (initiates contact, helpful, communicates effectively, displays interest in activities)	M	11
Krantz (1987)	*Female:* Physically attractive	M/F	5
Coie and Dodge (1988)	Prosocial Cooperative Good leader Socially skilful	M	6–8

	Few academic problems Non-aggressive		
Dubow and Cappas (1988)	Highly adjusted Low behaviour problems	M/F	8–10
Gelb and Jacobson (1988)	Uses group-oriented statements during group entry	M	9
Boivin and Begin (1989)	High self-esteem	M/F	8–9
Dodge, Coie, Petit and Price (1990)	Engages in social conversation Assertive behaviours Successful group entry More dyadic play (play involving another person) Less group play Displays happy, positive affect during interaction	M	6–8
Nowicki and Duke (1992)	Good at understanding non-verbal emotional information in faces and tones in voice	M/F	6–10
Adams and Roopnarine (1994)	Facially attractive Positively reinforces others Socially skilled Purposive Confident in social interactions Viewed as initiator Verbally fluent Self-assertive Energetic Little aggressive behaviour	M/F	4,9 & 12
Mendelson, Aboud and Lanthier (1994)	Generates many responses to social problems	M/F	5
Wentzel and Asher (1995)	Helpful to others Academically successful	M/F	11–13
Smith, Winningham and Haro (1999)	Social problem-solving skills	M/F African American children	3–4

Studies conducted outside North America

Spence (1987) Australia	Social-cognition skills (affective role taking and decoding of emotion from facial expression) Physically attractive	M/F	3–5

Table 5.1 Continued

Author(s)	Characteristic	Sample Gender	Age (years)
Studies conducted outside North America			
Chen, Rubin and Sun (1992) People's Republic of China	Sociability-leadership Shyness-sensitivity	M/F	7–10
Cillessen, van IJzendoorn, van Lieshout and Hartup (1992) Netherlands	Cooperative	M	5–7
Schaughency, Vannatta, Langhinrichsen, Ially and Seeley (1992) Argentina	Negatively correlated with attention problems, sluggish tempo and language-processing difficulties	M/F	7–10
Dekovic and Gerris (1994) The Netherlands	Helpful Cooperative Sympathetic Sensitive towards peers Takes others' perspective Understands the nature of interpersonal relationships Aware of others' needs Empathic towards a child in distress Maturity in reasoning about social world	M/F	6, 8, 10
Erwin (1994) England	Provides effective solutions to hypothetical social dilemmas Involved in more peer interactions Positive interaction style Gives reinforcement to peers	M/F	5–6
Hortacsu (1994) Turkey	Academically successful	M/F	10

Bonn and Kruger (1996) South Africa	Provides suggestions and guidance in difficult situations Explorative Engages in social conversation with peers Engages in role/pretend play and in organized games Initiates positive interactions (affectionate, caring and share) More compliant to peer's requests	M/F	8–12
Attili, Vermigli and Schneider (1997) Italy	Prosocial	M/F	7–8
Tassi and Schneider (1997) Italy	Task-oriented competitiveness (non-hostile competition with the goal of improving one's performance)	M/F	8–9

one's physical attractiveness or athletic ability. Within the realm of social behaviours, peer-directed aggression and social withdrawal have been studied most frequently as indicators of social incompetence.

Aggression as an obstacle to peer acceptance

Although Table 5.2 shows quite clearly that, although children can be rejected by their peers for a myriad of reasons, aggression is by far the most frequent. Detailed studies have indicated that at least half of the children who are rejected are aggressive (Cillessen, IJzendoorn, van Lieshout and Hartup, 1992; French, 1988). Ledingham (1999) cautions that, because there is so much overlap between peer rejection and aggression, many of the longitudinal studies that purport to investigate the consequences of peer rejection may actually be portraying the effects of aggression. She speculates that aggression may be a more potent predictor of later maladjustment than is rejection by peers. There is some evidence for her contentions. Several careful studies have been conducted in order to distinguish the consequences of being rejected by peers, being aggressive, and being both. Cillessen, IJzendoorn, van Lieshout and Hartup's (1992) longitudinal data collected in the Netherlands showed that children who are both rejected and aggressive were much more likely than non-aggressive rejected children to be rejected by peers again at the time of follow-up. Longitudinal studies conducted in the Southern United States by Coie, Terry, Zabriski and Lochman (1995)

Table 5.2 Personal and behavioural characteristics associated with rejection by peers

Author(s)	Characteristic	Sample Gender	Age (years)
Studies conducted within North America			
Green, Vosk, Forehand and Beck (1981)	Inattentive-passive Hyperactive Poor academic achievement	M/F	8
Dodge, Coie and Brakke (1982)	Peer-directed aggressive acts Low academic performance Engages in inappropriate solitary activity (clowning, daydreaming, walking aimlessly) Approaches peers during class time	M/F	8–10
Rubin, Daniels-Beirness and Hayvren (1982)	Agonistic behaviour (rough and tumble play, negative peer interchanges) Aggressive, hostile or hyperactive behaviours Agonistic solutions to social dilemmas	M/F	3–5
Coie and Kupersmidt (1983)	Displays solitary inappropriate behaviour Engages in less parallel play (participant engages in independent/similar activity in the vicinity of peers) Disruptive Start fights	M	9
Dodge (1983)	Less attractive Poor leader Inappropriate behaviours (inappropriate play, hostile verbalizations, exclusions of peers, hitting peers) Less social conversation Less cooperative play Aggressive Rough and tumble play	M	7–8

Dodge, Schlundt, Schocken and Delugach (1983)	Disruptive entry behaviours into peer group Negative responses to statements initiated by the peer host	M/F	5 & 7
Ladd (1983)	Aversive exchanges with peers Engages in unoccupied behaviour (participant is alone at a considerable distance from peers and appears to be doing nothing), parallel play, onlooking behaviours Less helpful and cooperative Less time participating in prococial or relationship-enhancing interactions (cooperative play and social conversation)	M/F	6–11
Carlson, Lahey and Neeper (1984)	Aggressive Disruptive Irritable Less helpful Changes subject during interaction Less knowledgeable about joining group activities Less likely to share Dishonest Tends not to participate Unable to wait turn Less adept at explaining things to others	M/F	7 & 10
Asher and Wheeler (1985)	Loneliness	M/F	8–11
Cantrell and Prinz (1985)	Physically aggressive Verbally aggressive Disruptive Inattentive Less helpful and cooperative Restless Bossy Unhappy Immature Socially isolated Over-sensitive Nervous Inattentive Over-active	M/F	8–11

Table 5.2 Continued

Author(s)	Characteristic	Sample Gender	Age (years)
Burleson, Applegate, Burke, Clark, Delia and Kline (1986)	Underdeveloped communication skills	M/F	6 & 8
Feldman and Dodge (1987)	*Male:* Displays deviant patterns of processing social information Generates fewer competent responses in problem situations Generates aggressive responses in problem situations *Female:* Generates a greater proportion of passive responses	M/F	6,8 & 10
Coie and Dodge (1988)	Less helpful and cooperative Aggressive Disruptive Academic difficulty Engages in solitary behaviours Off-task during class time	M	6–9
Dubow and Cappas (1988)	Academic difficulty Higher degree of behaviour problems Adjustment problems	M/F	8–10
Rubin, Hymel, Lemare and Rowden (1989)	Aggressive Disruptive Sensitive isolated (withdrawal) Perceived by peers as preferring to play alone	M/F	9
Dodge, Coie, Petit and Price (1990)	High rates of solitary focused behaviour Reactive aggression Instrumental aggression Few positive social interactions with peers (cooperative play, social conversation or leadership behaviour)	M	6 & 8

French (1990)	Socially withdrawn	F	8–10
	Anxious		
	Academic difficulty		
	Low academic task		
	orientation		
	Behaviour disorders		
	Low self-control		
	Hostile isolation		
Johnstone, Frame and	Lower academic ability	M/F	7–10
Bouman (1992)			
Rubin, Chen and Hymel	Aggressive	M/F	11
(1993)			
Wentzel and Asher (1995)	Low self-assurance	M/F	11–12
	Start fights		
	Low academic ability		
	Disinterest in schoolwork		
	Not independent		
	Impulsive learner		
	Inconsiderate		
	Not compliant		
	Displays indesirable forms		
	of classroom behaviours		
Crick, Casas and Mosher	Relational aggression	M/F	4–6
(1997)	Overt aggression		
Parke, O'Neil, Spitzer	Less prosocial	M/F	5–7
Isley, Welsh, Wang, Lee	Physically aggressive		
Strand and Cupp (1997)	Verbally aggressive		
	Disruptive		
Smith, Winningham and	Poor cognitive-language	M/F	3–4
Haro (1999)	skills	African American	
		children	

Studies conducted outside North America

Spence (1987)	Behaviour problems	M/F	3–5
Australia	(acting-out)		
Chen, Rubin and Sun (1992)	Aggressive-disruptive	M/F	7–10
Peoples' Republic of China	behaviour		
and Canada			
Cillessen, van IJzendoorn,	Aggressive	M	5–7
van Lieshout and Hartup (1992)	Impulsive		
The Netherlands	Disruptive		
	Dishonest		
	Hypersensitive		
	Non-cooperative		
	Shy		

Table 5.2 Continued

Author(s)	Characteristic	Sample Gender	Age (years)
Schaughency, Vannatta, Langhinrichsen, Lally and Seeley (1992) Argentina	Learning difficulty (linguistic information processing deficit) Inattentive Sluggish tempo	M/F	7–10
Dekovic and Gerris (1994) The Netherlands	Chooses own needs over needs of others	M/F	6–11
Hortacsu (1994) Turkey	Low academic achievement	M/F	9
Chen, Rubin and Li (1995) People's Republic of China	Aggressive	M/F	7–10
Bonn and Krueger (1996) South Africa	Aggressive Disruptive Rule violator Parallel and solitary play Immature forms of play Oppositional Ignores others Refuses to comply with others requests	M/F	8–12
Attili, Vermigli and Schneider (1997) Italy	Aggressive Less cooperative Uninvolved in social interactions	M/F	7–8
Tassi and Schneider (1997) Italy	Other-directed competitiveness (competition where the goal is to show that one is better than others)	M/F	8–9
von Salisch and Uhlendorff (1998) Germany	Angry, aggressive behaviour	M/F	8–14

and by Kupersmidt and Coie (1990) indicated that aggression was more closely associated with subsequent juvenile delinquency than was rejection. It remains possible, of course, that peer rejection is a better predictor of other outcomes that were not assessed in those and similar studies.

The unambiguous findings that aggression is the leading correlate of peer rejection do not mean at all that every aggressive child is rejected by all or most of his or her peers. If that happened, the aggression might in fact diminish because it would be discouraged by the peer group. However, the general rejection of aggressive classmates by most children often propels them toward cultivating associations with cliques of anti-social peers who value both their company and their aggression (Cairns and Cairns, 1994).

One limitation of previous studies in this area is their almost exclusive focus on overt aggression. The research programme of Crick and her colleagues has demonstrated the importance of studying relational aggression along with the overt forms of aggressive behaviour (e.g. physical, verbal aggression) that have traditionally been the subject of investigations in this area. Relational aggression consists of behaviours such as threatening to terminate a friendship in order to attain a goal, or excluding peers from activities in order to get back at them (Crick, Bigbee and Howes, 1996). Grotpeter and Crick (1996) compared the friendships of relationally aggressive (i.e. inflicting harm through the manipulation of others' peer relationships, e.g. spreading rumours), overtly aggressive (physical or verbal aggression) and non-aggressive children. Grotpeter and Crick reported that the friendships of relationally aggressive children included more instances of relational aggression and more frequent intimate exchanges than those of other children, whereas those of overtly aggressive pupils involved less intimacy and a greater frequency of overtly aggressive acts against other peers. The friendships of aggressive and non-aggressive students were similar in many respects, including comparable degrees of conflict, effective conflict resolution, caring and validation, help, and companionship. Tomada and Schneider (1997), in a study conducted in Tuscany, confirmed that relational aggression was frequent among Italian girls in middle childhood. They found that boys used both overt and relational aggression, indicating that relational aggression should not be considered the female form of aggression. Nevertheless, they insisted that it is important to study relational as well as overt aggression, because if researchers include only overt aggression in their studies, they will often conclude that females are not aggressive. Recent research with 7–8-year-old children in Minsk, Belarus confirms that overt aggression occurs almost exclusively among boys, whereas verbal and relational forms of aggressions were far more frequent among girls (Alexandrovna, 1999). These cross-cultural extensions of the work of Crick and her colleagues indicate the potential importance of studying relational aggression in various cultures, because cultural prohibitions against self-expression by females may differ, as may cultural condoning of overt aggression by males. Little is known about the friendships of relationally aggressive children and youth in most cultures, nor about the role of friendship in sustaining this form of aggression.

Bullying is a particularly vicious subcategory of aggression that has aroused particular concern around the world. Smith et al. (1999) published an interesting compendium of research on bullying in 15 European countries, Canada, the United States, Japan, Australia, New Zealand, and the developing world. As noted by Slee (1999), an Australian researcher, people in many countries often believe for a while that bullying is only a problem elsewhere, only to be awakened by a shocking and saddening incident of bullying close to home. Bullying is aggression directed repeatedly and specifically towards a specific victim who is, in most cases, known to be weaker than the bully. Bullies exploit their stronger status to prove their own strength or to exact possessions from the victim (Olweus, 1999; Smith et al., 1999). Questionnaire responses from around the world indicate than anywhere from approximately 5 to over 40 per cent of children report that they have been bullied (Björkqvist and Osterman, 1999; Fonzi et al., 1999). More convincing are direct observation studies of children's playgrounds such as those by Pepler and her colleagues in Toronto, who observed, on the average, an incident of bullying every 7 minutes (Craig and Pepler, 1997). Bullies are often rejected, on the whole, by their peers (Coie, Dodge and Kupersmidt, 1990; Slee, 1999) but may still abuse victims in an attempt to cultivate reputations of strength. Sometimes, their bullying may make them solidly popular within a minority subgroup of antisocial peers, even if they are despised and feared by most others (Boulton and Smith 1994; Slee, 1999). Sutton, Smith, and Swettenham (1999) observed that, in contrast to the popular stereotype, many bullies are not socially unsophisticated individuals. Many bullies need and have strong understanding of others and their thinking, without which they would be less efficient at selecting vulnerable victims and manipulating people. Thus, bullying is surely anti-social, but may not be indicative of social incompetence. In retort, Crick and Dodge (1999) cited studies showing that bullies are deficient in many basic social-cognitive processes.

Shyness and social competence

The recent distinction among subtypes of shyness/withdrawal is important in light of definitions of social competence that are based on the fulfilment of one's own social goals. Some shy individuals may be 'loners' who are truly happiest on their own and feel no anxiety about the lack of company. According to goal-driven definitions of social competence, those persons cannot be considered incompetent, because they are, in essence, capable of meeting their own goals. However, a shy person who is stymied by his or her shyness, who harbours the elusive personal goal of being accepted and experiences anxiety because that goal is not attained, would logically be considered to be socially incompetent.

For many years, shyness or social withdrawal was not viewed as particularly maladaptive and did not appear linked to later problems (Kohlberg, LaCrosse and Ricks, 1972; Parker and Asher, 1992). However, recent studies suggest that social withdrawal may in fact be a risk factor in children's development, in addition to causing the anxiety and unhappiness probably felt by many withdrawn children. Progress in the study of social withdrawal is impeded by conceptual and measurement problems. The term 'withdrawal' is used interchangeably with such descriptors as isolation, inhibition, solitude, reticence, shyness, neglect, unsociable, avoidant, and self-conscious. It is unclear whether social withdrawal is a unidimensional or multidimensional construct, that is, whether children identified as exhibiting socially withdrawn behaviour are a homogeneous or heterogeneous group. References to subtypes such as active and passive shyness (Litwinski, 1950), and fearful and self-conscious shyness (Buss, 1985), have emerged that have implications for the study of childhood shyness. Asendorpf (1986) proposed a definition for situational shyness as an ambivalent affective state of approach-avoidance conflict during social encounters that leads to a mixture of wary and sociable behaviour. According to Asendorpf, this distinguishes between shy children who want to interact but are anxious, and introverted children who have little interest in social interaction.

Rubin (1993) suggested that some forms of withdrawal, while normal at some ages, may be problematic at other ages. Although there is little consistency in the names of the subtypes used by various authors, there are some commonalities in their properties. *Fearful shyness* (Buss, 1985) or unfamiliar-inhibited shyness (Asendorpf, 1986) is characterized by an early onset during the toddler years, a possible biological pre-disposition towards inhibited behaviour; social wariness especially in novel, unfamiliar situations; and a propensity to withdraw from the peer group to engage in solitary, passive play. *Self-conscious shyness* (Buss, 1985) or social evaluative inhibition (Asendorpf, 1986) typically emerges between 4 to 6 years when the child acquires cognitive awareness of the self as a social object, and is accompanied by social anxiety.

The potential risk posed by shyness and withdrawal was not evident in early longitudinal studies for several reasons. First of all, the subtypes of social withdrawal discussed above were not differentiated. Second, most of the major studies were limited to outcomes that were not likely to follow a childhood characterized by shyness — outcomes such as delinquency, discharge from military service, or school dropout, rather than outcomes such as depression or unhappiness that would relate more logically to a history of shyness (Parker and Asher, 1992). In recent years, however, several more focused studies have emerged, and have demonstrated consistently that shy, isolated, anxious youngsters are more likely to experience feelings of loneliness, depression, and self-deprecation several years after the shy/withdrawn behaviours were first observed by researchers (Hoza, Molina, Bukowski, and Sippola, 1995; Hymel, Rubin, Rowden and LeMare, 1990; Renshaw and Brown, 1993; Rubin *et al.*, 1995). In interpreting longitudinal data on the consequences of social withdrawal in childhood, it is important to consider the age at which both the withdrawal and its subsequent outcomes are assessed. Shy behaviour in young children may not be stable, and may not even be noticed by other children. However, by early adolescence, peers are very aware of shy youngsters in their midst, and often subject them to ostracism (Hodgens and McCoy 1989; Younger, Gentile and Burgess, 1993).

Models of social competence: a brief guide for the perplexed

There have been several valiant attempts at integrating all the diverse behaviours and abilities that have been subsumed under the rubrics of social skills or social competence; Gresham's (1986) model, mentioned earlier in this chapter, is perhaps the best-known effort of this kind. However, there still is no consistency in authors' use of the terms 'social competence' and 'social skill', which is not surprising. The definition one favours depends on the reasons for one's interest in studying peer relations. Those who work with pre-delinquent youth, for example, might identify with a model of social competence that emphasizes conformity to the norms of society. They might find little logic in defining social competence in terms of the social goals of the anti-social participants in their studies or intervention programmes. On the other hand, someone interested in social competence as a means of achieving happiness in life would probably resist a definition of social competence based on conformity, and would be keenly appreciative of a definition based on individual aspirations. Given this diversity in perspectives, the only viable means of facilitating communication among users of these concepts is to ask that they accompany the expressions 'social competence' or 'social skill' by some explanation of their usage of the terms.

6   Techniques for assessing children's peer relations

This chapter contains descriptions of the major tools used to assess social competence: sociometrics, direct observation, reports by adults and self-reports by children. The purposes, advantages and disadvantages of each are considered. Recent innovations have enabled researchers to probe social interactions that occur in places previously considered out of reach.

There is no perfect way of gathering information about children's peer relations, which is not to say that the methods available are equally good. Amazingly, virtually all of the tools used in present-day peer-relations research were known in Moreno's time and were described and debated before 1950 in the journal called *Sociometry*. Of course, very substantial technical improvements have been made to each method in the intervening half century. The major techniques are peer reports or sociometrics, direct observation of children's social interaction in a variety of settings, reports by adults who know the children well and self-ratings by the participants in the research.

Sorting out the validity and usefulness of the measures can be a confusing and frustrating exercise, but one that must be undertaken whenever one tries to compare different studies in the field, design a new study, or interpret a study one is reading. This task is made more trying by the fact that the different sources of information – peers, teachers, parents, observers and participants – will, more often than not, provide somewhat discrepant information about the same children. As will be illustrated by a few examples in the following paragraphs, even a slight change in the wording of a question may affect the results. One fundamental principle of research design must always be remembered: a study is no better than its measures, however brilliant the underlying theory.

There are several ways of deciding among the potentially useful instruments for the assessment of children's peer relations. One way is to assign a premium to one of the methods on the basis of its nature. Following a tradition established by Moreno, information provided by peers is often considered more valuable than any other method. Peers are assumed to be in the best position to evaluate the relationship behaviours of others from the perspective of potential relationship partners. Although Moreno's dedication to sociometrics pervaded his career and his writings, he did toy with all of the other methods – direct observation, reports from informed persons in the social network and self reports – at different points in his career. He found some correspondence between these methods and sociometrics, but also many appreciable differences and concluded that observations and the other methods provided superficial information that would not reveal the 'deep structure' of a social group. The 'alternative' or 'supplementary' methods could be useful, however, in circumstances where the 'real test' (sociometrics) could not be administered (Moreno, 1960).

This premium on sociometrics has survived to the present day in many circles. However, some investigators trained in behavioural psychology place a premium on direct observation because of its inherent nature. When the social interaction being described occurs in front of one's own eyes, there is no denying that it happened. Given sufficient time and appropriate equipment, the event can also be described in as detailed a manner as is prescribed by the researcher, who can also direct the attention of the observer towards a particular aspect of the social interaction.

Moreno (1953; 1960) is also responsible at least in spirit for another way of deciding among the competing measures of social competence by introducing the distinction between 'descriptive sociometry' and 'diagnostic sociometry'. This distinction can be taken a bit further to justify learning about the structure of a group, including the identities of the individuals it rejects and who may be in need of assistance, by means of sociometrics. The other methods, including but not limited to direct observation, are used to complement the sociometrics by permitting a greater understanding of the processes associated with the acceptance and rejection of individuals. Finally, in order to understand these processes best, one has to do something to try to improve them, perhaps by changing the behaviour of an individual who is rejected by his or her peers:

> We cannot adequately comprehend the central direction of an individual in his development either through observation, for instance, a child, through watching its most spontaneous expression, its play life, or through partnership [observing as a group participant in order to learn about the individual's relationship style]. We must make him an experimenter.
>
> (Moreno, 1960, p. 101)

A third basis for deciding among the measures of children's peer relations is to consider the purpose of the study being planned or interpreted. Some measures may be best in particular situations and not in others. Teachers' and peers' ratings, for example, might be particularly useful in a study of bullying behaviour at school. In that situation, one might not want to go to the expense of observing children's play directly, because one might observe for weeks and still miss the few but psychologically important incidents of bullying that occurred in the school toilets or on the way home from school.

Advances in research methodology provide yet another perspective useful in gauging the value of the different measures, one that was introduced to methodologists in the 1950s (Campbell and Fiske, 1959), but is featured more prominently in studies appearing since 1980. The multi-method approach assumes that each method available for studying a particular social or psychological process is of some value, but that each is also hampered by some bias or error in measurement. Therefore, it is important to measure the same processes by several measures. In a study of children's social behaviour at school, for instance, one might use teacher ratings, peer ratings and direct observations. Hopefully, each of the measures would provide similar information about how disruptive, friendly and cooperative each of the pupils is. Measurement problems would be evident, on the other hand, if the same pupils were rated positively by teachers, for instance, on all of the traits or characteristics being studied, but not rated positively on any of them by other pupils. That might happen if the pupil is particularly proficient at academic subjects, which might please the teacher so much that it affects all aspects of his or her perception of the pupil.

If the different methods provide the same information about individuals, this bolsters confidence that the study is authoritative in explaining the process it seeks to explicate. Often, however, the different measures will lead to contradictory conclusions. A child who seems to be shy according to his or her peers may seem less so in data obtained from teachers. In that situation, frustrating as it can be, there may still be an important story to tell, perhaps that the child's 'shyness' is not evident in all situations, but only during social play outside of the classroom where the teacher is less directly involved.

The 'real test'

Sociometry has always been based on the assumption that human beings cannot like or love each other equally, even if some might wish that they do, should or could. Therefore, studying patterns of preferences among the companions of children or adults is assumed to be a useful study of a process that is universal and natural. Both children and adults are assumed to be conscious of their preferences for play and work companions, even if they are not conscious of the reasons for their preferences (Northway, 1967). In other words, by asking children or adults to indicate which schoolmates or workmates they prefer to associate with, researchers are not creating patterns of acceptance or rejection, like or dislike. They are only measuring patterns that already exist within play or work groups. It is important to remember that sociometric methods cannot measure a group's collective opinion about any individual, but can only provide a global picture about how well that individual is liked by each of his or her associates (ibid.). Indeed, some children, called 'controversial', can be liked by many and also disliked by many.

Within most children's peer groups, some children are popular or well liked by most of the other children, whereas other children are unpopular or disliked by their peers. During the last two decades, innovative classification systems developed by Coie, Dodge and Coppotelli (1982) and by Newcomb and Bukowski (1983) have made it possible to develop a more fine-grained identification of children's social status among their peers and to assess more accurately the consequences of rejection and acceptance. These classification systems stem primarily from Peery's (1979) taxonomic model, which is built upon the distinct dimensions of *social preference* and *social impact*. Social preference refers to the extent to which children are liked or disliked by their peers. Social impact represents how noticeable in a group the child is or by how the group is influenced by the presence or absence of the child. Of course, a child can be noticeable because others either value or dislike his or her companionship. Therefore, social preference is the clearer of the two dimensions and is used more frequently in analyses.

The dimensions of social preference and social impact can be determined by the use of positive and negative sociometric nominations. Negative nominations – asking children to indicate which of their associates they would be least likely to choose as play or work companions – were used in the very earliest sociometric tests. However, 'last choices' were often omitted from research conducted in the 1950s and 1960s, because some researchers found that they resulted in negative comments in the group (Northway, 1952). Furthermore, remembering that one of the main uses of sociometrics in the earlier years was in the study of leadership (see Chapter 1), many of the earlier users of the technique found no pressing need for negative nominations: 'Insofar as most people are not actively interested in those with whom they do not associate, the question itself was artificial' (Northway, 1952, p. 7). As discussed later in this chapter, any negative comments about the 'last choices' appear to have no enduring negative consequences. Last choices are now included more routinely because they enable a far more precise designation of the individuals who are at risk because they are actively disliked by many of their peers, as Moreno and other pioneers intuitively sensed (Kidd, 1951; Moreno, 1960). As discussed later in this chapter, very careful research has since confirmed that being actively disliked is stable over time and uniquely linked to maladjustment (Asher and Coie, 1990).

Moreno (1960) maintained that it was wrong to indicate to respondents exactly how many choices they should make. He believed that some individuals had one very important best friend and few others; these should not be forced to name three or five. Other people may really have five or more people in their social environments with whom they would genuinely wish to play or work. Some versions elicited anywhere from one to eight choices of play or work partners, or 'as many as you like' (Northway, 1952). As sociometrics became more widespread, a concern arose that because of the different questions being asked and, especially because of the different number of nominations allowed, the results of different studies were not really comparable (ibid.). Since then, researchers have asked children to identify the three or five children from their class or grade whom they would most and least like to have as play or work companions (e.g. Coie, Dodge and Coppotelli, 1982; Newcomb and Bukowski, 1983).

Today, many researchers are questioning the practice of arbitrarily pre-determining the number of peers that children may designate as peers they like or don't like to play with (i.e. typically three or five). The use of unlimited nominations is spreading rapidly mainly, not only because it permits children to make the number of choices that corresponds best with their social realities, but also because the inclusion of a peer on a particular child's list does not depend on the nomination of other peers (Parkhurst and Asher, 1992). In other words, if a child equally likes to play with four peers and is only allowed to identify three, the inclusion of the first three will arbitrarily force the absence of the fourth peer from the list of nominees. The fourth peer may be almost as popular or rejected or controversial as the third, but the researcher will never know that. In early sociometric research, the wording of the question used in eliciting the choices, including any restriction on the number of choices, was left to each investigator, who was presumed to be able to design the question best on the basis of the group being studied.

In contemporary sociometrics, most researchers ask children to indicate the classmates with whom they would or would not choose to play or work. It has been pointed out, however, that the exact wording of the question may colour the findings more than is sometimes thought. Vaughn and Haager (1994), who study the peer relations of children with learning disabilities, pointed out that some children with learning problems might not really be disliked, but still may not be chosen as partners to work with on school assignments. A male student who is not athletically inclined might be the 'last choice' as a play partner, but might not be totally ostracized if he has other positive attributes.

Based on his or her social preference and social impact scores (the number of positive and negative nominations received), each child is classified as belonging to one of the following groups: (a) *popular* (having many positive nominations and few negative nominations – which translates into high preference and high impact scores); (b) *neglected* (few positive and few negative nominations – average preference and low impact scores); (c) *rejected* (few positive and many negative nominations – low preference and high impact scores); (d) *average* (average amount of positive and negative nominations – average preference and impact scores); and (e) *controversial* (many positive and many negative nominations – average preference and high impact scores) (Coie, Dodge and Coppotelli 1982).

Some sociometric instruments involve *peer nominations* (e.g. Coie, Dodge and Coppotelli 1982) whereas others are based on *peer ratings* (e.g. Asher and Dodge, 1986); there has been considerable debate about their relative merits (see, e.g. Asher, 1985 or Frederickson and Furnham, 1998). Nominations, consistent with the original practices of Moreno and his contemporaries, have already been described as involving the naming of individuals who correspond to characteristics indicated in the question asked. In contrast, as depicted in Figure 6.1, children who participate in sociometric ratings are asked to rate each of their associates, often on a scale of 1 to 5, in terms of a question such as 'How much do you enjoying playing with each of the following classmates?' Rating scales have a number of attractive features. First of all, information is obtained on all members of the group, not just the extremes. Perhaps because of this, sociometric ratings are more stable over time than nominations, though nominations are indeed quite stable (see below). Second, rating scales are better if one wants to use the direct question 'How much do you like each of the following?' in sociometric procedures. As noted by Vaughn and Haager, that is the clearest sociometric question and the most likely to lead to clear information about social relationships. However, most researchers would not want to use that question in nomination format, where negative nominations would be elicited by the blunt 'Name the classmates you do not like'. In completing rating scales, children are free to not rate anyone as a classmate that they do not like or do enjoy playing with, by avoiding the lower extremes of the rating scale. The latter is an advantage only if, in reality, the respondent enjoys playing with all of his or her classmates; it is all too easy to avoid indicating dislike when it is really there. For that reason, nominations are believed to be better than ratings in identifying children who are at risk because of peer rejection (Asher and Taylor, 1981; Gresham, 1981). Another decided disadvantage of rating scales is research time: it takes children much longer to go down a list of all their classmates and assign ratings to each one than it is to name the few associates who match a specified characteristic.

Psychometric properties and main characteristics of nominations

Measures of sociometric acceptance and rejection have been shown to be quite stable, especially for short-term intervals between measurements. Researchers have frequently obtained short-term stability correlations ranging from .60 to .80 (e.g. Asher and Dodge, 1986). The majority of studies that have investigated the long-term stability of sociometric nomi-

10. Social Skills Training Research

Name _____

EXAMPLES: How much do you like to play with this
                     person at school

	I don't like to				I like to a lot
Louise Blue	1	2	3	4	5
Russell Grey	1	2	3	4	5
John Armon	1	2	3	4	5
Andrea Brandt	1	2	3	4	5
Sue Curtis	1	2	3	4	5
Sandra Drexel	1	2	3	4	5
Jeff Ellis	1	2	3	4	5
Bill Fox	1	2	3	4	5
Diane Higgins	1	2	3	4	5
Harry Jones	1	2	3	4	5
Jill Lamb	1	2	3	4	5
Steve Murray	1	2	3	4	5
Jo Anne Norman	1	2	3	4	5
Pam Riley	1	2	3	4	5
Jim Stevens	1	2	3	4	5

HOW MUCH DO YOU LIKE TO PLAY WITH

THIS PERSON AT SCHOOL?   1   2   3   4   5

                          I don't   I like
                          like to   to a lot

Figure 6.1 Sample rating-scale sociometric measure (Source: Asher, 1985)

nations (e.g. Bukowski and Newcomb, 1984; Hymel, Rubin, Rowden and LeMare, 1990; Roff, Sells and Golden, 1972) have indicated slightly lower stability coefficients than those pertaining to short-term stability. For example, Hymel, S., Rubin, K.H., Rowden, L. and LeMare, L. (1990) reported a stability coefficient of 0.56 for ratings of peer acceptance conducted three years apart (age 7 years to age 10).

The classification of children in the various social status groups (i.e. popular, average, neglected, rejected and controversial) is less stable than the overall stability of nomination scores (e.g. total liked most nominations, total liked least nominations, social preferences scores). For instance, Terry and Coie (1991) compared the classification outcomes using four similar but distinct formulae peer status for classifying, those of Coie, Dodge and Coppotelli (1982), Newcomb and Bukowski (1983), Asher and Dodge (1986) and French (1988; 1990). The first two of these systems feature positive and negative nominations, the third is computed with the scores from a five-point rating scale, whereas the final system involves a cut-off score applied to positive nominations only, as could be computed with many data collected in the 1950s and 1960s, when many researchers used positive nominations only. In general, the authors found only moderate agreement between the different classification systems, with considerable confusion between the neglected and rejected peer status groups, as well as between the popular and controversial groups. Nevertheless, the one- and two-year stability of status classification for the various measures was roughly the same. Stability coefficients for all four of the procedures ranged from low stability for the average (ranging from k $=0.01$ to k $=0.20$ across the four methods), neglected (k $=0.01$ to k $=0.20$) and controversial (k $=0.04$ to k $=0.17$) peer status groups, low to moderate stability for the rejected group (k $=0.19$ to k $=0.41$), to moderate to good stability for the popular group (k $=0.20$ to k $=0.52$). Thus, there appears to be greater stability in the more general peer nominations for acceptance and rejection than for membership in social status groups. For that reason, global acceptance and rejection scores, 'Liked Most' and 'Liked Least' are preferable in many analyses. The stability of rejected status may be sufficient to indicate that peer rejection poses a long-term risk for children's adjustment, as many have emphasized (e.g. Asher and Coie, 1990). However, since many children may be rejected only at some points in their development, Vitaro and his colleagues have suggested that researchers interested in studying rejection as a risk factor should use longitudinal data that permit the identification of children who are chronically rejected by their peers at several measurement points (Vitaro, Gagnon and Tremblay, 1990). Chronic ostracism by peers has been shown in several studies to increase the odds of later behaviour problems (DeRosier, Kupersmidt and Patterson, 1994) and the risk of boys' developing feelings of loneliness and depression (Burks, Dodge and Price, 1995), over and above the odds of a maladaptive outcome by children rejected only at a single point in time.

Ethics in sociometric nominations

Although sociometric measures are among the most widely used assessment tools in peer relations research, there has been considerable debate concerning the possible negative consequences of their use with children. As discussed above, in order to achieve a more precise peer status categorization when conducting peer-relations research, it is important to include negative peer nominations ('Name the children you do not like to play with'), along with positive nominations ('Name the children you like to play with'); otherwise the identities of children at risk of maladjustment because of rejection by peers will not be determined. Despite their importance in determining peer status, it is these negative peer nominations that have sometimes brought researchers, ethics committees, parents and school boards to question the appropriateness of sociometric measures (Bell-Dolan, Foster and Tishelman, 1989; Bell-Dolan and Wessler, 1994). The major concerns are that by asking children to identify the peers that they do not like, researchers may implicitly encourage participants to make negative statements towards their peers (Hayvren and Hymel, 1984) and to perceive or interact with unpopular and rejected peers in an even greater negative manner (Asher and Hymel, 1981; Foster and Ritchey, 1979).

Given the importance of gauging the risks involved in conducting research, especially with children, some researchers have studied in very careful and systematic ways the effects of sociometric measures on the children participating in their studies (e.g. Bell-Dolan, Foster and Christopher, 1992; Bell-Dolan, Foster and Sikora, 1989; Hayvren and Hymel, 1984). Generally, these studies have found no support for the contention that sociometric measures place children at greater risk than they encounter in everyday life. After children participated in sociometrics, no increase in negative peer interaction was noticed by trained observers (Hayvren and Hymel, 1984) or by parents and teachers (Bell-Dolan, Foster and Christopher, 1992). In all studies on the effects of sociometrics, the majority of children reported that they enjoyed participating in the research. In one particular study (Bell-Dolan, Foster and Christopher, 1992), in which 13 girls (7.5 per cent of the participants) had learned that a peer had identified them on the negative question nomination, only one of the 13 stated that she did not enjoy participating in the research. Thus, the limited data available on the effects of sociometric testing on children clearly suggest that the benefits of this type of research outweigh the potential risks. However, proper steps must be taken by researchers in order to make sure that a minimum amount of distress is present (i.e. no more than in the children's other daily activities, such as chores and homework). Bell-Dolan and Wessler (1994) provide suggestions on how to minimize risks. For example, it is advisable to add distractor questions such as 'Who is the tallest pupil in the class?', 'Who is the best in arithmetic?', 'Who tries hardest at sports?' so that the questions about disliking are imprinted less prominently in memory. In Schneider's own research in Canada, sociometric data are not collected on a group basis, although that method would save time. Children are brought individually to a small seminar room in their schools when they participate. If only sociometric data are collected during these individual sessions, the added privacy costs only a few minutes per child of research time.

Observational methods

Peer nominations and peer ratings have been the most important source of data about children's peer relations since research in the area started. However, researchers as early as Moreno were concerned that information from peers was very global in nature, indicating who is liked by whom, for example, but failing to supply detailed information about the social interactions of either the person being rated or the person providing the information about one of his or her peers. Thus, the founder of sociometrics was well aware that sociometrics had its shortcomings and tried direct observation to fill in the missing information. Moreno (1960) abandoned his own flirtation with direct observation once he reached the conclusion that the information gains from direct observation were more superficial than he hoped. He then began to stress the importance of having some relationship with the persons being observed, of observing as a participant in a group rather than a 'scientific spy' (1953, p. 101), but did not pursue participant observation very much in his own work or training.

Observation flourished, however, in the laboratory schools in the United States and Canada that were set up with the help of the Rockefeller Foundation in the 1920s. Those schools were set up at several universities in order to enable researchers to learn about children's development in a more intensive manner than they could as guest observers in other settings. Some of the laboratory schools are still in operation, for example, the laboratory school at the University of Toronto. Detailed sociometric records were collected at the laboratory schools, but the very nature of the schools lent itself to an emphasis on direct observations of the children as they interacted at play or at work. Often, the researchers believed that knowledge about child development at that time was too limited to serve as a guide for the observations. Therefore, they often used no categories or codes while observing and had no specific hypothesis in mind. They hoped that the running narrative logs of children's behaviour that they compiled would be useful in illuminating the course of child development and, therefore, they wanted to make sure that nothing of potential importance would be missed. Many of the observers wrote down every event in the child's school day.

In the end, many of the running narratives were too complex and too disorganized to analyse and were relegated to archival storage after little or no use. The sociometrics, which consumed a small fraction of the research time of the laboratory schools, were the primary measures reported in the journals of the time in articles about the children in the laboratory schools, along with IQ tests and personality scales. However, as interest in behavioural approaches to children's problems increased in the 1960s, observational methods acquired a new lease on life. Direct observation was assumed to be the only acceptable method for studying the problems and tracking changes in the patterns of reinforcement that sustained them. The laboratory tradition that gave rise to behaviourism emphasized objectivity and direct observations were assumed to be less biased than verbal reports from anyone (Hops, Davis and Longoria, 1995).

In the early stages of inquiry into a specific issue, fairly informal observation methods are still used and are often appropriate. For example, much has been learned about the nature of young children's interactions with their friends from Corsaro's (1988) and Rizzo's (1992) extended observations in kindergarten classrooms in the United States and Italy. Their observations went on for many months and were unstructured: Children were observed in no fixed sequence and the observers had no fixed set of behaviours to look for. Because of this, their results may have been coloured by their own subjective perspective and their own biases – and by the limitations of human perception and memory, which can result in overlooking an important feature of the behaviour being observed. However, previous knowledge did not provide an adequate basis for a formal, structured observational system. Had Rizzo adopted a pre-determined list of behaviours to observe and observed the children in a pre-determined order, their study probably would have contributed less than it did.

Once there is a sound theoretical basis for developing an observational method, however, it becomes important to convince the research community that the observations have been conducted in an objective manner and to describe very clearly exactly what has been observed. This makes today's observational data very different from the disorganized narrative logs that were collected in the university laboratory schools years ago. The categories of behaviour being observed must be defined so that the results of one observational study can be compared with the results of another. Without such definitions, what is considered a 'fight' or 'row' or an 'aggressive' act by one observer may bear very little resemblance to another observer's idea of the same phenomena. An example of a set of definitions for observation categories appears in Table 6.1 (see page 121) which depicts a classic set of observational categories that has been in use since the 1930s (Parten, 1932) with some modifications. An observer using the system would have to decide how to code the social behaviour of children being observed at regular, pre-specified intervals, perhaps every 10 seconds. It is important to sample enough behaviour to get a representative picture of the typical social behaviour of individuals and of the group. As an example, the children in a group might be observed one at a time in random order for 2-minute intervals each, for example, for six minutes a day (i.e. three 2-minute intervals) for 20 days, so that a total of 120 minutes of observation would be tallied for each child. The first decision to be taken at each interval when using the Parten system is whether or not the child being observed is engaged in play. If so, the observer must code, at each interval, both an association category, which tells whom the child was playing with (alone, a single peer, or a group) and a cognitive category, which describes the nature of the play. Non-play activities are coded as well.

The Parten system used as an example in the previous paragraph is a time-sampling procedure, because the children's behaviour is observed, in rotating order, for specific intervals of time, with coding used to describe their play at each interval. Time-sampling methods are not very suitable for counting specific incidents that have discrete beginnings and ends, such as fights. Event recording involves maintaining a running tally of the number of such phenomena. Duration and latency recording can be used if one is also interested in timing the length of episodes such as fights (Barton and Ascione, 1984; Merrell and Gimpel, 1998). A combination of these methods is often necessary to describe complex patterns of social interaction.

Nothing more sophisticated than paper and pencil are needed to complete these recordings. However, sophisticated software is now available for entering the data mechanically into a computer-readable file. Live observation is very common, but videotaped observation permits the observers to review the data as needed. Special video equipment with slow-motion and pause features enables more precise coding that includes subtle features of human interaction that are difficult to observe at full speed.

Observation codes much more detailed than the Parten system have been used in some influential research. Many of these involve sequence analysis (e.g. Bakeman and Gottman 1997), which attempts to provide a slow-motion 'replay' of critical exchanges within relationships. Sequence analysis is often invaluable in tracing the reactions that a specific behaviour tends to elicit from a relationship partner. However, in sharp contrast with the many detailed, second-by-second methods in observational research, some simpler codes are sometimes used because the microscopic observation of behaviour in great detail can obscure the overall quality of a relationship. For example, Kerns, Klepac and Cole (1996) had observers watch several minutes of the interactions of friends and then rate the children's friendships on 1 to 5 (or, sometimes 1 to 3) point scales for the features she needed to investigate in her study, such as responsiveness, intimacy, criticism and balance of power.

No matter how simple or complex the observational scheme, no matter where the observations are conducted, it is essential to demonstrate inter-rater reliability, to show that different observers code the same behaviour in the same way. Sophisticated statistical formulae have been developed to calculate inter-rater reliability and prove that the agreement among observers is greater than one would be expected to occur by chance (Bakeman and Gottman, 1997). Obviously, observations of what is supposed to be hostile aggression, for example, would be of little scientific value if, within the same study, three different observers could not agree as to which of the incidents they observe constitute hostile aggression. It often takes considerable time for observers being trained for a study to achieve inter-rater reliability. Understandably, this can be frustrating for enthusiastic observers who want to begin the actual data collection.

Table 6.1 Codes used in an observational study of the social play of young gifted children

Association categories	Cognitive categories	Other activities
Solitary – Child plays alone with toys different from those used by other children; no attempt at verbal communication with peer	*Functional* – Simple muscular activities, repetitive muscular movements with or without objects	*Reading* – Child reads printed page or book or is being read to
Parallel – Child plays independently, but in close proximity to other children; plays with toys similar to those of other children, but with no common purpose or shared play object	*Exploratory* – Focused examination of physical properties of an object	*Conversation* – Child talks to other person, answers questions, offers suggestions, or listens to peer doing same
Group – Plays with other children; clear indications of communication, common goal, joint game, or shared play activity	*Construction* – Use of play materials or objects to construct or create something	*Unoccupied/Transition* – Child is not engaged in an identified play activity, may be in transition between activities
	Manipulative – Child moves all or part of an object, game, or toy, in a manner that reflects clear understanding of its purpose or a clear new purpose, but without creating a new object or assuming a dramatic role	*Onlooker* – Child observes other children at play
	Dramatic – Child takes on a role, pretends to be someone else, or imitates a person	
	Games with rules – Child is engaged in a recognizable game with established or fixed rules	

Source: Adapted from: Schneider, Daniels, (1992) Peer acceptance and social play of gifted kindergarten children. *Exceptionality* 3, 17–29. By permission of Springer-Verlag Publishers.

Despite the recent innovations in observational technology, there remains a lingering doubt as to how the presence of observers affects the behaviours. Children seem to get accustomed to the presence of observers after a short period and obvious reactions to the observers' presence seem to dissipate. However, there is no way of escaping the reality that the presence of the observer will affect the behaviour being observed to some degree. The observer or the observer's surrogate (e.g. the tape recorder) are always present and may lead the children being observed to display their most admirable traits and stifle their shortcomings (Sillars, 1991). Nevertheless, it is difficult to stage a style of interacting that is totally unfamiliar for extended periods of time and it is unlikely that children being observed even attempt to. Despite the inevitable reactivity to the observer, researchers are able to capture by direct observation many of the most unattractive aspects of children's social behaviour as well as their more pleasing features.

There are many advantages to observing children in the settings where they normally interact with each other, especially the obvious fact that the observations are conducted under normal conditions typical of children's lives. However, some of the most influential studies of children's peer relations have featured observations in groups set up by the experimenters, especially studies of the peer relations of aggressive and rejected children (e.g. Dodge, Coie, Pettit and Price, 1990). Artificial as they may be, these contrived playgroups can be very useful because they permit the intensive, efficient observation of specific situations of interest. For example, one could set up a playgroup with one aggressive, one shy/withdrawn and two other children. It is true that interactions between aggressive and shy children do take place on school playgrounds and elsewhere from time to time, but one might have to wait so long to find such exchanges in the midst of so many other social contacts that it might not be feasible to station observers to watch them. Another situation that is typical of children's social interactions but that may be easier to observe in a contrived setting is when two children who already have a relationship with each other deal with the approach of a third child (Nadel and Tremblay-Leveau, 1999). In yet another important example, Coplan et al. (1994) used contrived playgroups as part of a study that investigated different forms of solitude in preschool children. They combined two 15–minute unstructured free play periods with a variety of structured tasks including 'show-and-tell' speeches. Children were asked to stand up one by one and tell the group about their last birthday party. This procedure enabled an important contribution to the literature on the subtypes of shyness during childhood.

Observational data are rich. Observers learn first hand and in living colour about children's peer relations played out in behaviours ranging from generous and helpful all the way to vicious and vindictive. However, this comes at a price. Conducting and coding observations are slow, costly and painstaking processes that cost many times more than any of the other assessment methods considered in this chapter.

Children's self-reports: a distorted mirror?

Some peer-relations research relies on children accurately responding to self-report measures referring to various aspects of their behaviour with peers. Unfortunately, the accuracy of self-report measures is often questioned (Furman, 1996); the prevailing consensus is that children may not be the most reliable informants on their own behaviour. Many children may harbour no active wish to deceive when completing self-reports on their interactions with peers, but their self-reports may be distorted because the children may be unaware of shortcomings in their own behaviour, or may be unable to compare their own behaviour with that of the typical child at their stage of development. Aggressive and rejected children, in particular, are known to underestimate their problems and provide in their self-reports inflated impressions of their social competence (e.g. Patterson, Kupersmidt and Griseler, 1990).

Despite these reservations about self-reports on behaviour itself, self-reports can be invaluable in providing valuable information concerning children's feelings, thoughts and impressions. Useful data have been gathered by many researchers using self-report measures for topics such as feelings of loneliness and social dissatisfaction (e.g. Asher, Hymel and Renshaw, 1984; Asher and Wheeler, 1985), feelings about friendships (e.g. Bukowski, Boivin and Hoza, 1994; Parker and Asher, 1993a), goals and strategies for peer interaction (e.g. Renshaw and Asher, 1983; Rose and Asher, 1999), social cognitions (e.g. Crick and Dodge, 1994), etc. For example, it is through the use of self-report measures that researchers have found that aggressive children often have the biased belief that other people are intent on causing them harm (Crick and Dodge, 1996; Dodge and Coie, 1987). It is also through the use of self-report measures that Rose and Asher (1999) have shown that children who have friendships of poorer quality tend to endorse more social goals involving revenge than do children who have friendships of greater quality. Self-reports are the best source of information about children's feelings of loneliness and about children's confidence in their abilities to be effective in social situations. Thus, although self-report measures may lack reliability or accuracy when an objective report of the child's social behaviour is desired, it is important not to underestimate their relevance to many aspects of the study of children's peer relations. Only children know what is happening inside their private mental space and, therefore, they are the best source of information about their thinking with regard to social situations.

Information from individuals in the child's social world

One alternative to the high cost of observations is to obtain reports from people who spend extended periods of time in interaction with the children one wishes to study and who know them well in a variety of situations. Therefore, reports about aggressive, withdrawn and socially competent behaviours of participants in research are routinely obtained from teachers, parents and peers. Each of these informants will rate any individual's behaviour through a particular lens. Teachers, for example, have experience with large numbers of children to use as a reference point. However, teachers cannot reasonably be expected to rate children's peer relations from the perspective of a potential friend, work companion, or relationship partner and their ratings of many of a child's traits may be coloured by the child's cooperativeness in class and academic achievement (Schneider and Byrne, 1987; White and Kistner, 1992). Parents know their own children intimately, which means that they may be aware of aspects of their children's social behaviour that teachers are unaware of. However, it is difficult for parents to be objective about their own children. Aside from the difficulty inherent in being objective about a loved one, parents may not have enough experience with children of a particular age to use as a reference point. In many cases, they may have little first-hand access to information about their children's social behaviour at school or in other community settings.

Sociometric choice ratings and nominations, the classic procedures for studying patterns of liking and disliking in groups that were discussed earlier in this chapter, are by no means the only ways in which researchers benefit from peers' familiarity with members of their social groups. Peer nominations and ratings are also used to inform researchers about the aggressiveness, withdrawal and socially skilled behaviours of their schoolmates. Peers can remember isolated events that have important repercussions for the reputations of individuals; such low-frequency events may not occur during the limited time observers can be present, or may be concealed from the observer. Importantly, peer ratings represent the social behaviour of an individual from the 'inside' perspectives of a member of the same age and social group and, therefore, a potential friend or enemy (Hymel and Rubin, 1985).

In both sociometric choice nominations and in peer reports of children's social behaviour, there is considerable variation among researchers using sociometric measures with regards to the reference group presented to the respondents. For example, one might obtain a different picture of the behaviour of a specific child if only schoolmates of the same gender were asked to rate it rather than all schoolmates; these differences are sometimes very substantial (Frederickson and Furnham, 1998). Peers are more likely to be aware of the behaviours of members of the same gender, because they associate with them more closely, but same-gender nominations and ratings pertain to fewer classmates and are often less stable for that reason (Foster, Bell-Dolan and Berler, 1986). In obtaining information about events that are highly noticeable to everyone, such as disruptions to the classroom, there may be little advantage to limiting the raters to classmates of the same gender as the child being rated. Same-gender ratings or nominations, however, may be necessary to learn about the more subtle aspects of relational aggression, such as spreading rumours or asking peers to stay away from a specific child.

Not surprisingly in light of their different perspectives, reports from teachers, peers and parents often provide discrepant information about an individual. The extent of the discrepancy depends on the particular behaviour being rated and the age and gender of the child participants. There may be greater agreement with regard to a very visible behaviour such as physical aggression than in reports about more subtle aspects of interaction (Schneider and Byrne, 1987). However, it is usually best to obtain reports from as many informants as possible and to interpret the information derived from each source with an understanding of the strengths and weaknesses of its particular vantage point.

Several of the major instruments for obtaining reports from informants are designed for use with several informants. These tools offer the advantage of having each of the informants rate the same behaviours using the same items as far as possible. Achenbach and Edelbrock's (1986) Child Behavior Checklist is used for parent and teacher reports and is accompanied, in forms intended for older children, by a youth self-report from. Slightly briefer and more focused on social interaction in the classroom rather than psychiatric disorder, is Gresham and Elliott's (1990) Social Skills Rating System. The best-known tool for collecting peer reports of children's social behaviour is the Revised Class Play (Masten, Morrison and Pellegrini, 1985). In completing the Class Play, children are asked to name the classmates who would best fill specific roles in a class play, such as the roles of a good leader, a person who gets into many fights, etc. The nominations are summed to derive scores for the aggressiveness, withdrawal and likeability of each child in the class. However, the method is due for substantial overhaul, because the items do not fully reflect fine distinctions that have emerged in recent research, such as the distinctions between relational and overt aggression or (Crick and Grotpeter, 1995) between different forms of shyness that are and are not accompanied by anxiety (Rubin and Mills, 1988).

Reports from teachers, peers and parents are, of course, accounts of the reporters' impressions of the child's reputation. Once an impression is formed, it may be hard to alter even if the child's behaviour changes (Hymel, Wagner and Butler, 1990). Therefore, it may be wiser to use direct observation, despite its cost, rather than reports from third-party informants if the purpose of a study is to track changes in children's social behaviour over time.

Studying peer relations in contexts that are difficult to access: peer relations research goes high tech

The methods discussed until this point have been known for half a century or more, although they have been fine-tuned extensively in recent years. Their limitations have also been known for some time and have inspired creative new methods designed to overcome at least some of the limitations of sociometrics, rating scales and direct observation. Several of the new techniques evolve from the painful realization that much of children's social lives unfolds in places where observers cannot easily venture and in the company of individuals who are not likely to complete sociometric scales or any other type of rating.

The experience sampling method (Csikzmentmihalyi and Larson, 1987) is a very useful way of studying children's daily activities and the fluctuations of their emotions in naturalistic settings. The experience sampling technique has been used primarily with adolescents, but successful use has been reported with children as young as 7 years old (Manning, 1990). Children carry electronic pagers with them, typically for one week. When signalled at random intervals by the experimenters, the children fill out reports about how they are feeling at the moment, what they are doing, what they are thinking of, etc., depending on the purpose of the study. The random time sampling allows for measurement that is far more precise than the data recorded in diaries or running logs of children's activities, although these 'low tech' measures have also proved useful and valid (Duck, 1991; Ladd and Golter, 1988; Schneider, Richard, Younger and Freeman, 2000).

Pepler and Craig (1995), who are Canadian researchers interested in violence in the schools, were concerned that traditional methods of direct observation were inadequate for their observations of school playgrounds, where they study incidents of violence. They believed that there were many incidents of verbal abuse, threats and aggression that occur so rapidly and are so concealed from adults that they would be missed by adults observing in the playground under the normal limitations of human vision and hearing. Furthermore, observers are unlikely to be able to capture verbalizations among children while observing a school playground without special equipment. This is a particular disadvantage in studying aggression among girls, who, when they are aggressive, tend to be verbally rather than physically aggressive (Björkqvist, Osterman and Kaukianen, 1992; Pepler and Craig, 1995). Therefore, Pepler and Craig developed a method for remote audiovisual observations, depicted in Figure 6.2, using microphones and video cameras to become able to see and hear all the events occurring on the playground. The children who are participating in the study wear a wireless microphone and a lightweight transmitter. The researchers who tune in can hear the conversation of the child wearing the microphone as well as those in his or her immediate proximity. Using the zoom lens of

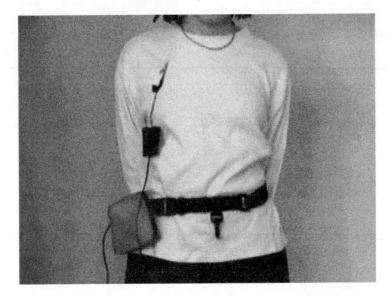

Figure 6.2 Remote observation of playground behaviour

the video camera, the researcher can add a simultaneous visual record of the same events. The audio signal is sent through the video camera in order to provide a simultaneous auditory and visual record of the same event that is preserved for later observation and coding. Although this apparatus is too expensive (about 700 US dollars [Pepler and Craig, 1995]) to provide for all the children on the playground, some degree of anonymity can be preserved by having the child whose behaviour is being recorded put the microphone and transmitter in a 'fanny pack'. Other children may be given 'fanny packs' of the same weight, so that the identity of the child under observation is not obvious. Pepler and Craig (1995) see as the major advantage of this method the possibility it gives to the children to interact with each other far away from the observers; at a distance, the more subtle observers' presence may have less of an effect on the children's behaviour than in traditional observational techniques.

Methodology in the third millennium

Research to date has resulted in the refinement of the mainstays of instrumentation in research on children's peer relations: sociometrics, direct observation, reports from peers and teachers and self-reports. The advantages of using multiple measures of children's social competence have become clearer than ever. Although using several measures is obviously more difficult than attempting to measure social competence by relying on a single source, the added time and expense bring an important dividend: they prevent the premature acceptance of ideas into the realm of accepted knowledge. Conclusions that have more to do with the weaknesses of the measurement tool than the topic at hand can misguide researchers, parents and teachers.

Recent technological innovations have made it possible to observe children interacting with other children from a distance and even in situations about the community where the observer is not present at all. The next chapter is devoted to children's relationships with their close friends; ways of assessing friendship are part of that discussion. However ingenious the recent technological advances for remote observations of children's peer relations may be, an important hurdle remains: measuring children's behaviours and emotions in natural settings where they normally interact with their close friends, in a way that minimizes any reaction to the presence of an observer. Electronic pagers and the type of data recording they prompt, would not capture the flavour of the interactions. At present, the technology for doing that exists only in James Bond films.

7 Relationships at the dyadic level

The reasons for the recent shift in attention from peer relations at a large-group level to the processes associated with more intimate friendships are discussed. Techniques for assessing these processes are then discussed. The chapter closes with a review of research documenting the harm that can result from the mutual friendships of anti-social children.

As was mentioned in Chapter 1, children spent vast amounts of time together in groups during earlier periods in the history of Western societies, even more than they do now. For much of the day, children provided for many of each other's physical and emotional needs, in situations where children now receive support from parents and teachers. Cross-cultural studies indicate that this social arrangement still prevails in many non-Western societies. In those circumstances where children live primarily in a world of children, 'friendship' is, as aptly put by Lopata (1981), just an ordinary relationship taken a bit further. However, in contemporary Western society, there are certain distinguishing features of close friendships that have been emphasized by philosophers and scientists alike. As noted by Ginsberg, Gottman and Parker, 'intimacy and affection are, of course, the hallmark of friendship at any age, the facet that most clearly distinguishes close friends from distant friends, acquaintances and activity partners' (1986, p. 10). The pivotal role of intimacy in friendship, typically seen as having its roots in Sullivanian theory (Sullivan, 1953; see Chapter 2), mirrors the reflections about friendship in age-old philosophical, literary and theological writings. This is perhaps most explicit in some of the writings of the Augustinian philosophers. Aelred, for instance, maintained that one owes loyalty, trust and support to all other humans; the essential difference between one's relationships with friends and acquaintances is that the friend is the person to whom one confides the secrets of one's heart (Entralgo, 1985).

Most psychological theories and many major authors in Western literature have insisted on the temporary nature of children's friendships, which cannot really be considered friendships at all because they change so quickly and lack depth. Traditionally, childhood relationships have been characterized as fleeting alliances precipitated principally by the momentary pleasure of sharing enjoyable activities. In their *Oxford Book of Friendship*, Enright and Rawlinson (1992) follow the path of friendship as a literary theme. Emphasizing the transient nature of children's friendships, the earliest citation claims that these fickle relationships ebb and flow according to changes in interest: Aristotle observed in *Nichomachean Ethics* that:

> their affection alters as their taste in pleasure alters and pleasure of that thought changes rapidly ... Consequently they form attachments quickly and break them off quickly, often changing over the course of twenty-four hours. But young people who are friends, unlike the old, do want to pass their time in one another's company; that is how their friendship is carried on.
>
> (Aristotle, transl. H. Rackham, 1945; 461)

However, Enright and Rawlinson do highlight some exceptions to the ephemeral quality of children's friendships; some citations allude to the trust, self-disclosure and intimacy associated with more mature relationships. Interestingly, these literary references closely mirror the trajectory of inferences about children's friendships in theories of personality and child development. However, in contrast to earlier theorists emphasizing the quick changes in children's friends, more recent evidence confirms that many children do have enduring relationships with friends, as will be discussed later in this chapter.

The beginnings of friendship in early childhood

Refuting the many claims that young children do not have friends in the true sense of the word is no easy matter; the inherent difficulties are reviewed in detail by Howes (1996). Children who are 2, 3, or 4 years old do not have the vocabulary to communicate to researchers who their friends might be or to describe the nature of any relationships they might have with them. In studying friendship among preschoolers, external sources of information must be used: reports from parents, impressions of teachers or caregivers, or observations of play behaviours. These sources do not provide ready access to the mental space of the children or of their possible friends, although they alone can construct the internal idea that they have a relationship as each other's friends. Nevertheless, some important conclusions can be drawn from the data that can be gathered.

First of all, by the time the child has reached 2 years of age, children who have the opportunity to play on a regular basis with peers do form specific relationships. In other words, they are able to select from among their group of peers an individual or set of individuals with whom they play more frequently and ask to associate with more frequently. They also respond more positively to invitations to play from that particular child or those children. Observations of the play of preschoolers indicate that children involved in specific relationships act out elaborate scripted play sequences by as early as 13–18 months; such scripts do not appear until the age of 2 years in the play of unacquainted children (Dunn, 1993; Howes, 1996). By the age of 2, children become involved in play sessions arranged by parents for children who the parents believe to be friends. (Ladd and Golter, 1988). According to the best data available, the specific relationships of children aged 2 to 4 years can remain stable for as long as one or two years (Dunn, 1993: Howes and Phillipsen, 1992; Unger, 1991, cited in Howes, 1996). This rate of stability (e.g. 75 per cent over one year among 2-year-olds in Unger's study) is essentially the same for children up to the age of ten (Berndt, Hawkins and Hoyle, 1986; Schneider, Fonzi, Tani and Tomada, 1997).

When playing together, toddlers who are friends display more complex and more mature play than others (Howes, 1996; Werebe and Baudonniere, 1991). Although most preschoolers ignore classmates who cry, friends are more likely to try to comfort each other if they cry (Howes and Farver, 1987). Importantly, friends are likely to experience distress should one of them move away or change preschools. When peers with whom children are well acquainted accompany them to new preschool settings, their adjustment appears to be smoother than that of children who make the transition alone (Howes, 1988).

Several characteristics of children's relationships correspond to the criteria often used to define adult relationships (Howes, 1996). Children, like adults, seek to satisfy their needs for companionship, affection and intimacy in their interactions with one another. Companionship can be operationalized as the close proximity that children maintain to their preferred play partners, the stability of their choices of playmates and simply having fun or playing together. There is evidence that children identified as friends display shared positive affect and that their social pretend play functions to explore trust and intimacy. Children's play activities indicate that they recognize the need for sensitivity to others if they want to solve problems (Howes, 1996). In addition, children of nursery school age have shown tendencies to organize into social peer groups for which 'friendship' is a basis for inclusion (Corsaro, 1981).

Thus, according to the best information it is possible to obtain, children as young as 2 years seem to have relationships that can be thought of as friendships. The quality of the play interactions between friends and friends' response to each other's distress can be interpreted as early signs of what Hinde (1979) considers the distinguishing feature of a relationship - mutual commitment.

What causes friendships to form and be maintained?

An impressive achievement of research on peer relations over the past thirty years has been the identification of certain fundamental characteristics of childhood friendship.

Proximity

Being in a location that is physically near one's friends is a main factor of friendship, for it increases the likelihood that children will become companions and reduces the effort needed to maintain the relationship (Clark and Drewry, 1985; Spurgeon, Hicks and Terry, 1983); this may be more important for younger children than their older counterparts due to their restricted mobility (Epstein, 1989). Evidence for the importance of propinquity comes from classic findings, known since Furfey's (1928) early work, in which children are found to be more likely to form friendships with peers from their own neighbourhood or school; this tendency is recognized readily by children themselves (Furman and Bierman, 1983; Spurgeon, Hicks and Terry, 1983).

Shared activities

The substance of childhood friendship is usually considered to be the sharing of common pastimes (Selman and Schultz, 1989), although the salience of this as the cement of relationships with friends decreases with age. For instance, shared play activity is more important in the relationships of preschoolers than older children. The relative importance of shared activities and interests decreases between the ages of four and seven (Furman and Bierman, 1983) and this continues into adolescence (e.g. Berndt and Perry, 1986; Bukowski and Hoza, 1989; Spurgeon, Hicks and Terry, 1983). Nevertheless, shared activity remains an element even of adult friendships, which are based in part on the common enjoyment of leisure time (Argyle, 1992; Argyle and Lu, 1990).

Similarity

According to literature on adult interpersonal attraction, similarity, particularly in values and attitudes (Duck, Miell and Gaebler, 1980; Ladd and Emerson, 1984) can reduce dissonance in a friendship and increase the chance of agreement (Berscheid and Walster, 1978). Similarity essentially enhances the compatibility that is integral to a relationship and compatibility, in turn, enables the mutual enjoyment of shared activities (Clark and Drewry, 1985). Studies of children's friendships highlight the importance of similarity. Children, at all ages, resemble their friends more than their non-friends in a number of respects (e.g. Erwin, 1985). This is not always a good thing. In a pioneering study conducted by Hartshorne and May in 1928, friends were found to resemble each other in deceitfulness. More will be said later in this chapter about the problems that result from aggressive children befriending each other.

Some evidence suggests that the dimensions of similarity change according to developmental stage. Emphasis on superficial similarities in age, race and physical appearance declines as children mature (Furman and Bierman, 1983; Ladd and Emerson, 1984). Similarities in tastes, interests and attitudes begin to take precedence (Berndt, 1982; McGuire and Weisz, 1982). This is evidence of a developmental shift that influences the types of similarities children look for in their friends. Although older friends may have more personality-related and less superficial commonalities than younger children, even in early adolescence, friends appear to be more similar in terms of age, sex, race (Berndt, 1982) and social status (Clark and Drewry, 1985).

Tangible support, instrumental assistance

Material or instrumental assistance — such as helping a friend by lending something he or she needs or wants — appears to be a key element of childhood friendship. Children report that they expect this type of assistance from their friends (Bukowski and Hoza, 1989; Hartup, 1989) and that they receive higher levels of tangible support from friends than from casual acquaintances (Berndt and Perry, 1986). Bukowski and Kramer (1986) found that, when evaluating the likelihood that two children will become friends, children consider levels of helpfulness or sharing. Children are more willing to share with friends than with non-friends, even if it means gaining less reward (Jones, 1985). Children between the ages of four and nine consider the ability of a friend to lend tangible support as especially important in the friendship. In early adolescence, the ability of a friend to stand up for his or her friend in a conflict with a third party achieves great significance. Indeed, this was found to take precedence over engaging in common activities, sharing secrets and discussing private matters in determining friendships for 12-year-olds (Bukowski, Newcomb and Hoza, 1987).

Of all the features of friendship, it is the support that friends provide at times of stress that is considered the link between friendship and general well-being, as introduced in Chapter 2. There has been some speculation that support from friends can help compensate for lack of support from siblings and parents. However, this has not been confirmed consistently in research. Stocker's (1994) study, conducted with 8-year-olds in the United States, did provide some support for the compensation hypothesis. Participating children who perceived relationships with both their mothers and their friends as lacking in warmth were found to be more maladjusted than children who perceived little warmth in only one of those relationships. Two other studies suggest, on the other hand, that support from friends cannot counteract lack of support from family members and vice versa. Research by East and Rook (1992), conducted with 12-year-olds in the United States, indicated that support from siblings did not compensate for lack of support from peers. A convincing study by van Aken and Asendorpf (1997), who examined the self-esteem of 12-year olds in Germany, demonstrated that lack of support from one parent could only be compensated by support from the other parent. Furthermore, lack of support from classmates was not compensated by supportive relationships with siblings or non-school peers. Despite the inconsistent findings of these studies, it is too early to discard the compensation hypothesis, especially because, of the three relevant studies, only one, by East and Rook, was conducted with children displaying atypical patterns of social behaviour. In the two other studies, many or most of the participants may not have had personal problems of sufficient magnitude to require social support in order to maintain their self-esteem. Hence, those two studies may not be as helpful in gauging the supportive properties of friendships, because most of the participants may not have been in need of support at the times they participated in the research.

Intimacy and self-disclosure

The intimate sharing of feelings is a characteristic of childhood friendship; there is more private discussion within close dyads than with non-friends (Waldrop and Halverson, 1975). Intimacy becomes quite important in middle childhood and early adolescence (Berndt and Perry, 1986; Bukowski and Kramer, 1986; Furman and Bierman, 1983; Sullivan, 1953). This increase may be based on the ability of youth of these age groups to take others' perspectives into account, as well as their growing awareness of individual differences in personality characteristics among their peers (McGuire and Weisz, 1982). Although it is probably more important to older children, intimacy may still be important to young children, who may be less likely to articulate intimacy-related behaviour when explaining their impressions and expectations of friendship to researchers. Some evidence of the intimacy in friendships of younger children comes from a study by Rotenberg and Sliz (1988), in which children aged five and seven conveyed a more personal audio-taped message to friends than non-friends. However, others have found that intimacy is not an important element of friendship until adolescence (Berndt and Hanna, 1995).

Trust

Studies of children from the age of six years (Shannon and Kafer, 1984) through middle childhood (Buzzelli, 1988) highlight the importance of trust in friendship. Research indicates, however, that expectations that centre on trust change with age. For instance, younger children tend to rely upon friends to play with them, guard secrets and fulfil promises (Bigelow, 1977; Rotenberg and Pilipenko, 1983). These expectations apply to adolescents as well, but, at that developmental stage, emphasis is also placed on honesty, genuineness and the ability to meet interpersonal needs.

Reciprocity

Children who are friends exhibit higher levels of mutual social responsiveness than those who are merely acquaintances. This can surface during play, for best friends tend to be more equal in assuming different play roles than non-friends (Hartup, 1989; Stoneman, Brody and MacKinnon, 1984). As children grow and become less self-centred, the expectation of reciprocity becomes increasingly explicit (Berndt, 1982). Rotenberg and Mann (1986) found that, when asked to judge the level of friendship between two age mates, 12-year-old children considered not only the amount of personal disclosure, but also the degree of mutual intimacy. Furthermore, as children mature, trust becomes more reciprocal in dyadic friendships (Rotenberg and Pilipenko, 1983).

Conflict, conflict resolution and competition

Conflicts do occur between friends, although, from middle childhood on, children are known to expect that friends will join them in resolving conflicts as quickly and amiably as possible (e.g. Berndt, 1982). Research results do not provide a precise, consistent image of how these expectations translate into behaviour in situations of potential conflict. Sullivan (1953) theorized that competition would lead to conflict and to the dissolution of friendship. However, some empirical findings indicate the diametric opposite, at least for males at certain ages (e.g. Berndt, Hawkins and Hoyle, 1986; Buhrmester, 1996; Hartup, 1992). Although he singled out competition more specifically than any other cause of the rupture of friendship, Sullivan (1953) acknowledged that some degree of competition may be normative in male friendship and may do no harm.

Everyday decisions, especially regarding such common dilemmas as what to do when only one of the two children can get the first turn or play with a toy designed for one player, lead to the juxtaposition of the individual interests of the two friends and, thence, to potential conflicts. According to some sources, the pursuit of individual needs has often been seen as permissible within the friendships of males only (e.g. Buhrmester, 1996; Maccoby, 1990). Children may also see the context of a close relationship as one in which they might expect to be allowed to pursue their own wishes without fear (Hartup, 1989) and to be accepted without the need to exert the effort inherent in being equitable in each instance. Despite this, reciprocity remains the basis of the relationship. There might be a tendency to concede to the friend's wishes when the inevitable problem arises (Jones, 1985; Morgan and Sawyer, 1967), as a token expression of friendship or, perhaps, out of apprehension of losing the friend. Jones (1985) found that, on occasions when friends wished to argue for their own interests, they felt a far greater need than non-friends to justify their own assertive behaviour to each other. In contrast, Hartup *et al.* (1993) found that this tendency of friends to offer more elaborate rationales applied to dyads of girls, but not to boys. This could reflect the frequent contention that girls are more reticent to promote their own interests in their close relationships (e.g. Buhrmester, 1996).

In an observational study of friends and non-friends negotiating how they might share a single toy, Fonzi, Schneider, Tani and Tomada (1997) found that friends worked harder to find a compromise and they displayed greater sensitivity in their discussions than did non-friends. Their most dramatic finding is the fact that the dyads of friends spent over twice as much time in their discussions as non-friends. Friends also responded to each other's proposals with far more novelty. They also tended to accept their friends' offers either partially or conditionally instead of totally accepting or rejecting their friends' offers. The greater elapsed time could be interpreted by itself in several ways. It might well mean that friends felt the need to offer each other more elaborate rationales for their positions than non-friends, as suggested by Jones (1985). It might also indicate that, in keeping with the findings of Tesser, Campbell and Smith (1984), friends stood their ground in order to avoid the deflating experience of losing to a close friend.

Dyads of non-friends often spend much time at the beginning of the problem-solving process determining their respective roles rather than tackling the problem (Azmitia and Perlmutter, 1989). Thus, although the findings are not entirely consistent, the overall picture is that friends work harder than non-friends to avoid turning everyday problems into heated conflicts. Summarizing current research on the significance of conflict in childhood friendship, Hartup (1992) maintained that it is the management of conflict, rather than the presence of conflict that is important for longevity and well-being of children's relationships with their friends.

The stability of the friendships of primary schoolchildren in a changing peer configuration

In theory, it is easier to study the stability of the friendships of primary schoolchildren than those of preschoolers because primary schoolchildren can describe their friendships much better. This provides the opportunity to study how friendships emerge, enhance and decline against the backdrop of a peer group context that rarely remains constant.

Children's school lives are punctuated by regular, predictable changes in their network of acquaintances and potential friends, above and beyond those changes that cannot be foreseen. They often form friendships at school; consequently, the network of acquaintances changes at the end of each school year, to a greater or lesser degree depending on the size of the community, the transience of its population and the organization of the school system. Even if regular contact between friends is still possible, the return to school after summer vacation may provide an opportunity to re-evaluate the relationship, consciously or unconsciously, after what is often a period of separation for some or all of the summer. Some friendships may wane as partners mature and change and as new opportunities for friendship with other children emerge; other friendships may be maintained or enhanced. Continuing or renewing a friendship within the somewhat altered peer-group configuration that emerges each school year may be an important step, not only for the individual relationships of children with their friends, but also in the developmental unfolding of the ability to form lasting, close relationships in general.

The life cycle of children's relationships

Considerable research has been conducted to determine how the nature of children's friendships changes with increasing age. In virtually all of the studies, each friendship is studied only at a single point in time. It is important to remember, however, that relationships with friends also change over time. The nature of developmental changes in children's relationships with their friends has received very little attention from researchers.

Developmental models of friendship maintain that relationships with friends undergo marked qualitative change over their life course. In developmental models, the processes related to initial attraction become less potent in cementing the relationship as it continues. Although a number of stage models have been proposed for relationships in general (e g., Altman and Taylor, 1973; Levinger, 1980; see Fehr, 1996), most of these pertain primarily to relationships between adults. However, a stage model for children's friendships is at least implicit in Selman's recent work on pair therapy (Selman and Schultz, 1990); its content essentially parallels both Selman's stage model for children's understanding of friendship (Selman, 1980) and most of the developmental models in the adult literature. The reciprocity of the relationship and in turn, the intimacy of the bond between the two friends, characterize the higher stages, replacing the more unilateral benefits obtained from the relationship that are essential elements of the earlier stages. Such unilateral benefits might include enjoyment of a leisure activity, for example. The intimate exchange that emerges at the higher stages is seen as the essence of friendship (e.g. Sharabany, 1994), consistent with some of the writings of philosophers and theologians, as noted above.

Ways of studying children's relationships with their close friends

It is essential to remember that children's friendships are private phenomena that often occur at times and in places where adults are not present. This reality imposes certain limitations on all available means for studying children's friendships. The most common methods employed by the widely cited early studies were essay techniques (e.g. Bigelow and La Gaipa, 1975), in which children and adolescents wrote about their conceptions of friendship, or interviews on the topic of friendship. Although these techniques may be of some value, essays and interviews are abstract methods in which certain elements of children's relationships cannot be captured. Because of their limited vocabulary, children may not be able to fully articulate or identify certain features of their friendships, even though these may be important dimensions of their relationships. It has been argued that a more direct approach is more useful. Gottman, (1983) for example, suggested that it was necessary to directly observe the interactions of children, instead of speculating about them through more abstract approaches; this enables the researcher to identify certain behaviour sequences that are crucial to the friendship. However, this may be difficult to implement with older children. Elements that are integral to the friendships of older children, such as self-disclosure, are usually kept from outside observers (Foster, Bell-Dolan and Berler, 1986). Researchers therefore have to assess the impact of their method on the results obtained. In light of this, it is often the case that children exhibit behaviour associated with a characteristic of friendship earlier than they articulate the importance of the particular characteristic (e.g. Rotenberg and Sliz, 1988).

Different methods are used in contemporary research in order to learn about different aspects of friendship. It is important to know which children are friends, how stable the friendship is and what kind of relationship they have. Furthermore, it is important to know something about each of the friends as individuals. As detailed later, friendship, which sounds quite benevolent, can be quite harmful if one befriends the wrong person. The reader is referred to Hartup's (1995) review article for convincing arguments in favour of measuring all of these facets of friendship.

Reciprocal sociometric choice was the traditional sociometric technique for identifying friends until recently. Users of these techniques, (e.g. Northway, 1952) from the early pioneers to many current researchers, rely on peer nomination as a main criterion for friendship. For instance, if Amy nominates Helen as a play or work partner and Helen chooses Amy, they would be considered friends. However, there is a certain limitation to this assumption, for the two children may choose each other even though their relationship is superficial. Peer nomination does not necessarily indicate that a friendship has the mutual trust, support and intimacy characteristic of a close childhood friendship. Error can also occur if a child is considered friendless when there is no reciprocal nomination, because that child may have friends outside the classroom.

There have been some useful improvements in sociometric techniques for measuring friendship. One of these is to phrase the stimulus question in terms of friendship rather than choice of play or work partner, using such questions as 'Who are your good friends among the children in this school?'. However, there is still ambiguity in sociometric techniques, for children may identify their friends according to their own interpretation of the meaning of friendship. Thus, the definition of 'friends' for one child may not be the same as the definition by which his or her friend lives. Because friendship is by definition characterized by the reciprocal commitment of two individuals to a relationship with each other, it is best to designate friends on the basis of mutual nominations by both. In some studies it is necessary to work with the nomination of only one friend, particularly those conducted with adolescents or those conducted outside of the settings where children meet their friends. This is less than ideal, because it does not permit a distinction between reciprocal friendships and relationships in which only one of two children considers the other a friend (Furman, 1996).

Another innovation is to retain the sociometric measures for the choice of play or work partners, but to accompany them with ratings of liking. In other words, in addition to indicating their choices of play or work companions, the respondents would be asked to indicate, perhaps on a five-point scale, how much they like each of their classmates or how much they enjoy spending time with each. Different researchers have used different combinations of unilateral nominations, unilateral ratings, reciprocal nominations and reciprocal ratings in designating children as friends for their studies. It is clear that each method will lead to the identification of different children as friends. Nevertheless, each method has its own valid purpose and the friends identified by each are likely to remain stable for several months (Erdley, Nangle and Gold, 1998).

In addition to identifying friends, it is essential to find out about the quality of their friendships. Some friendships are more intimate; others are more superficial. In some relationships, each friend has equal say in the decisions that the friends take together; in other friendships, one child dominates. Some friendships are characterized by many conflicts. Importantly, friendships differ in terms of how well and how rapidly conflicts are resolved. Several methods of assessing quality have been proposed, none of which are foolproof.

Friendship-quality questionnaires

Friendship quality questionnaires provide a standardized way of assessing friendship quality. Several scales have been developed, including the

Friendship Quality Questionnaire (Parker and Asher, 1993a) and the Friendship Quality Scale (Bukowski, Boivin and Hoza, 1994). The various rating scales have much in common, though they are not identical (see Furman, 1996 for a more detailed summary of the contents of the scales and their psychometric properties). The questionnaires include items pertaining to the defining features of friendship, many of which were introduced earlier in this chapter: similarity, companionship, help, support, conflict and conflict resolution. Although questionnaires are usually used with children aged 8 years old and older, Ladd, Kochenderfer and Coleman (1996) recently developed a structured interview version of a friendship questionnaire for use with children 5 and 6 years old.

In some situations, it is difficult to obtain ratings from both members of a friendship. However, assessing a friendship by means of the perceptions of only one of the two friends has many limitations, although a unilateral perspective on friendship quality is better than not measuring friendship quality at all. Just as marital or romantic partners may see their relationships differently, friends' perceptions of their relationships are not always similar. This does not necessarily mean that the questionnaires are not valid. The persons involved frequently have different views of the same relationship (Furman, 1996); these differences are an integral and intriguing aspect of the scientific study of friendship.

Direct observation

Another way of learning about the quality of children's friendships is by observing the friends in conversation at play. This is by no means easy, because it is not likely that an observer will be present during many of the critical moments of a relationship between friends, such as the expression of intimacy or the resolution of a conflict. The likelihood of an adult observer having access to such critical moments decreases as children get older. Observations of friends interacting at their preschools is very common in studies of younger children, whereas observations of friends of primary-school age or older in their natural play or school settings is quite rare.

John Gottman (1983) is one researcher who was indeed able to observe children in natural play settings. He analysed children's conversations with peers during play sessions at the children's homes. In one study, 13 children ranging in age from 3 to 6 years played host for one play session to either their best friends or to strangers. A subsequent investigation examined 3-year-old to 9-year-old children's conversations over the course of three play sessions. The dyads were recorded on audiotape while the children played in the room where the host child usually entertained playmates. Before the actual play sessions, the parents of the participating children were asked to habituate their children to playing in the presence of the tape recorder. This measure was presumably taken in order to reduce the potential for awkwardness during the play sessions and to encourage the children to behave just as they would have had no recording device been present. From these studies, Gottman generated important information about the social processes that lead to children's friendships.

Jeffrey Parker (1986) used a rather innovative technique to study children's conversations. Parker knew that it would not be possible to train preschool-aged children to act as confederates in his experiment because of the complexity of the confederate's task. Yet he wanted to maintain the rich, spontaneous nature of children's conversation while simultaneously exercising a degree of experimental control (Parker, 1986). Parker utilized a 2–foot-tall talking doll called Panduit to solve this problem. Panduit was small, green and dressed in silver clothing. The doll was immobile, but it stood upright and contained an electronic device that enabled an assistant hidden behind a two-way mirror to talk to the child under the guise of Panduit. Most children responded favourably to the doll (Parker, 1986). This study, similar to Gottman's (1983), provided significant insight into friendship development in children. Without the creative addition of the Panduit confederate, however, the undertaking would not have been possible.

In working with older children, some researchers have attempted to approximate the conditions of real-life friendship in the laboratory. For instance, Dishion and his colleagues (e.g. Dishion, Andrews and Crosby, 1995) invited predelinquent youth to bring their best friends to the laboratory. The friends were filmed while discussing how they would resolve various problems that have occurred to them: planning a common activity, resolving a conflict between themselves and resolving a conflict that they have had with other youth. Several other researchers have attempted to simulate conflict and conflict situations for friends. For example, Hartup *et al.* (1993) observed the interactions of pairs of friends in which each member was given a different explanation of the rules of a boardgame.

Integration of measures

Each of the measures discussed in this section provides useful information about an important aspect of children's friendships. Ideally, a single study should include as many of them as possible.

Individual differences in patterns of friendship

Gender differences

In literature on friendship, gender has received a considerable amount of attention. Studies of friendship selection reveal that there is remarkable consistency in choice of friends in terms of gender. Preschoolers frequently choose cross-sex friends, whereas elementary school and middle school children make almost exclusively same-sex friends. Studies show that the number of cross-sex choices increases with age for adolescents (e.g. Bukowski *et al.*, 1993; Eder and Hallinan, 1978).

Children's same-sex choices appear to be related to their preferred activities. For example, boys who prefer rough-and-tumble play and girls who dislike this type of amusement make more same-sex choices (Bukowski, Gauze, Hoza and Newcomb, 1993; Maccoby, 1988). Bukowski *et al.* (1993) found that there were also gender differences in the quantity of friendships. In their study, elementary school girls reported that they had fewer same-sex friends than boys; this sex difference peaked at approximately age 11. However, there were no gender differences in the number of reciprocated friendships or the stability of friendships yielded no sex differences. Gender differences have been found in the quality of children's friendships. Girls are more likely to report more intimate exchange, validation and caring, help and guidance, closeness and security (Bukowski, Gauze, Hoza and Newcomb, 1993; Parker and Asher, 1993b).

There has been some suggestion that changes in society affect gender differences in the nature of friendship and in children's accessibility to close intimate friendships. For example, Murray (1999), a columnist in the *American Psychological Association Monitor*, observed that in the United States, fathers tend to demand that their boys act 'tough' and that teachers discipline boys with little sensitivity. The mass media now convey images of male heroes as heartless killing machines, replacing the strong but sensitive figures such as the affable cowboy Roy Rogers of the 1950s. For these reasons, Murray maintains, a distrust of other males replaces intimate same-sex friendship as boys enter adolescence. Much more research would be helpful to determine whether Murray's contentions apply to other societies and, indeed, to confirm that they are true for the United States.

Cross-gender friendships

The overwhelming majority of friendships during middle childhood are with members of one's own gender. However, there are distinct advantages and disadvantages to having friends primarily of the opposite gender during the primary school years. Kovacs, Parker and Hoffman (1996) compared 8-year-olds and 9-year-olds with and without friends of the opposite sex. Those researchers found that children whose primary friendships were with members of the opposite sex were perceived by peers as more aggressive and less helpful. These children also tended to be less popular with peers of both the same and opposite sex. Teachers in the study sample rated children in the primary-opposites group lower for academic skills and for social competence. On the other hand, children with mostly opposite-sex friends had fewer stereotypes about gender roles than did children with mostly same-sex friends. They also tended to be better adjusted than children with no friends at all.

Friendship between older and younger children

Epstein (1989) has suggested that the choice of a younger friend may indicate social problems, or it may alternately be a healthy way to achieve balance. For instance, an older child who is physically smaller, cognitively slower, or who is less socially competent may benefit more from the friendship of a younger child than an age-mate (ibid., p. 168). Depressed, socially withdrawn and learning-disabled children (Osman, 1982) frequently select younger friends. Friendships between older and younger children are more difficult to study than same-age friendships, due to the restrictions imposed by the age make-up of the classroom.

Having the wrong friends: friendship and the adjustment of children and adolescents with anti-social behaviour patterns

It has often been emphasized that just having friends may not serve positive functions, because one can have the wrong friends or have troubled relationships with one's friends. Given the expectations that most children and adolescents have of their friends, one would expect aggressive youngsters to be systematically deprived of the benefits of friendship. Children with behaviour disorders tend to be disliked and rejected by their classmates (e.g. Cole and Carpentieri, 1990; Dishion, 1990; Gresham, 1982) and spend much less of their school time interacting with others and more of their time alone (Neel, Cheney, Meadows and Gelhar, 1992; Walker and Rankin, 1983). Thus, they may be excluded from the interactions that later crystallize into friendship. The very fact that their peers regard them as lower-status pupils could make them less attractive as candidates for friendship. Youngsters who break rules might also be excluded from extracurricular activities where friendships might develop and may alienate prospective friends by their behaviour.

According to Sullivan (1953) and Selman (1980), a true friendship between children in middle childhood or later can emerge only when the relationship progresses to the point where the members are able to share intimate experiences. Many relationships involving aggressive children and adolescents may never get to that point because of the inability to resolve the inevitable conflicts. According to most available research, these individuals are not proficient at generating appropriate solutions to problems or at seeing things from the perspective of another person (Richard and Dodge, 1982). The solutions they generate tend to be hostile and insensitive (Guerra and Slaby, 1989; Lochman and Dodge, 1994) and they tend to misinterpret the behaviour of others as having hostile intent (Dodge and Frame, 1982).

Therefore, it is not surprising that some studies indicate that aggressive children have fewer friends than do other children (Cairns et al., 1988;

Ray, Cohen, Secrist and Duncan, 1997). Nevertheless, it has been demonstrated clearly that even the most aggressive children do have friends (e.g. Dishion, Andrews and Crosby, 1995; Rys and Bear, 1997; Windle, 1994). Who are these friends? Consistent with the principle of homophily, according to which individuals form friendships with others who are similar to themselves (Berndt, 1982; Erwin, 1985), aggressive children tend to form friendships with other aggressive children. This has been confirmed many times, even for children as young as 4 years (Farver, 1996). In a study conducted with 886 boys from homes of low socioeconomic status in Montreal, Tessier, Tremblay and Bukowski (1994) found that boys formed friendships with peers who shared a similar level of aggressiveness. Similarly, homophily was found to be a factor in determining friendships between anti-social American boys with similar arrest records and levels of anti-social behaviour in a study conducted by Dishion, Andrews and Crosby (1995). Kupersmidt, DeRosier and Patterson (1995) also found that aggressive and rejected third- and fourth-graders often became each other's friends. Further confirmation of the homophily effect for friendships among elementary-school children was provided by Poulin *et al.* (1997), whose research featured multiple measures of different types of aggression in multiple settings.

Some North American studies also indicate the harm caused by mutual friendships between aggressive children and youth. Berndt and Keefe (1995) conducted a longitudinal study with adolescents in which it was determined that having friends who disrupted the class was associated with an increase in disruption later in the school year. In the Montreal study by Tessier, Tremblay and Bukowski (1994), aggressive boys who had aggressive friends displayed higher levels of delinquent behaviour in their self-reports than aggressive boys whose friends were not aggressive. Moreover, researchers have noted increases in aggression over time among children who have relationships with aggressive peers (e.g. Boivin, Vitaro and Hodges, 1998; Poulin, Dishion and Medici, 1998).

Little is known at this point about the precise mechanisms by which aggressive friends exacerbate each other's problematic aggression. Cooper, Brooks, LeCroy and Ashford (1994) speculated that one reason why delinquents sometimes seem to have close friendships may be because their good friendships are the result of lax parental supervision. They contend that lax supervision and the absence of parental monitoring may be the real risk factors, not the friendship itself. In a pioneering examination of conversation protocols, Dishion *et al.* (1997) found that deviant and violent talk was common in the conversations between aggressive male adolescents and their friends. In a study with elementary-school-age participants, Grotpeter and Crick (1996) found that engaging together in aggressive acts was a prominent feature of the friendships of overtly aggressive children.

Aggressive children and adolescents may also transmit their beliefs to each other. Children and youth may have to adopt the core attitudes and beliefs of friends or potential friends in order to remain a part of a particular social circle without experiencing high levels of cognitive dissonance. This may be especially true in the late elementary school grades, when students become quite concerned about their status among peers (e.g. Parker and Gottman, 1989). More information is needed about the effects of friends' interactions on thinking patterns and beliefs that may be related to aggression, particularly patterns of social problem-solving and maladaptive beliefs about aggressive behaviour. Investigators have consistently found that aggressive children and adolescents are more likely than non-aggressive youngsters to attribute hostile intent to ambiguous social behaviours, to set social goals involving revenge and domination, to generate fewer non-aggressive solutions to social problems, to evaluate aggressive behaviours positively and to lack confidence in their ability to implement non-aggressive strategies. Aggressive children and youth are also more likely than their non-aggressive peers to approve of aggressive behaviour (Huesmann and Guerra, 1997).

Enemies

In the traditional sociometric literature, saying that you would not want to play with someone was considered the same as saying that the person nominated was your enemy (e.g. Shantz, 1985). This parallels the common practice in that literature of equating friendship with saying that you would choose to play or to work with someone. However, just as it is important to distinguish between a friend and a best friend, it is important to distinguish among levels of disliking. One can wish not to play or work with someone for a variety of reasons, as enumerated in Chapter 5. Not all these reasons amount to the intense, extended loathing that characterizes hatred (Frude, 1993) and enemyship. Studying degrees of dislike is made difficult by the fact that children use the word 'hate' far too easily for their pronouncements of hate to be taken seriously (Frude, 1993).

Just as friendship has distinct qualities above and beyond preferential choice of work or play companions, there are, at least in theory, certain special properties of relationships between enemies. These have been studied to a limited extent in the literature on adult interpersonal relationships. Wiseman and Duck (1995) summarize some of the distinct properties of enemyship (a term they themselves had to coin). They make it clear that enemyship is not the same thing as rejecting a peer. Enemyship is, first of all, a relationship with a specific person, often one who has interfered with the attainment of one's goals. It is a fairly enduring relationship that often involves the conscious use of power against the enemy. Harsh feelings against enemies remain vivid after relatively long periods of time. In some but not all ways, enemyship is the opposite of friendship. People can rank their enemies as well as their friends, i.e. speak of worst enemies and best friends. Enemies try to make each other feel uncomfortable, just as friends try to make each other feel at ease. Enemies also strive to give each other a negative self-image, whereas friends try to be rewarding to each other and to enhance each other's feelings of self-worth. In describing their enemies, adults speak primarily of malicious actions, not of personal qualities. Both friends and enemies are likely to be members of one's own sex. Only a small minority of adults report having no enemies.

Surprisingly, there appears to be no systematic research about the number of enemies children have, the number of children who have stable enemies, or about the stability of enemyship in childhood. However, there have been a few studies of the basis for children believing that other children are their enemies. For example, Hayes, Gershman and Bolin (1980) asked preschoolers to indicate 'Whom do you dislike more than any one else?'. More boys than girls were named as enemies by children of both genders. The researchers asked the children to state the reasons for their dislike of their enemies. Aggressive behaviour and breaking rules were the most frequent reasons.

Hayes, Gershman and Halteman (1996) extended that research by comparing the reasons for enemyship provided by males at four developmental levels - preschool, primary school, early adolescence and young adulthood. Aggression and aberrant behaviour (e.g. 'he talks too loud') were given as reasons for enemyship at all ages. There were also some age-specific findings. Inappropriate play and breaking rules constituted a substantial basis for enemyship only during the preschool years. Early adolescents reported that their enemies were phoney. Both early adolescents and, especially, young adult men, also mentioned negative character traits, e.g. 'He is mean'.

What purpose is served by having enemies? Some psychoanalytic writers have taken up this question. Their answers have yet to inspire systematic research even with adults, so there is little conclusive evidence regarding the function of enemies in children's social lives. In terms of basic instinctual needs, having enemies has been linked to stranger anxiety in infants, which typically emerges at about the eighth month of life (e.g. Volkan, 1988). According to some speculations, stranger anxiety functions to help the infant learn the difference between close loved ones and everyone else and to learn the difference between good and bad. Based on the psychoanalytic writings of Melanie Klein, Fornari (1966; Volkan, 1988) maintained that the stranger becomes the infant's first enemy, even though the stranger has never attacked the infant in any way. The infant senses the enemy as a 'bad presence' that the infant tries to eliminate.

Displacement is another source in infancy of enemyship according to some psychoanalytic writings (Parens, 1979; Volkan, 1988). According to those sources, the infant develops a biologically-based aggressive drive that surges for some reason at about age 9 months. Afraid that any aggression towards an individual in the immediate environment might lead to the loss of the mother's love, the infant displaces or channels the aggressive impulses and needs enemies to serve as targets.

Enemies also have functions in the playgroups that emerge during the preschool and school years. Opposition to a common enemy helps solidify a group that otherwise might be torn apart by disagreements within it. Second, people are thought to have a tendency to attribute their own shortcomings to their enemies: 'enemies in effect serve as receptacles of the protagonists' own assimilated garbage, what they cannot or will not acknowledge about themselves' (Aho, 1994; p. 87). Aho also stated that well-adjusted individuals 'who have fully digested and assimilated their own garbage' (1994, p. 117) might have no need for enemies and, therefore, might refrain from creating them. Unfortunately, very little is known about what types of children (or adults) tend to have the most enemies or hate them the most. There is also virtually no concrete knowledge about the effects enemies have on children.

A few studies suggest that children, like adults (Wiseman and Duck, 1995), are very vigilant in the presence of their enemies. They seem to be constantly on the lookout for new offences and seem to believe in advance that they will have to defend themselves against counterattack. Ray and Cohen (1997) conducted a study in which they read to the 11-year-old participants a series of stories about children in situations where they might have been provoked by other children. In some of these stories, it was clear that the other child's act was intentional; in others, the act was plainly an accident. The most interesting stories, however, were about situations in which the intention of the other child could not be determined from the information provided. In some of the stories, the children were described as friends, in others as enemies (i.e. children who disliked each other). The children participating in the research were asked whether the child in the story had provoked the other child accidentally or intentionally. They were much more likely to believe that the child's provocation was intentional in stories where the children were enemies.

Enemyship also seems to affect children's use of language in everyday conversations. This was evident in an exploratory study by Bernicot and Mahrokhian (1988), who worked with Parisian children from 5 to 8 years of age. The children were asked to complete a set of unfinished comic strips in which the hero (Mickey Mouse or Donald Duck) had to make a request for information or for some action from either a close friend or a 'mean enemy'. The requests made to enemies differed dramatically from those made to good friends. The requests to enemies were phrased very carefully. They included elaborate reasons and justifications for the requests to enemies, as well as subtle but nasty innuendoes about the personalities of the enemies.

Further research on enemyship in childhood could be very profitable in explaining bullying and other forms of aggression in schools. In discussing the role of hatred in some forms of human aggression, Storr (1968) focused on the aggressor's need to compensate for past humiliations. That possibility and, indeed the full history of the relationships between aggressors and their victims, have not been studied sufficiently. Thus, there is a need for a dyadic perspective in studying both the positive and negative aspects of children's peer relations.

8 Peer relations of children with atypical patterns of development

Intellectual handicaps, behaviour disorders, learning disabilities and giftedness are all known to affect children's interpersonal relations. This chapter includes consideration of the mechanisms by which these atypical patterns of development influence peer relations. Research on the peer status of these individuals is reviewed.

As discussed in Chapter 1, the pioneers in peer-relations research during the 1920s and 1930s berated the psychoanalytic tradition for building its basic theories with insights gathered exclusively from the study of people who demonstrated atypical and problematic social behaviour. Since that time, the call for more research on normal populations has been heeded. Ironically, many scholars are now engaged in eloquent appeals for more and better study of children with atypical development. Although research on children with atypical development has not declined since the 1920s and has indeed mushroomed, most of the research has been conducted with the certain purpose of understanding the atypical populations and finding better ways of educating them, not with the primary aim of acquiring knowledge about the human species that could contribute to developmental theory. One of the major challenges faced by contemporary scholars of child development is how to integrate data obtained from atypical and typical populations in formulating and refining coherent theories. One of the most comprehensive and readable writings on that problem is a chapter by Burack (1997), who offers a number of useful analogies to illustrate the importance of data from atypical samples. He notes that in physics, for example, scientists have discovered how to slow the motion of atoms almost to a standstill; studying the atoms in that extreme and unusual situation has provided valuable insights into their essential nature. Studying persons who have had brain injuries has been a mainstay of research in the neurosciences. Although many of the most influential early theorists in child development assigned little value to the study of exceptions to their general rules, more recent scholars, led by Bronfenbrenner (Bronfenbrenner, Kessel, Kessen and White, 1986), argued against this general world view that they regarded as too broad to capture the realities of children in their social worlds. They advocated, with some success, greater attention to individual, environmental and social differences. This chapter - along with Chapter 9 on cultural differences and the discussions on gender differences in Chapters 2 and 7 - describes only some of the work that has been conducted to understand individual differences in children's social relations.

Equity theory (e.g. Hatfield, Utne and Traupmann, 1979) is a cornerstone of the literature on friendship in social psychology. According to different versions of that theory, a relationship will survive if both partners believe that they derive equal benefit from it, or if they each perceive that they get out of the relationship as much as they put in. In friendships between children with atypical patterns of development and peers with disabilities, there is unlikely to be strict equity. One of the friends needs more help and is often incapable of providing as much reward as the other. Thus, the study of the peer relations tests the limits of equity theories. Can they be stretched to apply to equity in a socialist sense - where each relationship partner contributes as much as he or she can and derives as much benefit as he or she needs?

The following pages provide an illustration of how children's peer relations are influenced by three atypical patterns of social interaction: those of children with mental retardation, learning disabilities and the potential for gifted behaviour. These three forms of exceptionality bring different features to interpersonal relationships. Mental retardation is often a very visible disability because it may affect physical appearance and because it is obvious to classmates that children with mental retardation do poorly at most academic tasks, in many games and in mastering the subtleties of interpersonal communication. Learning disabilities are more subtle because children with learning disabilities are not recognizable by their physical appearance and because they may do well at certain tasks, though they fail at others. Children with the potential for gifted behaviour often make themselves apparent to others by their proficiencies and talents, which are positive attributes but none the less attributes that may make them different from most of their peers.

Friendships of children with mental retardation

The friendships of children with disabilities test the limits of many of the theories discussed in Chapter 7. Similarity is a key characteristic of friendships of normally developing children. However, the classic finding embodied in the principle of homophily (see Chapter 7) that children select friends of the same gender, race, IQ, social status and/or academic achievement (Berndt, 1982) may not extend to similarity in disability status.

Indeed, Cuksts (1988) found that, in integrated classrooms, adolescents with physical disabilities harboured negative feelings about having friends who also had disabilities. The usual reasons for becoming friends may not apply to children without MR who do befriend children with MR despite the fact that the friendships are not reciprocal, shared leisure activities may be difficult and the friend with a disability may obtain much more support than the friend without a disability. In a friendship between a child with typical development and one with disabilities, the latter may have limited ability to partake in recreational activities and may not be able to 'give' as much as to 'receive'. This is documented by Cukst's (1988) finding that children with disabilities who were rejected by their peers did not report what they could contribute to a friendship, but did refer to their personal gains from friendship.

Crystal, Watanabe and Chen (1999) suggested that both age and culture should be important moderators of children's acceptance of peers with disabilities. In their view, members of collectivistic cultures (see Chapter 9), where people have a heightened sense of obligation to fellow group members, should be more accepting of individuals with disabilities than members of individualistic societies, such as the United States, where higher value is placed on independence, self-reliance and competitiveness. These authors also proposed that concern and empathy for peers with disabilities increase over the course of development from early childhood through adolescence. This is because such complex cognitive processes as abstract thinking and perspective-taking (the ability to understand the perspective of other individuals in a social situation [Selman, 1980]) are needed in order to process the concept of equality and to think of other persons in a non-stereotyped manner.

Sadly, there are few indications that children of any age or culture accept peers with mental retardation as readily as they accept others. Table 8.1 contains only studies of the actual peer acceptance of real children. In a number of other studies, children were surveyed about their general attitudes towards peers with mental retardation. The results of the survey studies are not always as negative as those of most of the real-life sociometric studies.

The studies listed in Table 8.1 are nearly unanimous, although it must be remembered that only two of them were conducted outside North America (Manetti, Schneider and Siperstein, 2000; Nabuzoka and Ronning, 1997). Only studies conducted since 1975 are listed, but the reader can rest assured that the same sad tale was told in studies published before that date, all of which were from the United States. As shown in Table 8.1, the researchers in a few of the studies wisely took into account the social behaviour of the children with mental retardation. Those studies suggest that children with mental retardation may not be doomed to peer rejection solely because they have mental retardation: They can achieve peer accep-

Table 8.1 Studies since 1975 on the social acceptance of children with mental retardation (MR) by their peers without mental retardation

Author	n	Age (years)	Measure(s) of mental retardation	Measure(s) of peer acceptance	Results
Strichart and Gottlieb (1975)	80	9–12	School decision	Amount of imitative behaviour by peers without MR Play with peers without MR	–
Ballard, Corman, Gottlieg and Kaufman (1977)	37	8–10	School decision	Sociometrics	+ with treatment
Reese-Dukes and Stokes (1978)	54	10–11	School decision	Sociometrics	–
Gottlieb, Semmel and Veldman (1978)	324	Mean: 11	School decision	Sociometrics	+ if competent – if disruptive
Marlowe (1979)	14	10	IQ, observation of habits	Sociometrics	–
MacMillan and Morrison (1980)	287	7–14	School decision, IQ	Sociometrics	–
Morrison, Forness and MacMillan (1983)	133	7–14	Psychological assessments, persistent academic failure attributed to substandard intellectual functioning	Sociometrics, observation, teacher ratings	–
Bender, Wyne, Stuck and Bailey (1984)	33	9–11	School decision, achievement testing	Sociometrics	–
Taylor, Asher and Williams (1987)	68	8, 9, 11	School decision, intellectual and academic deficits	Sociometrics, teacher ratings	–

Study	N	Age	Criterion	Method	Result
Gresham and Reschly (1987)	302	8–12	U.S. state guidelines	Sociometrics	–
O'Keefe, Saxon and Siperstein (1991)	320	8–11	School decision	Sociometrics	–
Siperstein, Leffert and Widaman (1996)	43	Mean: 11	IQ	Sociometrics, observations	NS; depended on social competence
Nabuzoka and Ronning (1997) (Zambia)	75	8–12	Assessed by a psychologist and psychiatrist	Attitude questionnaire	–
Manetti, Schneider and Siperstein (in press) (Italy)	197	9–11	Italian national guidelines	Sociometric ratings	–

Notes: +: Children with MR were better accepted than others.
  –: Children with MR were less accepted than others.
  NS: No significant difference in acceptance
Study was conducted in North America unless otherwise indicated

tance if their social behaviour is perceived as competent. Therefore, teaching socially competent behaviour merits high priority by the teachers and parents of children with mental retardation.

Children with learning disabilities

Although they are of average intelligence or higher, children with learning disabilities have specific deficits in some of their academic subjects areas, or in processing information of some specific types (e.g. visual symbols or spoken language). These problems are thought to be associated with neurological dysfunctions, although it is not common to diagnose brain damage in each individual case. The nature and definition of learning disabilities have been debated extensively (see Polloway, Patton, Smith and Buck, 1997).

Wiener (1987) summarized the theories that have been proposed to account for the problems faced by children with learning disabilities in their relations with peers. One possibility is the *discrepancy hypothesis*, according to which children with learning disabilities are disliked because they lack abilities that are valued by their peers and that children without learning disabilities are more likely to possess. Depending on the peer group, such abilities could include proficiency in academic subjects, physical attractiveness, general intelligence, or athletic ability. In contrast, the *psychological processing deficit* hypothesis holds that the peer-relations problems of children with learning disabilities stem from the same basic perceptual, cognitive and language-processing deficits that cause their difficulties in academic subjects. Those deficits may affect the ability to understand the intentions of others, to read other people's emotions and to react to them in a manner that is appropriate to the situation. In a somewhat similar vein, the *strategic deficit hypothesis* holds that, just as children with learning disabilities lack the strategies needed to approach academic problems actively and competently, they lack the strategies needed to tackle and resolve social problems. Finally, the *differential treatment hypothesis* links the social problems of children with learning disabilities to differences in the way adults or peers interact with them. For example, teachers who are aware of the learning-disabled status of some of their pupils might treat them as they would treat children younger than the level of the classroom and peer group.

In a more recent formulation, San Miguel, Forness and Kavale (1996) proposed a *psychiatric comorbidity hypothesis* to account for the peer-relations problems of children with learning disabilities. According to that hypothesis, the difficulties are attributable to the very high rates of depression and attention problems among children with learning disabilities. Both depression (Ederer, 1990) and attention problems (Landau and Moore, 1991) have been linked to the social rejection of children by their peers.

Table 8.2 depicts the results of recent studies on the peer acceptance of learning disabilities. As shown, most studies indicate that children with learning disabilities are rejected by their peers. The results of earlier studies are, unfortunately, no more encouraging. Of course, these results do not mean that every child with learning disabilities suffers rejection by peers. Researchers are continuing to study the peer relations of children with learning disabilities in order to find out which types of learning disability are associated with social success and social failure.

Children with special academic talent or exceptional creativity

Friendships between gifted children and their non-gifted peers are characterized by an inequality that is somewhat different in complexion from the relationships between children with and without disabilities. In some situations, gifted children can bring greater reward to their relationships with non-gifted peers than can their friends who do not share their special talents. This may occur to the extent that the 'Terman myth' is not a myth. Terman, an eminent American psychologist who conducted longitudinal studies of children with high IQs from the 1920s to the 1960s believed that high IQ would enable children to be better than others at virtually everything — school, sports, moral character, friendship and, later, marriage. Accordingly, they should be better than their non-gifted friends at many of the activities that are valued in the peer group, which should make them popular. They should also be better at using their intellectual abilities to solve problems that arise within their relationships (Terman and Oden, 1959).

However, there are other situations in which the Terman myth may be less applicable to the peer relationships of gifted children. A lot depends on whom one regards as gifted. If by 'gifted' one means children who fall in the top 2 or 3 per cent of the distribution of IQ scores (i.e. IQ greater than 125 or so), that means that in a primary school of 400 pupils, there would be ten or so gifted children. Those ten might share the interests of the group and be popular among them because of the things that they do well. However, if by gifted one means a one-in-a-thousand genius, things could be quite different. That exceptional individual may be very different from his or her schoolmates. Like the gifted child at the top second or third percentile of IQ scores, the prodigious child displaying rarer levels of high ability is able to answer the teacher's questions very readily and do well on tests. However, that child's capacities and needs are far beyond the level of the regular academic programme; his or her interests may be very different from those of most peers, who may have difficulty understanding him or her and who may find the very talented child somewhat strange. The one-in-a-thousand genius may be bored and alienated.

Table 8.2 Studies since 1980 on the social acceptance of children with learning disabilities by their peers without learning disabilities

Author	n	Age (years)	Measure(s) of learning disability	Measure(s) of peer acceptance	Results
Garett and Crump (1980)	200	9–11	School decision	Sociometrics	–
McMichael (1980) (UK)	198	5	Reading and vocabulary tests	Sociometrics	–
Prillaman (1981)	390	6–11	IQ, achievement test scores, psychological deficits	Sociometrics	NS
Horowitz (1981)	188	Mean: 9	School decision, IQ, achievement test scores, teacher observations	Sociometrics	NS
Johnson and Johnson (1983)	71	9	School decision	Peer attitude scales, observation	NS
Bursuck (1983)	24	8–9	School decision based on diagnostic test battery	Sociometrics, friendship nominations	NS
Sainato, Zigmond and Strain (1983)	46	9–13	Achievement test scores, IQ	Sociometrics, observation	NS
Levy and Gottlieb (1984)	68	8–10	Identified by child study team as perceptually or neurologically impaired	Sociometrics, observation	–
Marotz Ray (1985)	664	8–11	School decision	Sociometrics, teacher ratings, observations	–
Flicek and Landau (1985)	220	8–11	School decision	Sociometrics	–
Gresham and Reschly (1986)	200	Mean: 9	State guidelines, IQ, achievement test scores	Sociometrics	–

Study	N	Age	Definition	Measure	Result
Gottlieb, Gottlieb, Berkell and Levy (1986)	74	8–10	Identified by school	Sociometrics	–
Hoyle and Serafica (1988)	233	Mean: 10	School decision, IQ, achievement scores	Sociometrics	–
Kistner and Gatlin (1989)	713	8–10	School decision, IQ, achievement scores, evident mental deficit	Sociometrics	NS
Bursuck (1989)	32	7–9, 11	IQ, achievement test scores	Sociometrics	–
Vaughn, Hogan, Kouzekanani and Shapiro (1990)	249	3–5	Identified by the school district as having a discrepancy between IQ and achievement test scores and an information processing deficit	Sociometrics	–
Stone and La Greca (1990)	547	9–11	Evidence of a disorder in one or more basic psychological processes, academic achievement below student's IQ not due to other handicaps	Sociometrics	–
Ochoa and Palmer (1991)	793	9–10	IQ, language and achievement scores	Sociometrics	–
Vaughn, Haager, Hogan and Kouzekanani (1992)	249	5–9	Identified by school district, discrepancy between IQ and achievement tests, evidence of processing deficit	Sociometrics	NS
Juvonen and Bear (1992)	255	8	State criteria, discrepancy between achievement and intelligence scores, IQ	Sociometrics, friendship nominations	NS

Table 8.2 Continued

Author	n	Age (years)	Measure(s) of learning disability	Measure(s) of peer acceptance	Results
Vaughn, McIntosh, Schumm, Haager and Callwood (1993)	220	8–15	Identified by school district	Sociometrics, friendship nominations	NS
Nabuzoka and Smith (1993) (UK)	358	8–12	IQ, medical and psychological assessments	Sociometrics, peer ratings	–
Bear, Juvonen and McInerney (1993)	46	10	Identified by school board, IQ, achievement test scores	Sociometrics	NS
Sale and Carey (1995)	634	6–10	Identified by school special education services, clinical judgements	Sociometrics	–
Pearl, Farmer, van Acker, Rodkin, Bost, Coe and Henley (1998)	1538	9–11	School decision	Social cognitive maps, peer behavioural assessments	–
Margalit (1998) (Israel)	187	5–6	Psycho educational team, IQ, language and/or perceptual delays	Sociometrics, friendship nominations	–

Notes: –: indicates that children with learning disabilities were rejected by peers.
NS: indicates no significant differences in peer acceptance of children with and without learning disabilities.
Study was conducted in North America unless otherwise indicated

Similar ostracism may be the fate of the child whose giftedness is defined in terms of exceptional creativity rather than high IQ. By definition, creativity means the ability to see things in novel and often different ways; the novelty may be welcomed by peers in some cases, but the differences may not be valued. Furthermore, in order to translate their creative potential into an enduring contribution to science, the fine arts, or literature, creative children must withdraw for extended periods of time in order to develop their talents and produce their creative products. A musically precocious child cannot at the same time play football and compose a symphony or practise the violin. A budding writer cannot always afford to take the time away from the novel he or she is writing in order to join schoolmates who are listening to rock music, even if he or she shares that interest or would feign to in order to be better accepted. Going even further is the belief, widespread among artists and musicians, that truly creative persons must suffer in order to reach the pinnacle of their creative potential (Andreasen and Canter, 1975). Being rejected by peers is indeed a sure way of suffering.

It has been traditional to study the lives of the gifted through historical records and biographical accounts. As noted in Chapter 1, those sources provide very limited information about social relations. This applies even more to biographies of eminent persons, because the biographers typically pay the most attention to the early signs of greatness, eminence and creativity. Schneider (1987) surveyed autobiographies rather than biographies, based on the assumption that early peer relations have a far more enduring impression on a person writing his or her own life story than a biographer chronicling the personal life of a famous person. Schneider found clear but brief accounts of early relationships at the beginning of most autobiographies. The social competence depicted in them varied enormously by the discipline in which the individual achieved eminence. The childhoods of about half of the outstanding writers were marred by loneliness and/or peer rejection. The early histories of musicians and visual artists were quite similar to those of the writers. In contrast, scientists and political leaders appear to have fared quite well in their relations with childhood friends.

One would not have the impression from Table 8.3 that many gifted children do other than superbly in relating to others. Studies conducted before 1980 convey a similar impression. It is worth noting that, in at least one major study, by Solano (1976), gifted boys were found to be popular while gifted girls tended to be rejected. Nevertheless, in general, the Terman myth is not devoid of a substantial grain of truth. However, a glance at the table will reveal that giftedness was defined in almost every study either by high IQ or by high academic achievement. This is partly because it is very difficult to measure creativity with as much precision. Furthermore, in order to achieve the sample size needed for the study, most researchers defined the top 1–3 per cent of the population as gifted. As detailed by Schneider

Table 8.3 Studies since 1980 on the social acceptance of gifted children by their non-gifted peers

Author	n	Age (years)	Measure(s) of giftedness	Measure(s) of peer acceptance	Results
Maddux, Scheiber and Bass (1982)	110	10–11	IQ, achievement test scores, teacher referral	Sociometrics	11-year-olds: NS 10-year-olds: –
Barnett and Fiscella (1985)	35	3–6	IQ	Observer ratings	+
Carter and Kuechenmeister (1986)	470	8–10	School decision	Sociometrics, parent and teacher ratings	NS
Adler, Mueller and Ary (1987)	868	8–13	School decision	Sociometrics	+
Eccles, Bauman and Rotenberg (1989)	735	7–14	IQ	Sociometrics	+
Schneider, Clegg, Byrne, Ledingham and Crombie (1989)	213	10	IQ	Sociometrics	+
Lupkowski (1989)	35	3–5	IQ, achievement test	Parent questionnaires, observation	NS
Luftig and Nichols (1991)	496	11	IQ, achievement testing, marks, teacher and parent nominations	Sociometrics	+
Schneider and Daniels (1992)	58	5	IQ	Sociometrics, teacher ratings, observation	Boys: – Girls: NS
Cohen, Duncan and Cohen (1994)	255	Mean: 11	IQ, school marks, portfolio of superior ideas and accomplishments	Sociometrics	+

Study	N	Age	Identification	Measure	Result
Farmer and Farmer (1996)	96	8–9	School decision	Sociometrics	+
Udvari and Rubin (1996)	123	8–14	School board decision, Teacher and/or parent nominations	Sociometrics	NS
Galloway and Porath (1997)	23	Mean: 10	IQ	Teacher and parent ratings	+
Pearl, Farmer, van Acker, Rodkin, Bost, Coe and Henley (1998)	1538	9–11	IQ	Peer interviews, Peer behavioural assessments	+

Notes: +: Gifted children better accepted by their peers
−: Gifted children less accepted by their peers
NS: No significant difference in acceptance between gifted children and non-gifted children.
Study was conducted in North America unless otherwise indicated.

(1987), peer rejection would probably be much more common had the researchers focused on highly creative children rather than those with high IQs, or on the top 0.1 per cent of the IQ range.

Conclusions: exceptionality and children's peer relations

It should be noted that much of the research documenting the peer rejection of many children with disabilities is by now very dated. Hopefully, as more generations of children go through their school years in contact with children with exceptional patterns of social development, some of the stigma associated with disability will lessen. This might occur because children may get used to seeing children with disabilities as peers who belong to the same group, with learning needs that are among the responsibilities of their own teachers. However, within the reality of schools as captured by most research, the examples of children with mental retardation, learning disabilities and gifted potential illustrate that children's friendships have difficulty overcoming the obstacles of dissimilarities between friends and inequalities in friends' abilities to provide for each other a rewarding relationship. If the advantages intended by those who advocate educating children with exceptionalities in normal school settings are to be realized, much more will have to be done in than is currently attempted in most places to help cement rewarding relationships between children with and without disabilities. Some practical ways of doing this are discussed in Chapter 11.

9 Cultural differences in peer relations

Characteristics of cultures are thought to affect the relationships of individuals within them. This chapter contains a review of research documenting this, with emphasis on the complex and multicultural composition of most contemporary Western societies. Research documenting cultural differences is summarized.

Cross-cultural comparisons of social behaviour can help identify the origins of social competence. Research can attempt to link the characteristics of a society to the social behaviour of its members. Such efforts have often been successful, as shown by some of the studies mentioned later in this chapter. However, cross-cultural research is also very revealing even if it emerges that a particular aspect of children's social relations is no different in different cultures. In this way, universal, species-wide aspects of social behaviour are discovered. Results have indicated that there are a small number of 'scripts' for social interaction that are enacted by children of many different and distinct cultures (Whiting and Edwards, 1988). Children in all cultures appear to possess a desire to become capable individuals and to learn about themselves and social interactions (Edwards, 1986). Differences in culture can affect the ways in which children express their deep-seated need to become socially competent and the ages at which important milestones occur.

Research into the link between culture and children's peer relations draws on two main bodies of literature. The first compares features of one culture, such as its religion, economy, or ideology, with the same features of other cultures; cultures are regarded as separate and distinct. Effective use of this approach involves broad sampling of cultures that vary along a specific dimension. For example, one might wish to study cultures that vary in their levels of aggressive behaviour in order to see whether the general aggressiveness of a culture translates into approval of aggression by children. However, there are many challenges in trying to conduct comprehensive cross-cultural comparisons, which require excellent communication between researchers in different places. Human and material resources must also be available at each data collection site. Comprehensive, cross-cultural sampling has been achieved more often in studies of adult inter-personal relations, although it is increasingly being applied to research with children.

A second body of literature examines the relations between people from different subcultures coexisting within the same majority culture. Such interaction is common in many Western countries, which are the hosts of immigrants in unprecedented numbers. Throughout the twentieth century, individuals fleeing economic or political stress sought shelter in North America, Western Europe, Australia and other Western societies. However, there is also increasing movement of populations across borders as the result of such political and economic unions as the European Union and the North American Free Trade group. These social and political changes provide increasing opportunities to study such phenomena as inter-racial and inter-ethnic friendship, gauging the influence of culture on children's preferred relationship partners. There have been numerous studies on this topic and this may be due in part to the widespread media coverage of the events leading to the racial desegregation of American schools and of vio-lence between young people of different cultural origins in Britain, France and Germany.

Individualism/collectivism

A fundamental distinction among cultures is whether they can be charac-terized as individualistic or collectivistic (Hofstede, 1983). Collectivistic cultures place importance on group identity over the individual autonomy associated with individualistic cultures. Individuals from collectivistic cul-tures also work towards a common goal and assume greater collective responsibility for the welfare of group members. This is often translated into the sharing of child-care responsibilities and collective child-rearing.

The English-speaking countries of Canada, Great Britain, the United States and Australia represent the most individualistic societies (Hofstede, 1983). Children in these nations are raised under a belief system that emphasizes personal autonomy and individuality to a far greater degree than almost all Third World cultures or even those of continental Europe. Because they rely less on common, shared opinions, people in individualis-tic cultures tend to hold more discrete, idiosyncratic beliefs about others. Urban areas are usually more individualistic than rural locations in a given region (Madsen and Shapira, 1970). Immigration usually involves moving from a collectivistic society to one characterized by individualism (Triandis *et al.*, 1988).

Recent findings have indicated that there may be enormous within-society variations in collectivism/individualism. For example, urban Koreans who are working towards industrialization in their collectivistic culture are also known to be highly individualistic (Cha, 1994). Indeed, it is common for societies to have both individualistic and collectivistic characteristics. For example, Indians living in India and abroad have been shown to have collectivistic ideals concerning family relations and an individualistic orientation towards interpersonal relationships and economic activity (Sinha and Tripathi, 1994). Some research indicates important differences among cultures that have often been lumped together as 'individualistic'. North Americans have been shown to value the pursuit of individual interest, whereas Western Europeans value egalitarianism and harmony, even though they also value individual autonomy (Schwartz and Ros, 1995, pp. 111–12). In a discussion of the dynamic interplay between collectivistic and individualistic forces within cultures, Philipsen (1987) emphasized that cultures are in constant evolution and do not remain fixed in terms of their individualism or collectivism. He also insisted that in order to understand a culture completely, the researcher must understand not only how collectivistic or individualistic it is, but must also understand the forces within the culture that work to make it collectivistic or individualistic. Competing forces are at work in many societies, pulling them toward greater individualism or greater collectivism.

Personal identity is defined more extensively by membership of a cultural group when there is extensive contact between different cultural groups; this especially applies to multicultural societies (McGuire, McGuire, Child and Fujioka, 1978), particularly among minority groups (e.g. Hewstone, Bond and Wan, 1983; Hofman, 1985). Research has explored the cultural indentities of children in numerous cultures. Results from studies in which a collectivistic minority is surrounded by a majority culture indicate two opposite tendencies. One contention is that if surrounded by a majority, minority parents will cling to their own cultural identity and protect their children from assimilation by infusing cultural values. However, a different outcome may occur, in which the parents teach their children the skills necessary to succeed in the majority culture (Ogbu, 1981). This may involve adopting different parenting styles in order to impart the competencies necessary to thrive in an individualistic society.

Gudykunst and Ting-Toomey (1988) maintain that individualism/collectivism is not the only dimension that influences social relationships in a society. For instance, Hall (1976) proposed another cultural distinction by differentiating between high-context and low-context cultures. In a low-context culture, such as English Canada, individuals openly communicate information about relationships to each other. In high-context cultures such as China, Japan and Korea, this information is inferred from the context or situation. Thus, in a high-context society, a child may have to learn the skills necessary for this type of deduction. In order to be socially competent, the child must use intuition and knowledge of a situation instead of relying on direct messages used during social interaction. Although the skills necessary for social competence in high-context cultures emphasize interpretative ability, the ability to understand and interpret social situations remains essential in a low-context culture (see, e.g. Argyle, Furnham and Graham, 1981).

The combination of individualism/collectivism and low/high context as cultural characteristics can influence the nature of interpersonal relationships (Gudykunst and Ting-Toomey, 1988). There may be a need to preserve one's public image in individualistic, low-context cultures, whereas individuals living in collectivistic, high-context cultures may focus on the collective image of their group. Although maintaining an individual public image may also be a priority, individuals in a collectivistic society will try to ensure that their public image does not conflict with the norms and standards of their community. Research into this and other areas of social development should recognize the interplay between developmental and cultural differences, as culture may be more apparent in certain developmental stages. For example, adolescents are often depicted in the media as having far greater concern about their public images than either younger children or adults.

Tolerance of ambiguity and diversity

Cultures also differ in their levels of tolerance of ambiguity in relationships and diversity in behaviour (Hofstede, 1979). In cultures where there is little tolerance of a departure from the norm, there is pressure on parents and children to conform and thus eliminate behaviour which does not adhere to social norms. As well, a child may be encouraged not to associate with others who display atypical behaviour, thus learning to reject non-conformists. A child may therefore adopt a formal set of rules for social interaction in order to avoid uncertainty. These individuals may in turn encounter higher levels of stress and more emotional displays in their interpersonal relationships.

Cultures may also be characterized by the distance between individuals with high and low power. Hofstede (1980, 1984) adopted power distance as a cultural characteristic and found that individuals in certain cultures readily accept an unequal distribution of power. Children from these high-power-distance cultures may be more likely to value conformity, assume authoritarian beliefs and obey adults without question.

Rules

Argyle (1983, p. 123) defined a social rule as 'a shared belief that certain things should or should not be done' within the confines of a particular setting. Social rules apply to all situations and the breaking of a rule most often leads to some form of repudiation by peers. Cultures may differ according to what rules apply to different situations. For example, Japanese adults are expected to restrict emotional display and defer to others far more than their British counterparts (Argyle *et al.*, 1986). Within a culture, different rules may apply to different settings; there may be fewer rules governing certain types of relationships than others. Rules also exist for relationships between children and adults. These probably vary with age, culture and setting, but there are currently few data on cross-cultural differences in the rules that apply to children's social relations.

Until the past few years, it was quite common to find articles in child development journals that reported comparisons of the behaviours of children in different countries, but did not explain the reasons for the comparison in any great detail. In recent years, however, there has been greater emphasis on research that is undertaken for a sound theoretical reason that is articulated very clearly in advance, for example, to study the effects of individualism or collectivism on the competitive behaviours of children. Not all interesting cross-cultural research can be reviewed in this chapter. The selection below represents the cross-cultural comparisons of children's peer relations that have been studied most extensively.

The peer relations of East Asian children

The most extensive data base on the peer relations of children in non-Western countries is from East Asia, especially China. There are many reasons why data on Chinese children are particularly valuable, aside from the obvious fact that so many of the world's children live there. Chinese society is relatively homogeneous — there are few internal differences in ethnic or cultural origin. Furthermore, social class differences are less pronounced in China than in most other countries. In contrast, many comparisons between different Western countries, for example the United States and the United Kingdom, are complicated by the fact that the populations of both countries are comprised of citizens of many cultural origins and distinct social classes, each of which have differing values and priorities. Finally, the literary, philosophical and religious roots of Chinese people's expectations of others are documented very completely and articulately. Longitudinal studies are facilitated by the fact that there is very little population mobility (Chen, Rubin, Li and Li, 1999).

China differs greatly in terms of individualism/collectivism from the countries of North America and Western Europe, with China occupying the collectivist end of the spectrum (Triandis, 1990). This contrast is often used to account for differences in social relations in these two societies. The collectivism inherent in Chinese culture is seen as providing a structure for social behaviour, because interaction among individuals accords with the needs and expectations of the group. According to Yang (1981), the Chinese anticipate the reactions of others and model their behaviour accordingly. Related to this is Toupin's (1980) observation that Chinese society places great value on the rejection of verbal aggression, avoidance of direct expression of feelings and avoidance of confrontations. Verbal conflict and direct confrontation run contrary to the Chinese notion of 'face' (Chiu, Tsang and Yang, 1988). The importance of conflict resolution through mediation and bargaining is reflected in China's non-adversarial or inquisitorial procedural model of community justice (Cloke, 1987; Leung, 1987).

Buddhism, Taoism and Confucianism make up the core of the Chinese belief system. Emphasizing harmony, social obligations and interrelationships, (Shenkar and Ronen, 1987), Buddhist, Taoist and Confucianist principles dominate and guide social relationships (Chao, 1983; Cryderman, 1992; Ryan, 1985). In Buddhism, the 'self' or ego is composed of social components that centre around the family, extended family, community and country (Ryan, 1985). Taoist principles promote the rejection of self-assertiveness and competitiveness (Ryan, 1985) and this may affect children's moral and ethical development by discouraging the fulfilment of their own goals at the expense of those of others. Confucianism asserts that there are four fundamental principles by which to live: self-cultivation, maintaining a harmonious relationship with the family, taking responsibility in community affairs and serving the country (Kong, 1985). In particular, self-cultivation advocates the perfection of interpersonal skills and the fulfilment of the role and moral obligations one has in the community (Kong, 1985; Shenkar and Ronen, 1987). It fosters harmonious family relations and the avoidance of role conflict. There is clear role differentiation within the structure of the Chinese extended family (Tsui and Schultz, 1988). Chinese people believe that this well-defined family structure provides for continuity in society, because successive generations are linked with their ancestors and each individual possesses a role in history (Kong, 1985). Parents adopt an authoritarian parenting style and emphasize proper conduct, as prescribed by Confucian principles, in the socialization of their children. They emphasize obedience, control and academic achievement.

Research on children's peer relations in China

Well-planned studies have enabled scholars to trace parallels between the core principles of Chinese society and the patterns of peer relations of its children. Space permits description of only a few examples. Chu (1979) investigated the susceptibility of Chinese and American children to interpersonal influence. Findings indicated that Chinese 8-year-olds were more conforming and more socially dependent than their American age-mates when asked to perform a series of ambiguous perceptual tasks. Furthermore, the Chinese children imitated popular and high-achieving participants more than the American children. Such behaviour may parallel the mutual interdependence and deference to authority figures that is integral to Chinese society.

In their observational study of cooperation and conflict among Chinese and Canadian 5-year-olds, Orlick, Zhou and Partington (1990) highlighted the mutual interdependence of Chinese children. They found that Chinese children engaged in more prosocial behaviour, such as helping and sharing, than the Canadian children. The Canadian children displayed less cooperative behaviour and 78 per cent of their behaviours involved conflict. Orlick, Zhou and Partington (1990) suggested that these cross-cultural differences are due to differences in the socialization of Canadian and Chinese children.

Despite the dramatic differences in the core values of the societies, there exist some important similarities between Chinese and Western children's peer relations. Chen, Rubin and Li (1994) found that helpful prosocial behaviour and aggression were correlated with social adjustment and social maladjustment, respectively; these results are analogous to findings with Western samples. However, the cultural meaning of shyness differs greatly, even though the behaviour of shy children is very similar in Chinese and Western cultures (Rubin, 1998). In a Canadian study shy and sensitive children, aged 7–9, were found to be rejected by their peers. However, there was positive correlation between shyness-sensitivity and peer acceptance for Chinese children aged 7–10 (Chen, Rubin and Sun, 1992); this is probably the only known research in any country in which shy children were shown to be popular. Chinese children who are shy might be well liked by their peers because being soft-spoken, well-mannered and academically inclined is considered virtuous in Chinese culture (Chen, Rubin and Li, 1994). Nevertheless, by the age of 12, shyness and sensitivity in Chinese children are associated with peer rejection, as in most other countries (Chen *et al.*, 1999). This finding may have occurred because different expectations are placed in China once one reaches adolescence. High levels of academic pressure are placed during secondary-school selection procedures (Dong, Yang and Ollendick, 1994). Pressure from within the school system may reflect the expectation that older children become more independent, responsible and self-controlling. For all these reasons, assertiveness and maturity regarding interpersonal relations may be prerequisites for successful social adjustment in older children in China as elsewhere (Chen, Rubin and Li, 1994). Although these expectations are also found in Western cultures, age differences in the Chinese data pertaining to the shyness-sensitivity dimension raise the possibility that there is a later age for the developmental shift towards valuing assertiveness in the Chinese sample. It is also possible that the valuing of shyness by younger children is not general in Chinese society, because recent data on children from Chinese families with more formal education than those studied by Chen and his colleagues fail to corroborate the finding that the peers of young Chinese children value shyness and reserve (Hart *et al.*, 1998). To the extent that the peer groups' valuing of shyness in the early primary-school years applies to most of China, it has broader implications for cross-cultural research on children's peer relations. The effects of collectivism/individualism may be more evident at particular ages or stages and may be reflected in the ages at which important transitions in the expectations of groups or individuals take place.

Comparisons of Latin American children and children in the more individualistic Western societies

Studies of Latin American children constitute another substantial contribution to the cross-cultural literature on children's peer relations. Latin American society, like East Asian society, is highly collectivistic. As in East Asia, the extended family is a prominent feature of daily life and the prominent source of social support and guidance. However, comparisons between Latin American and North American or Western European children do not provide quite as clear a contrast as the East-Asian studies, for several reasons. For the most part, Latin Americans share many of the religious beliefs of North Americans and Western Europeans and share much of their cultural history. Most Latin American countries are not characterized by internal differences in cultural origin to the same degree as the United States or Canada, but many of them are more heterogeneous than China, Japan, or Korea. Lower socioeconomic classes predominate in Latin America, though there are often drastic discrepancies in living conditions between the lower classes and the small middle-class and upper-class groups.

One of the earliest cross-cultural studies, by Kupersmidt and Trejos (1987), was motivated by the desire to find out whether, in spite of the collectivism of a society, individual children were still targets of rejection by their peer groups at school. Kupersmidt and Trejos investigated the peer relations of Costa Rican children. They administered a group sociometric interview to 328 primary schoolchildren divided into 3 different age groups. Because of its 40-year history of political neutrality, non-violent changes of government and lack of a formal standing army, Costa Rica presents researchers with an opportunity to study a level of collectivism that is unique from other collectivistic Latin American countries. Like the majority of Hispanic countries, Costa Rican culture places importance on traditional sex roles and on family relations over peer relations.

Kupersmidt and Trejos found that, on identical peer nomination instruments, there was a similar proportion of popular children among Costa Rican and US samples (11 per cent and 13 per cent, respectively). There were also similar cross-cultural results for peer rejection, as 11 per cent of Costa Rican children and 15 per cent of American children were rejected by their peers. However, Kupersmidt and Trejos found that there were different specific behaviours affiliated with peer rejection. For example, in Costa Rica, peer rejection is often associated with withdrawal from group activity, but this was not indicated by American children. This difference may be connected to the distinction between collectivistic and individualistic societies. Collectivism emphasizes the importance of the collective experience of society and therefore refusal to participate in a group event may be considered offensive to the group. In contrast, individualistic societies may regard non-participation as an individual's personal right; the group, therefore, does not take offence and reject the non-participant. Regardless of the greater commitment to the group, children from collectivistic cultures do still like and dislike particular individuals, as occurs in less collectivistic societies.

DeRosier (1989) examined Costa Rican children's attitudes towards their network of intimate relationships. She studied 148 Costa Rican primary schoolchildren, the majority of whom were from working-class and middle-class households. After administering Furman and Buhrmester's (1985) Network of Relationships Inventory to gauge children's perceptions of the people in their lives who provide social support, she compared the Costa Rican results with American data from Furman and Buhrmester's original study. Results indicated that Costa Rican children rated most people in their personal network (i.e. siblings, parents, best friends, teachers) more positively than did their American counterparts. Also, the Costa Rican children reported that their relationships were less conflictual. As suggested by DeRosier, these positive attitudes towards others are connected with the prosocial, cooperative nature of the surrounding Costa Rican culture.

In terms of levels of intimacy in specific relationships, the Costa Rican children reported that they received the most companionship from their mothers and siblings. In contrast, American children felt that their best friends provided the most companionship. Both groups reported the lowest levels of companionship from teachers. Teachers were also consigned the 'least affectionate' by American children. However, the Costa Rican children felt their relationships with their best friends deserved the rating of least affectionate. They also reported higher levels of conflict and lower levels of satisfaction with this relationship. Cultural ecology may thus determine the role of individuals within a supportive network, as well as the relative importance of peer relations. Compared to others, DeRosier's study is of particular value, for it addresses the nature of more intimate relationships instead of group peer relations.

Comparisons of US and Mexican children have been invaluable in understanding how the competitiveness of a society is mirrored in competition among children. In his classic studies, Madsen found that Mexican children exhibited a high amount of cooperative behaviour. In one experiment, Kagan and Madsen (1971) tested Anglo-American and Mexican children on a device designed to reward children for cooperative interaction; competition did not lead to rewards. They found that, among pairs of 7-year-old to 9-year-old children, Mexican children were the most cooperative, Anglo-American children were the least cooperative and Mexican-American children displayed an intermediate level of cooperation. In another study, findings indicated that Anglo-American children more often than their Mexican counterparts responded with conflict during an antagonistic social encounter (Kagan and Madsen, 1972). In a similar study, results showed that, when using the marble-pull game, there was an increase in non-adaptive competition with age for Anglo-American children (Madsen, 1971). Kagan and Madsen (1971) hypothesized that levels of cooperation and competition are influenced by whether subjects have a strong group orientation or a strong individual orientation. Applying Piagetian developmental theory, Madsen (1971) suggested that, although older children should be able to recognize that competition is more adaptive and thus exhibit more rational problem-solving behaviour the 'I' orientation and desire to compete are so strong among these older Anglo-American children that they prevent the cooperative interaction that would lead to mutual rewards.

Taken together, research conducted in China and in Latin America has demonstrated that children's peer relations mirror to a considerable extent the individualism or collectivism of the societies in which they live. Both China and Latin America provide very sharp contrasts with the individualism of North America and Western Europe. However, there is also some value in comparing societies that are indeed individualistic and collectivistic, but not as totally dissimilar as, for example, the United States and China. The Mediterranean cultures of Europe are often considered more collectivistic than the Northern European countries (Georgas et al., 1997). Goudena and Sánchez (1996) conducted an interesting comparison of the peer interactions of 5-year-olds in Andalucia, Spain and Holland. The collectivism of Andalucia compared even to Northern Spain has been documented in several studies published in Spanish journals. The research conducted by Goudena and Sánchez is particularly valuable because it featured direct observation of the children at play. There were some important differences. Dutch children interacted more extensively in pairs and in small groups, whereas Spanish children interacted more frequently with large groups of peers. Even when they were not playing, the Spanish children were more involved in conversations with peers and in watching groups of children at play than were their counterparts in Holland. There were also some unexpected similarities, especially the fact that the probable collectivism of the Spanish children did not translate into more positive judgements about their peers.

The differences found by Goudena and Sánchez, like the differences that have been found between North America and both China and Latin America, are probably attributable to differences in individualism/collectivism. However, this should not be assumed. In a world where many societies are changing very rapidly and coming into greater contact with one another, it is important for researchers to measure directly the individualism or collectivism of the communities they study, rather than making assumptions based on the general literature on the particular society.

An explicitly collectivistic subculture: the Israeli kibbutz

There have been copious studies on the psychological adaptation of children on Israeli kibbutzim. Individuals living in these collectivistic communities share their possessions and work responsibilities with each other and are permitted to leave whenever they wish. Kibbutzniks' group orientation does not lead to isolation, for they maintain contact with the surrounding, less collectivistic Israeli society. Because membership is by choice, a kibbutz is an excellent setting to study collective ideology.

Schools on kibbutzim emphasize cooperation more than the European-style schools in surrounding Israeli cities. During the period in which most research was conducted, children were raised in a children's house but still maintained contact with their families. In the past two decades, there has been a growing trend towards more family-oriented living arrangements. There are many possible implications of the structure of the kibbutz for children's social relations. Because children have more contact with caregivers than parents in the collective environment, there may be an effect on the early formation of parental attachment relationships. This could in turn affect the children's formation of subsequent relationships.

How, then, is this collective upbringing reflected in children's behaviour? There have been numerous observational studies of the social play of kibbutz and non-kibbutz preschoolers. Levy-Shiff and Hoffman (1985) compared the free-play of kibbutz and urban children. All participants were Israeli-born children of European descent. They found that kibbutz-raised children displayed more group interaction, less competition and less emotional expression and affection than their non-kibbutz counterparts. The kibbutz children essentially replaced physical aggression with verbal confrontation. This type of behaviour may be a predictor of future social adjustment patterns of children. Indeed, adult kibbutzniks are often characterized as group-oriented and emotionally detached.

Hertz-Lazarowitz, Fuchs, Sharabany and Eisenberg (1989) found that kibbutz children exhibited higher levels of social interaction than city children, in both traditional and more participation-oriented classrooms. There have also been indications that kibbutz children are more cooperative than non-kubbutznikim. Shapira and Madsen (1974) observed children's level of cooperation when attempting the marble-pull task. Participants were kibbutz and Tel-Aviv city children aged 4 to 11 years. They found that, at all ages, kibbutz children exhibited less competitive behaviour and more cooperation to achieve a common goal than the urban children. However, all children displayed increased levels of competition as they got older. This trend occurred at a slower pace in the kibbutz children, for, even at the age of 11, they were still quite cooperative at the marble-pull task compared with the city children. In Sharabany's (1982) study, kibbutz and Tel Aviv children were asked to share information about their social contacts. Results indicated that kibbutz youngsters had more social contacts than the city children. However, the children also had less concern for peer group sanctions and identified less with their peer group than their city counterparts. In another study, similar structured self-report instruments indicated that anxiety about social relations or general, manifest anxiety appears to be no higher or lower among kibbutz children and preadolescents (Ginter, Lufi, Trotzky and Richmond, 1989). Findings such as these illustrate the kibbutz youth's greater involvement with their peers, as well as their emotional distancing from peers.

From the beginnings of the kibbutz movement in the early twentieth century to the 1980s, most kibbutz children slept in children's houses, but had contact with their parents for several hours during the day. This arrangement was instituted in order to promote self-reliance, equality of the sexes and commitment to collectivistic principles (Aviezer, van IJzendoorn, Sagi and Schuengel, 1994). Some recent studies indicate that these communal sleeping arrangements may have had a negative effect on parent–child attachment. For instance, Sagi et al. (1982) found a large number of insecure attachment bonds (see discussion of attachment theory in Chapter 3) among children who slept in collective environments; they suggest that this may reflect the inconsistent nature of mothers' care. In collective sleeping arrangements, infants began at six weeks of age to sleep in children's houses and are monitored by unfamiliar, rotating caregivers at night. Some researchers suggest that the unavailability of a consistent, responsive, maternal caregiver at night conflicts with the availability of the mother during the day in influencing attachment patterns.

Sagi et al. (1994) examined the impact of collective sleeping on mother–child attachment. They maintained that the social ecology of the communal sleeping environment creates obstacles for mothers and their children. Their study indicated that the attachment representations of children in collective sleeping arrangements did not relate to those of the mother; they concluded that the intergenerational transmission of attachment is greatly influenced by the context and is therefore not a universal feature. They assert that communal sleeping deviates from evolutionary adaptation. There was no difference in mother–infant interaction, infants' disposition, or other variables, between the two groups. However, among home-based infants, 80 per cent were securely attached, whereas only 48 per cent were securely attached among communal-based infants. The researchers maintain that mothers were continuously inaccessible during the night and that this conflicted with their availability during the day; this may have created a pattern of inconsistent interaction for the child.

Researchers also examined children's attachment to their primary caregivers, the metaplot in the communal children's houses. Oppenheim, Sagi and Lamb (1988) studied mother–child attachment in kibbutzim using the Strange Situation classification. Results indicated that future development of the children was unrelated to the attachment of infants to their mothers and fathers. However, there was a relationship between infant-metapelet attachment and future development, emphasizing the importance of these primary caregivers. For instance, Oppenheim, Sagi and Lamb report that those infants who were securely attached to their metaplot were both more independent and more concerned about other people than were their counterparts with insecure attachments to their metaplot.

It is most fortunate that researchers capitalized on the opportunity of studying communal sleeping arrangements before the practice was abandoned. The value of research on kibbutz children lies not in determining whether a kibbutz community raises better or worse socially developed children. Instead, research of this nature illustrates the way in which a collectivistic subculture may influence children's peer relations.

Cultural dimensions of childhood aggression

An important reason for studying children's peer relations in different cultures is to determine whether attitudes towards aggression among adults in a society translates into greater and more problematic aggression by children. The Zapotec communities in Oaxaca, Mexico, provide an interesting opportunity to examine the connection between adult aggression and children's aggressive behaviour with peers. The Zapotec, who rely heavily on agriculture, are organized into small, separate communities. The rate of aggression varies widely between these communities. For example, in the 24 Zapotec communities studied so far, the annual homicide rate ranges from 4 to 123 per 100,000 people. It is not surprising, then, that attitudes towards violence vary as well. In the less aggressive communities, play fighting among children is looked upon with disfavour. However, the more violent communities are characterized by rough play even among adults, as well as the corporal punishment of children. Fry (1988) studied the behaviour of 24 children, aged 5 to 8 eight years, from two Zapotec communities with different levels of normative violence. Observations were restricted to incidences of serious fighting, play fighting and threats. Results indicated that there was twice the rate of play aggression in San Andres (a pseudonym) than in the less violent community of La Paz (6.9 incidents per hour versus 3.7 incidents per hour, respectively). Researchers observed lower rates of more serious aggression in both communities. Nevertheless, San

Andres children still exhibited a higher rate than their La Paz counterparts (0.7 incidents per hour versus 0.39 incidents per hour, respectively). Older San Andres children engaged in serious play fighting more frequently than younger children, whereas in La Paz, the rate of serious play aggression was lower for the older children than the younger children. Small correlations were found between serious fighting and play fighting, showing that children tend to engage in either one or the other, for the most part. The results of this study imply that aggression, which does indeed occur across cultures and may have some evolutionary purpose, is significantly modified by the cultural context. The findings also support Smith's (1989) contention that children prepare for their future adult roles within their communities by play fighting.

Italian studies are an excellent source of information about cultural differences in aggression, especially with regard to differential expectations for boys and girls (Schneider, 1971). As detailed below, traditional Italian society condoned aggression by males but not by females. Relevant data are available from major urban settings regarding the behavioural correlates of peer status in Italian preschools (Fonzi, Tomada and Ciucci, 1994) and Grade 2 classrooms (Attili, Vermigli and Schneider, 1997). These studies, which were conducted with large samples, used measures similar to those used in most American studies. The results indicate that both the pattern and strength of the behavioural correlates of peer acceptance in Italy are very similar to those of most other countries, with correlations every bit as strong as those found in studies conducted in North America with both preschoolers and elementary school-age children. There are some indications, though, that, unlike the results of studies conducted in Central and Northern Italy, youngsters in Southern Italy perceive some forms of aggression as typical of peers they consider sociable (Casiglia, LoCoco and Zappulla, 1998). These data, combined with those from other countries, support the conclusion that there are many invariant aspects of peer acceptance in children's groups, despite plausible reasons for cross-cultural differences. Cross-cultural similarities indicate that aggressive/disruptive behaviour is linked with peer rejection, whereas prosocial behaviour is associated with peer acceptance. Aggressive/disruptive behaviour is associated with rejection by peers, but prosocial behaviour is linked with their acceptance.

In their study of aggression among children in small Central Italian towns, Tomada and Schneider (1997) attempted to replicate Crick and Grotpeter's (1995) findings which indicated that American boys displayed higher levels of overt aggression and lower levels of relational aggression than girls. As discussed in Chapter 3, overt aggression refers to physical and verbal expressions of hostility aimed directly at another person. Relational aggression, often referred to as covert aggression, involves displays of aggression involved in interpersonal relationships, such as spreading rumours or excluding another child from a playgroup (Crick and Grotpeter, 1995; Lagerspetz, Björkqvist and Peltonen, 1988). Overt aggression is common in Italian playgrounds: Genta *et al.* (1996) found there to be significantly more bullying among elementary schoolchildren in Central Italy than in Norway, England, Spain and Japan. Thus, the display of aggression among Italian males may still be considered normal, just as it was even encouraged among adolescent boys in traditional Italian villages as a display of their sexual prowess and preparation for their future patriarchal roles. Overt aggression is discouraged among Italian girls (Maraspini, 1968; Schneider, 1971). Tomada and Schneider (1997) analysed peer nominations for aggressive and prosocial behaviour provided by Italian elementary school teachers and students. They found that, contrary to their hypothesis, Italian girls did not have higher levels of relational aggression than boys; boys had higher levels than girls of both relational and overt aggression. However, the gender gap was narrower for levels of relational aggression. Therefore, despite the fact that Italian boys seem as relationally aggressive as Italian girls, it is still important to study relational aggression in Italy. That is because almost no girls were found to be physically aggressive. If relational aggression is not taken into account, one would arrive at the erroneous conclusion that aggression is relatively absent among females in Italy. Comprehensive studies comparing larger samples from a greater number of countries could determine the importance of studying relational aggression in other societies.

The Six Culture Project (Whiting and Edwards, 1988; Whiting and Whiting, 1975) undertook the task of identifying cross-cultural differences in children's early social development. Researchers conducted direct observations of mothers and their children, aged 2 to 10 years in India, Okinawa, the Philippines, Mexico, Kenya and the United States; they coded mother and child interaction, as well as social relations between children. Researchers were knowledgeable about each culture; this added to the merit of the study. The study was chronicled in a detailed, two-volume account, which included descriptions of each culture's living arrangements, economy, child-rearing practices, social support network and type of responsibilities given to children.

The Six Culture Project highlighted some important cultural differences between the countries studied. For example, school-age children in cultures with universal education had more extensive contact with peers, especially with same-sex peers. In Nyansago, Kenya, where only one out of the 22 children studied attended school, results indicated the lowest amount of peer contact. Rarely did any of the children in the study display aggressive behaviour and this was especially true among girls. The highest ratings of aggressive behaviour were given to children in Khalapur, India; this culture also practised the most corporal punishment of children. Children from Mixteca, a Mexican Indian community, displayed similarly high levels of aggressive behaviour; this community is also characterized by high levels of adult aggression. Boys from cultures that provided segregated, competitive schooling displayed high amounts of rough-and-tumble play. Children who exhibited the most nurturing behaviour with same-sex peers tended to live in cultures in which children are expected to help care for siblings.

Osterman *et al.* (1994) conducted a cross-cultural study of aggression and victimization in children belonging to five different ethnic groups. Data were collected from 8-year-old children in Turku, Finland (Swedish and Finnish speakers), Chicago, the United States (Caucasian and Afro-American) and Warsaw, Poland. Using the Direct and Indirect Aggression Scales (DIAS) (Björkqvist, Lagerspetz and Osterman, 1992), the researchers found that Afro-American children had the highest levels of peer- and self-nominated aggression. They attributed this to the violence that existed in the Afro-American children's Chicago communities. Although scores for boys did not differ significantly across cultures, there was significant variation among girls' scores. For instance, Polish girls indicated high levels of aggression in self-reports and this was confirmed by peer reports. Such high levels may be attributable to the tradition of opposition to foreign power that has long existed in Poland (Osterman *et al.,* 1994). Aggression also seemed acceptable among Caucasian girls from Chicago. The Afro-American girls had the highest scores of aggression. Farver *et al.* (1997) also found high levels of aggression among American children. In their cross-cultural study, 30 4-year-old children from Sweden, Germany, Indonesia and the United States were asked to construct stories using toys with aggressive and non-aggressive cues. American children's stories incorporated more aggressive content, words and characters than stories of their Swedish, German and Indonesian counterparts. In their stories the American children also handled situations using aggression to a greater degree than the stories of non-American children. Farver *et al.* suggested that high rates of crime and violence in the United States influence the development of aggression in children. They added that, in highly individualistic American society, socialization of children emphasizes competition, independence and emotional indifference to the needs of others. The greatest difference in aggression occurred among American and Indonesian children. This may reflect cultural differences in child-rearing practices and tolerance for aggressive behaviour. Farver *et al.* point to Triandis' (1990) finding that Indonesian society is characterized by collectivism and disdain for aggression. Compared with American children, Indonesian children are not encouraged to become independent and competitive, but are taught to value harmony, cooperation and the importance of community and family. This study highlights how levels of aggression in children's narratives may reflect cultural characteristics.

Huesmann, Lagerspetz and Eron (1984) conducted a cross-cultural study to determine if there were cultural differences in the correlation between television viewing and aggressive behaviour for children in the

United States and Finland. Primary children were tested and interviewed in each of three years. The longitudinal results suggested that the viewing of television violence was related to aggression and predicted future changes in levels of aggression by American girls and Finnish and American boys. The strength of this relation depended on both the intensity of the violence and the amount of viewing time. For American children, both these factors were equally important, whereas violent content was more important for Finnish children. The television violence-aggression correlation was intensified for boys the more they identified with the television characters. Television violence is regulated in television programming in Finland and much of the violence viewed is imported. Huesmann, Lagerspetz and Eron (1984) postulated that Finnish children therefore may not relate to the violent shows or think they are real.

In another study, Eron and Huesmann (1987) examined the relationships between television viewing, peer ratings of aggression and peer popularity among Israeli kibbutz youth and Israeli city children. They also collected data from children from Australia, the United States, Finland and Poland to form a cross-cultural comparison. There were many common findings among the different samples studied. Aggression, as rated by peers, was stable over a 3-year period and aggression was negatively correlated with popularity in all samples, consistent with the conclusion presented in Chapter 3. However, there was cross-cultural variability in the degree to which aggression could be predicted by the viewing of television. This was especially evident for the viewing of violent programming. This correlation was rather weak for the kibbutz children; this may be due to the regulation of television viewing by kibbutz caregivers. Metaplot (caregivers) typically discuss the special implications of violence after the children watch television programs of this sort. It might also be possible that the impact of violent television on children is weakened by the collectivistic nature of kibbutz society.

Cross-cultural differences can affect the level of tolerance for atypical behaviour and these different thresholds may determine how adults react to aggressive behaviour in children. Schneider, Attili, Vermigli and Younger (1997) compared the beliefs of Italian and Canadian parents about aggression and social withdrawal. They hypothesized that Italian mothers would consider aggression to be more worrisome and that English-Canadian mothers would have stronger emotional responses to social withdrawal. They also studied ratings of mothers with children who were identified as withdrawn or aggressive. Results indicated that the Canadian mothers did indeed consider social withdrawal to be more problematic than did their Italian counterparts. However, both samples indicated that aggression was generally more worrisome than withdrawal. The researchers encountered some interesting gender differences, for the intensity of the Italian mothers' emotional reactions to withdrawal by girls were lower than reactions to this behaviour encountered in boys; this gender difference was not found in Canadian samples. A higher proportion of Italian mothers felt that problem behaviours in children were caused by stable, internal factors such as personality traits. However, Canadian mothers tended to believe that children's behaviour could be easily changed. This difference may be connected to Italian villagers' belief in the role of fate and luck in children's future success (Maraspini, 1968). Behaviour is therefore not considered to be modifiable by parenting skills. In contrast, Canadian mothers seem to be more likely to believe that parental intervention and disciplinary style can modify the behaviour of the child. This study provides insight into the way in which cultural characteristics can influence parents' attributions of their children's behaviour, as well as their level of tolerance for social withdrawal and aggression.

Weisz, Suwanlert, Chaiyasit and Weiss (1988) also studied tolerance thresholds for over-controlled (e.g. shy, withdrawn) behaviour and under-controlled behaviour (e.g. aggression), in research conducted in Thailand, Jamaica and the United States. The majority of Thais subscribe to Thai Buddhism's teaching that, although some degree of unhappiness is universal, this is not a permanent part or reflection of one's personality. The study involved Thai and American teachers and parents reading two vignettes, each of which provided an example of the behaviour patterns studied. They were then asked to rate the seriousness of the behaviour, as well as whether it was unusual or not. Additionally, the parents were asked to report the level of concern about the behaviour they would experience if they were the protagonist's parent or teacher, the likelihood of a change in the behaviour, what had caused the behaviour and what they should do about it. Results indicated that Thai subjects rated over-controlled and under-controlled behaviour less seriously than their American counterparts. In comparison to the American respondents, the Thai participants also rated these behaviour patterns as less worrisome to a teacher or parent, less unusual and more likely to improve on their own. Thai and American psychologists reported equal levels of concern about the problem behaviours. The psychologists' level of concern was greater than Thai parents and teachers, but lower than that of all American subject groups. Thais attributed under-controlled and over-controlled behaviours to faulty child-rearing more often than Americans did; Americans tended to attribute these behaviours to environmental stressors, such as an unsettled day in the family and internal, personal conflicts. Both cultures, however, felt that under-controlled behaviour was more worrisome than over-controlled behaviour.

French, Setiono and Eddy (1999) studied aggression among childhood peers in Indonesia. Indonesian Javanese society is extremely collectivistic (Hofstede, 1991) and emphasizes cooperation, conformity and harmony (Koentjaraningrat, 1985). Using the individualism/collectivism paradigm,

French, Setiono and Eddy hypothesized that aggression would be associated with high negative sociometric status in both the United States and Indonesia, but that this would be particularly pronounced in the latter country. They also predicted that social withdrawal would be associated with high social status for American children but not for their Indonesian counterparts. Results indicated the expected association of aggression with negative sociometric status. French, Setiono and Eddy suggest that this may reflect the characterization of aggression in childhood as an element of disorder in relationships (see Patterson, 1982), rather than an individual phenomenon. Results also suggested cross-cultural similarities in terms of the relationship between sociometric acceptance and reciprocal friendship. However, in American samples, those children who were aggressive did have peer groups and friends, whereas this was not found for Indonesian children. In Indonesia, aggressive children rarely had friends. The finding that there were fewer reciprocated friendships in Indonesian children may reflect the collectivistic ideology, for harmonious peer groups are commonly valued over a small amount of close friendships (Noesjirwan, 1978).

Research has focused less on the cross-cultural differences in school behaviour thresholds of schools and teachers; the concept of 'threshold' refers to the level of disruptiveness or other atypical behaviour that leads adults to conceive of the behaviour as unacceptable or problematic. Walker and Lamon (1987) investigated such thresholds in their comparison of American and Australian primary school teachers' standards and expectations of children's behaviour. Findings indicated that both samples rated similar behaviours as troublesome. American teachers were far less concerned about the children's problem behaviour than about a lack of social skills; this gap was narrower for Australian teachers. Australian teachers placed more emphasis on the importance of classroom decorum. For example, they gave more negative ratings to children's extraneous comments during lessons and discussions. Both samples had similar and higher thresholds for atypical social behaviour when working with pupils having behaviour disorders or disabilities. The results of Walker and Lamon's (1987) study are indeed interesting, but a wider cross-cultural comparison of numerous nations would prove even more valuable.

The challenges in conducting cross-cultural comparisons

The studies discussed in this chapter bear witness to the talents of the researchers in overcoming the many obstacles inherent in comparing data from different societies. Scanning the results makes it look deceptively simple to compare the peer relations of children in different countries. To begin with, such research requires in-depth knowledge of each of the countries to be compared. Such in-depth knowledge may reveal, first of all, that the issue to be studied is of greater importance to only some of the societies to be targeted. In almost every country, there are internal distinctions, such as in ethnicity, socioeconomic status, or gender, that may turn out to explain more differences in core values and social behaviour than the contrast to another country. An added complication is the near impossibility of translating questions without losing some of the original meaning. Furthermore, participants in different countries may feel differently about being involved in research. Some may see this a source of novelty and honour; others may regard it as an intrusion on their privacy. Researchers and their students in different societies will also differ in research training.

None of the existing studies on cultural differences in children's peer relations have overcome all of these problems. Nevertheless, the growing research base does indicate some important and logical differences in peer relations between differing societies, in such key areas as the peer acceptance of shy children and the extent of competition between children. Other studies serve the other purpose of cross-cultural research: to show how children are the same in different societies. The nearly universal peer rejection of children who display hostile aggression is an example of this.

10 Cultural imprints on children's friendships

Children in different societies differ in the extent to which they depend on close friends for social support. In cultures where extended family ties are strong, children may be able to depend on cousins and other relatives for assistance and companionship in times of stress. Children in collectivistic societies may not have to negotiate individual friendships as much as children in many Western countries do. This chapter provides a review of theory and research linking features of culture to features of children's friendships. The extent and significance of inter-cultural friendship in multicultural societies are also discussed.

Almost all published research on children's friendships has been conducted in individualistic cultures, especially the United States. Little is known about the functions of friendships between children in collectivistic cultures, which predominate in Asia, Africa, and Latin America. As detailed in the previous chapter, people in collectivistic societies derive much of their sense of personal identity from their membership of a larger collective unit, such as their communities, extended families, or nations. Despite the possibilities that the functions of friends are not identical in all societies, and that children's behaviour with friends differs across cultures, enough data do exist to indicate, at the most fundamental level, that children around the world regard friendship as an intimate relationship based on reciprocal personal commitment. Explorations of children's concepts of friendship have been conducted not only in the United States (e.g. Berndt, Hawkins, and Hoyle, 1986), but also in Canada and Scotland (Bigelow and La Gaipa, 1975), Iceland (Keller and Edelstein, 1990), Germany (Hofer, Becker, Schmidt, and Noack, 1990, cited in Krappmann, 1996), and China (Keller, Schuster and Edelstein, 1990, cited in Krappmann, 1996). These interview studies reveal very few important differences between cultures in children's basic conceptions of friendship.

Although social organization may not diminish children's basic need for friends or the quality of their friendships, cultural differences may exist in terms of people's expectations of their friends. Not surprisingly, in certain collectivistic cultures, the extended family may provide much of the supportive role that friendship assumes in North America, as in DeRosier's (1989) study of the social networks of Costa Rican children, or in Westen's (1995) study of Canadian children of East Asian origin. In some societies, friends may tend to provide more tangible, practical help than anything else; in others, friends may provide more emotional support and guidance (Cohen, 1966; Krappmann, 1996). Krappmann (1996) offers some interesting speculations about the possible constraints on children's friendships in collectivistic cultures. Out of necessity, more of his arguments are based on theory and on research conducted with adults rather than on studies of children's friendships.

One of the most important issues is the leeway for voluntariness of interpersonal affiliation in a culture, because the voluntary nature of friendships is at the heart of many concepts of friendship. The social organization of some societies restricts the number of individuals with whom a child or adult has regular contact, thus restricting the possibility of forming friendships. This is especially the case in isolated fishing or agricultural villages (documented, for example, by Edelstein [1983] in Iceland). In some cultures, the basic social structure and patterns of economic activity dictate the identities of the peers one encounters in everyday life; it is not always possible to arrange more extensive companionship with a peer with whom one wishes to cultivate a friendship.

Aside from the general structure of social and economic life in a society, it is important to consider the interplay of family life and social life with peers. Although families are important to children everywhere, the extended family unit is a far more prominent element in people's daily lives and thinking in most of Southern Europe, Asia, Africa, and Latin America than it is in North America or Northern Europe (Stanton, 1995). In the more family-oriented societies, members of extended families, including grandparents, aunts, uncles, and cousins, provide a great deal of emotional support, practical assistance, and advice. One might suspect that people need friends much less in those societies than in places where individuals must form voluntary relationships with friends in order to receive the social support they need in moments of stress.

However, a society characterized by rich family life does not have to be a society characterized by impoverished social life with peers. It could also be argued that strong bonds with kin do not preclude high-quality relationships with others (Kirchler, Pombeni, and Palmonari, 1991), and that the high-quality interaction style learned in relating with one's kin might even be generalized to other close relationships. This could be one of the reasons why Schneider, Fonzi, Tani, and Tomada (1997) found that the friendships among 8-year-old girls in Italy, a very family-oriented country, were significantly more stable than those of their counterparts in Ontario, though there were no parallel findings for boys. They also found that, for both genders, there was less discrepancy in the Italian sample between the two friends' ratings of the quality of their relationship. This suggests that the communication between friends is of higher quality. Schneider, Fonzi, Tomada and Tani (2000) compared, using direct observation, the behaviours of Italian and English-Canadian 8-year-olds in situations of potential conflict with their friends. While playing the car-race, a fast-paced, competitive game with their friends, the Canadian children committed significantly more infractions of the rules. Italian friends were also found to be more involved in the race. Schneider, Fonzi, Tomada and Tani also videotaped the Italian and Canadian friends in a simulated negotiation sequence. The friends where shown a Kinder egg, a chocolate egg with a toy hidden inside, and were asked to discuss how they would share it. In discussing how they might share a single Kinder egg, Italian youngsters made fewer proposals in all, but none the less were able to achieve a greater discrepancy between initial and final negotiating positions, suggesting superior skill at negotiation and compromise. The authors speculated that the differences between the Italian and Canadian children's performance might be attributed to the Italian children's exposure to compromise within relationships as result of their more extensive contact with extended family members. The differences might also be attributable to the great emphasis placed by Northern Italians on teaching children how different people have different perspectives on social situations and problems.

Another interesting comparison of children's friendships in different cultures comes from research conducted in East and West Berlin shortly before and shortly after the reunification of Germany. Children's daily lives were very different in these two parts of the city during the period during which the research was conducted, including important differences in many aspects of schooling and family life that seem to have affected both children's opportunities to befriend each other and the nature of their friendships with other children. In East Berlin at the time, children spent most of the day, including the afternoon hours after the regular school day, under adult supervision in schools or day-care centres. An explicit norm of cooperation was emphasized by the adults who provided supervision. In implementing this ideology, the adults praised whatever cooperative behaviour they saw, criticized any conflictual behaviours as immature, and resolved disagreements between children. In contrast, parents in West Berlin had the primary responsibility for structuring their children's social lives in the afternoons after school. The school authorities of West Berlin shared the goal of promoting mutual helpfulness, but the school personnel did not promote a fixed ideology nor did they monitor pupils' social behaviour with anything approaching the vigour of their colleagues in the Eastern section of the city (Oswald and Krappmann, 1995).

Perhaps because they were provided with so much emphatic discussion about the responsibilities of peers, primary schoolchildren in East Berlin were found by Krappmann, Uhlendorf and Oswald (1995) to have more mature concepts of friendship than children of the same age in West Berlin. There were both similarities and differences between the two cultures with regard to their actual friendships rather than abstract concepts of friendship, as described in detail by Little, Brendgen, Wanner and Krappmann (1999). Despite the more mature concepts of friendships among the young East Berliners, friends in both East and West Berlin often disagreed with each other about the quality of their friendships. Furthermore, children in East Berlin reported greater conflict with friends than children in West Berlin, perhaps because the pupils in East Berlin had become keenly aware of conflict after hearing it discussed and criticized so extensively, but remained unskilled in resolving conflicts, which adults did for them. Children in East Berlin also reported having less fun with their friends, perhaps because the active monitoring of their play inhibited horseplay and joking. Nevertheless, there were no differences between the two cultures in the closeness perceived in the relationships with friends. In addition to the lessons to be learned about the effects of culture on children's friendships, the research in Berlin is useful in illustrating the apparently universal importance of closeness in friendship. It also demonstrates that in friendships as in many other aspects of children's lives, abstract concepts often fail to correspond to observable behaviour.

Using a very different method to study cultural differences in children's ideas about friendship, Pinto, Bombi and Cordioli (1997) studied children's pictorial representations of similarity in friendship. The participants in the study were children from five different parts of the world that were known to differ in terms of the individualism/collectivism of adults, peace/war, and ethnic homogeneity/heterogeneity. The five areas studied were Rome, Villafranca (a smaller town in Italy), the Bolivian town of Camiri, the Bolivian forest village of Ipitacito del Monte, and Beirut, Lebanon. Pinto, Bombi and Cordioli hypothesized that friendships in collectivistic cultures would emphasize sharing and mutual affinity, whereas those in individualistic cultures place importance on maintaining a personal sense of uniqueness. They predicted that, according to this paradigm, children from Ipitacito del Monte, a highly collectivistic culture, should create more similar pictorial representations of themselves and their friends. Pinto, Bombi and Cordioli maintained that people living in environments characterized by war may display radical judgements about strangers and may develop defensive attitudes. Accordingly, they predicted that children from Beirut would draw two friends as very similar. They asserted that multi-ethnicity can have positive or negative outcomes in terms of tolerance levels. They speculated that children from Camiri, in which integration has been positive, will not feel as much of a need to represent similarity as an aspect of friendship as their counterparts in Beirut, where there is religious division. Results indicated that children from Ipitacito del Monte exhibited the greatest overall degree of similarity in their pictorial representations of themselves and their friends; this was especially true for the younger children. Pinto, Bombi and Cordioli concluded that dimensions of individualism/collectivism are the only ones they studied which affect similarity between friends. It is interesting to note that in Lebanese samples, children tended to differentiate between themselves and their friends using dimensions in space, emphasizing a hierarchical nature of their friendship. This suggests that, in an area marked by war, the ability to protect may be more important than similarities in age or other personal characteristics (Pinto, Bombi and Cordioli, 1997). Intensive observations by Corsaro (1985) of the interactions of preschoolers in the United States and Italy indicate that children in both countries use very similar strategies to protect the exclusiveness of their friendships and the private, shared play spaces of friends.

Despite the difference, some functions of friendships may apply to all cultures. For example, friendship may afford a protective environment in which one can discuss topics that are prohibited or would be considered deviant in discussions with other people (Hollander, 1958; Krappmann, 1996). Krappmann (1996) suggests that friends may help each other to deal with the shortcomings and dissatisfactions that result from the nature of the social and economic structure of the surrounding society, whatever that social or economic structure may be.

Inter-ethnic and inter-racial friendship

The enrolment of immigrants from previously unfamiliar cultures in the urban schools of North America, Western Europe, and Australia has given researchers an opportunity to study the relations between different racial and ethnic groups. Additional opportunities for studying cross-cultural contact in schools resulted from the racial desegregation of US schools and from the desire to facilitate the academic progress of children of Middle Eastern origin in Israel. Social reflection theories maintain that children become prejudiced because they learn that society values different ethnic groups differently; they may also become prejudiced due to their parents instilling prejudicial attitudes in them. Psychodynamic explanations assert that children become prejudiced because their parents punish expressions of hostility. Children therefore displace this hostility onto lower-status minority ethnic groups. Cognitive-developmental theories maintain that prejudice reflects the young child's egocentrism (Aboud and Doyle, 1995).

Children encounter others who may differ from them in many respects, such as race/ethnicity, gender, and age; such variables are often used by children when choosing or rejecting friends. Because similarity is often an important prerequisite for interpersonal attraction, (Hallinan and Williams, 1987) many conjecture that children will often choose friends who are of the same ethnic or racial group. Many studies have found this to be the case for majority group students (e.g. Braha and Rutter, 1980; Clark and Ayers, 1992; Denscombe, Szulc, Patrick and Wood 1986; Howes and Wu, 1990). This preference was weaker in minority students according to most but not all studies. The low incidences of cross-race or cross-ethnic friendship choice must indicate that race or ethnicity plays a prominent role in friendship selection. The high degree of own-group preference, even in very young children (Braha and Rutter, 1980; Jelinek and Brittan, 1975), has surprised many researchers. Although most of these studies were conducted in the United States, the results of research from Britain, Australia, and Israel are generally similar to the pattern of US findings.

It is a belief among some social psychologists, sociologists, and school administrators that the mixing of different races or ethic groups in classrooms and in the school as a whole will foster the formation of inter-ethnic/racial friendships among students (Hallinan and Teixeira, 1987a). However, such beliefs have not always proved true, and in some cases hostility and tension have only increased due to the proximity of different races and ethnic groups (Amir, 1969). School organization may affect cross-ethnic/cross-race friendship selection, acceptance, communication and aggregation. Schools may pose a barrier to the formation of inter-ethnic/inter-racial friendships by imposing contexts, such as ability grouping, that limit opportunities for association among different groups.

There is variation in the extent to which the racial composition of the class or school affects friendship choice. Hallinan and Smith (1985) found that the numerical minority group had more cross-race friendships than the majority group. Interestingly, Hallinan and Teixeira (1987b) found that the cross-race friendships of blacks were not affected by racial composition, whereas the likelihood of a white child choosing a black classmate as a friend increased the more black children there were in the classroom. Denscombe (1983), however, found that whites showed more ethnocentrism in a school with a higher ratio of minorities to whites than they did in other schools. There have been many descriptive accounts of the 're-segregation' which may occur in racially diverse schools with a substantial proportion of minority students (e.g. Schofield, 1995).

Among the school variables that can promote or inhibit friendships between pupils of different racial and cultural origins, the practice of separating students by levels of academic ability has received the most attention. Hallinan and Teixera (1987a, 1987b) found that being in the same ability group had a significant positive effect on white students' choice of black students as friends. Although findings from one of their studies indicates a small negative effect on blacks' choice of white friends (Hallinan and Teixeira, 1987a), those from their other study did not indicate any significant effect of ability grouping on cross-race friendships of black students (Hallinan and Teixeira, 1987b). Damico and Sparks (1986) found that whites talked more often to black school-mates when there was no ability grouping than when the school employed ability grouping. Uniting black and white students in the same group for instruction affected white students' inter-racial friendships more than it affected racially mixed friendships of black students. Similarly, Hallinan and Teixeira (1987b) suggest that classroom structure affects the cross-race friendships of white children more than black children.

Hallinan and Teixeira (1987b) found that white students were less likely to choose black classmates as friends in competitive classrooms where marks were compared and emphasized; there was no effect on black students' choice of white friends. In classrooms where there was an emphasis on basic skills and understanding of the curriculum, whites were less likely to choose blacks, but blacks were more likely to choose white classmates as friends (ibid.). In classrooms where there was considerable student initiative and enthusiasm about learning, blacks were more likely to select white students as best friends, and there was a weak positive effect on the inter-racial choice of whites (ibid.). Hallinan and Williams (1987) concluded that the inter-racial friendships of blacks were more responsive to classroom climates that affected status hierarchy than were the inter-racial friendships of whites.

Allport maintained that, 'equal-status contact between majority and minority groups in the pursuit of common goals' (1954, p. 281) is a condition for mutual acceptance. Slavin (1979) examined the effects of cooperative learning groups on cross-ethnic/cross-racial friendship selection. (Cooperative learning was discussed in Chapter 4.) The cooperative learning groups in Slavin's study were composed of students of different ethnic/racial groups and differing scholastic capabilities. Students were assigned the responsibilities of tutoring and quizzing their peers, and the group was rewarded for the achievement of its members. Every student in the group was given an equal opportunity to add points to the group's score by improving his or her previous performance (Slavin, 1979). Results of Slavin's study indicated a statistically significant effect for the cooperative learning context on the number and proportion of cross-race friends selected. Similarly, Zigler (1981) found that more casual cross-ethnic friendships were formed in the cooperative learning group than in the regularly instructed control group. Only until 10 weeks after the experiment ended was there a treatment effect on close inter-racial friendship. Nevertheless, cooperative groups did have positive effects on students' interaction with peers of a different race.

Should society or schools be disturbed by the findings that children tend to choose friends of their own cultural or racial group? This depends on how one views race and ethnic relations. Lundberg and Dickson asserted that 'a certain amount of ethnocentrism is a normal and necessary ingredient of all group life,' and it is 'therefore, not in itself necessarily to be regarded as a problem' (1952, p. 34). However, others may be disturbed by the prevalence of ethnocentrism in race relations and may not agree with this opinion.

There is evidence that ethnocentric friendship extends well beyond the borders of the multicultural societies where most of the classic studies were conducted. For example, ethnic homogeneity in friendship has been found in Czech society. In a study of the ethnic characteristics of friendship among Czech Gypsy minority and non-Gypsy majority students, Rican (1996) confirmed findings of ethnocentrism prevalent in many American and Western European studies. Rican maintains that research into this area is warranted in Czech society, which is plagued by ethnic tensions. Results from this study indicate that Gypsy and non-Gypsy children tended to provide more positive sociometric nominations of peers from their own respective ethnic groups; this has also been shown by Kundrátová (1995).

Expanding knowledge about children's friendships around the planet

As in research about most other aspects of children's peer relations, the studies discussed in this chapter demonstrate both important differences and equally important similarities in children's friendships in different cultures. In many important studies published recently, researchers have wisely attempted to link some known characteristic of the cultures studied to multiple aspects of children's friendships, instead of just measuring children's friendships in different countries without a clear reason to justify the cross-cultural comparisons. Hopefully, more studies of this type will continue to emerge.

11 Facilitating children's peer relations

This chapter contains descriptions of the various techniques developed to enhance peer relationships both for entire school populations and for children with intellectual and behavioural exceptionalities. The evidence for their effectiveness is reviewed. Traditional social skills training is considered, as are more recent interventions designed to facilitate friendships at the dyadic level. The chapter closes with a discussion of the value of multi-pronged interventions that involve individuals as well as their peers, families, and schools.

As discussed in Chapter 1, researchers studying children's peer relations have always considered it part of their mission to apply what they learn to the prevention and correction of peer relations problems. As early as the 1930s, brief, focused efforts were made to improve the acceptance of rejected children. Some of the early interventions went no further than teaching young children the proper rules of games, and such skills as assembling designs with coloured blocks, learning stories that popular children enjoyed, and assembling picture puzzles. Unsophisticated as it sounds, that intervention did succeed in getting peers to increase their acceptance of children whom they had previously rejected. At the same time, Moreno's psychodrama became standard feature of care in psychiatric facilities and institutions for delinquent youth.

However, most of the techniques in current use originated later in the century, during the heyday of behavioural psychology in North America in the 1960s and 1970s. In its purest form, behaviourism defined overt behaviour, and overt behaviour only, as the subject matter of psychology (Wolman, 1973). Some behaviourally oriented practitioners began applying the basic principles and procedures of behaviour modification to interpersonal skills and behaviours. Stated very simply, these procedures entail creating an environment where behaving appropriately leads to more rewards than behaving inappropriately does.

However, social skills training was developed mostly by psychologists trained within the behavioural model who participated in several transformations that amount to something of a retreat from its purest interpretation. One of these new slants of behavioural theory was the introduction of the notion of 'skill', as chronicled by the theorist E. Lakin Phillips (1979), who proposed that social skills form a nexus between the individual and the environment (the word 'nexus' means connection or link). Classical behaviourists had no need for a concept other than reinforcement to link individuals to their environments. Struggling to insert the notions of nexus and skill into a behavioural model that he did not wish to destroy, Phillips insisted that social skills were largely understandable by means of observable behaviour, although by skills he meant capacities that could be inferred from behaviours and not behaviours themselves. Examples of the social skills he emphasized were the 'skills in managing oneself, in dealing with others, in aligning situations so as to reduce friction and optimize problem solving' (ibid., p. xii). Importantly, social skills training was only to be considered successful if it led to appreciable improvement in observable behaviour, which is probably the majority position to the present day. None the less, in order to do anything substantial with the notion of 'skill', at least a change in the emphasis or spirit of classical behaviourism was needed. Although Phillips insisted that social skills were modifiable by changing the reinforcement patterns in individual's environments, the direct regulation of reinforcement is quite peripheral in many of the techniques he promoted with great vehemence, including teaching children systematic ways of solving problems (discussed later in this chapter) and of coping with frustration.

Phillips' stance typified that of many colleagues at the time who had been trained in behaviourism in the truest Skinnerian tradition. In their first years of university, they had read Skinner's *Walden Two* (1948), the novel in which he describes his vision of Utopia. In *Walden Two*, rewards are distributed systematically in an environment that is totally controlled, but in the most benevolent way. For example, gardening, which is inherently rewarding, earns few points per hour, whereas rubbish collection yields a high points-to-hours ratio.

Along the same general lines, behaviour therapists set up token economies in schools and hospitals in order to improve the social behaviour of pupils and residents. Proper social skills are often targeted in token economies (e.g. MacDonald and Sherman, 1987). Proper behaviour earns tokens; improper behaviour leads to a fine. The tokens can be redeemed for privileges or desired objects. There is no doubt that token economies are effective. Therefore, they are still used, and are certainly better than punitive institutional practices that are less effective. However, as token economies proliferated, a sad realization emerged: the improvement in behaviour often failed to transfer once the child left the setting where the tokens were distributed so systematically (Levine, Fasnacht, Funabiki and Burkart, 1979). Many of the real-life classrooms, communities, and homes to which the children were re-integrated are run by individuals who do not share Skinner's (1948; see previous paragraph) vision of Utopia as *Walden Two*. Not all parents and teachers want to control the contingencies of reinforcement so carefully, and not all are able to. Therefore, without abandoning the principles of the behavioural movement, and certainly without discarding its research tradition, many scientists and practitioners were ready for some alternative modes of intervention.

Bandura's reciprocal determinism (1978) brought substantial changes to the behavioural tradition, which had previously wanted to consider little or none of any processes that might occur between the environment and the learning it engenders. Several elements of Bandura's model inspired many of the major contemporary techniques of social skills training in current use with children. One of these elements is observational learning — the fact that children can learn things by watching and imitating others. Observational learning often occurs in the absence of any tangible reinforcement at the moment of observation, but is enhanced if the person being observed appears to be reinforced for the behaviour he or she is modelling.

Cognitive abilities and beliefs also form important parts of Bandura's model of reciprocal determinism. As illustrated below, many techniques in children's social skills training deal with such cognitions and beliefs as children's understanding of other people and their intentions, children's beliefs about what is right or wrong in a social situation, their abilities to plan their social behaviour, their satisfaction with what they have done, and their beliefs in their own effectiveness in social situations. All of these derive directly from Bandura's social-learning approach, and, although they have been adopted by many who were trained in the pure behavioural model, these techniques could not have emerged from Skinner's behavioural (stimulus-response) theories.

As social skills training expanded and enthusiasm for it grew, it became apparent that its success was not unlimited. The limits of social skills training would probably never have been discovered had it not been for the strong research tradition in the study of peer relations. As discussed in Chapter 1, this field has always been characterized by an insistence that ideas be proven scientifically before they are admitted to common knowledge and that intervention techniques be proven successful before they are adopted in clinical and educational practice. Careful assessment of the success of an intervention includes finding out whether it works in different settings, whether the improvement it generates will be maintained over time, and whether it can work with individuals who chronically display dysfunctional social behaviour. Children's social skills training measured up only partially to this very demanding yardstick. As aptly put by Beelmann, Pfingsten, and Loesel (1994), who conducted a meta-analysis of the more recent social skills training studies, it is not that social skills training is any less effective than it once was, only that researchers are asking it to do more. Although social skills training is not always equal to the challenge of effecting permanent cross-situational change for children with the severest difficulties, it is important to remember that it does have an established record of some success (Schneider, 1992). In appraising its usefulness, its low cost and ease of use in schools, recreational centres, and therapeutic milieux should be taken into account.

In any case, in their search for ways of improving the peer relations of the children who are at greatest risk, in ways that will last and be evident in many parts of their social worlds, many contemporary authorities are re-appraising the wisdom of an exclusive focus on teaching skills to the child. Returning somewhat to their conceptual roots, they are now exploring the benefits of a more comprehensive system of intervention that indeed includes skill training for the child, but also includes training for parents and teachers, and, often some attempt at tapping the change potential of the child's peer group. Some examples are described below, after a capsule description of the major techniques used in training children's social skills.

Basic methods: structured learning

Social skills training can be implemented for primary prevention (i.e. before any problems have been observed) in whole classrooms or in small groups for secondary prevention — with children who already are begin-ning to show signs of maladaptive patterns of relating to peers. The whole-class format avoids stigmatizing any individuals by assigning them to special groups. The small-group format provides for more individualized attention, just as individualized remediation is often provided to children who have difficulty with their schoolwork. In some cases, especially with adolescents, bringing aggressive children together in groups can backfire because the members of the group encourage each other's maladaptive behaviour (Dishion, McCord and Poulin, 1999). There is no reason to believe that this occurs any more or less in social skills training groups than in any other form of group counselling or therapy. Some success in over-coming this problem has been reported by including children with both competent and incompetent social behaviour in the training groups (Bierman and Furman, 1984).

The basic steps in implementing structured learning are described in detail by Cartledge and Milburn (1995) and by Goldstein (1999). As recalled by Cartledge and Milburn, observational learning, according to Bandura's social learning theory, does not occur to any appreciable extent as a result of casual exposure to a model. Rather, optimal imitation of mod-els happens when the observer pays attention to the model, understands the salient features that are to be imitated, encodes these features for future reference, and is convinced that there is some incentive for imitating the model. Therefore, the elements of structured learning are designed around these conditions.

The first step is providing a rationale in order to motivate the trainees. This can be done by using stories, folktales, or anecdotes that illustrate how children are better off if they behave in a socially skilled manner. It is important to select skills in which the trainees are deficient and which will be important to them to succeed socially in their daily lives. The skills are taught one by one. First, the skill must be presented in sufficient detail for the trainees to appreciate the important elements. Often this is taught by breaking the skills down into 'skill steps'. For example, the skills steps used to teach the skills of introducing oneself in Goldstein's (1999, p. 164) structured learning model are:

1. Decide if you want to meet the person.
2. Decide if it is a good time.
3. Walk up to the person.
4. Introduce yourself.
5. Wait for the person to tell you his/her name. If he/she doesn't tell you, ask.

Once the skill has been explained, it must be modelled. Puppets, videotapes, adult demonstrations, and live demonstrations by peers or older children have all been used successfully. Sometimes, both a positive and a negative modelling display (i.e. depicting correct and incorrect performance) are provided to ensure that the trainees understand the important points of the skill, although there is always some chance that some children will imitate the negative model.

It is important for the trainees to rehearse performance of the skills they have been shown by the model. This is often done through role plays, which can be videotaped. The videotapes can be played back to the trainees, who can then be given feedback by the other children or by the adult leader regarding how close their performance approximates the model (Ladd, 1981; Schneider and Byrne, 1987). Guided imagery can also be used in rehearsal; the trainees are instructed to imagine themselves implementing the skill properly, followed by a pleasant outcome (Cartledge and Milburn, 1995).

Appropriate imitation of the skills must be reinforced. In some cases, verbal praise is all that is needed. In other situations, especially in groups of children with behaviour disorders, tangible reinforcers are used, to reinforce both imitation of the model and cooperation with the smooth running of the group. The reinforcers may be points that can be redeemed for a special privilege, favoured activity, or small gift.

Basic methods: social problem-solving

Problem-solving interventions represent a major application of the 'cognitive revolution' in psychology, which has raged since the 1970s. Social problem-solving techniques have been used very extensively in primary prevention programmes designed for whole schools. Elaborate curricula, including stories, games, and teaching materials have been developed to make it easier for teachers to implement this form of intervention (Elias *et al.*, 1997). Problem-solving techniques evolved from research into the problem-solving styles of aggressive children. Those youngsters have been found to believe that they have few alternatives to aggression in dealing with provocations. This is made all the worse by their tendency to be on the look-out for provocation and to interpret as provocations behaviours that other children would not interpret as containing hostile intent (e.g. Dodge and Tomlin, 1987). Aggressive children are also more likely than others to believe that an aggressive solution is perfectly legitimate in response to such provocation.

The problem-solving sequence typically taught is depicted in Figure 11.1. The first step in implementing problem-solving training is getting the trainees to recognize that they have a problem (Cartledge and Milburn, 1995; Meichenbaum, 1975). Through guided discussions, the children learn to recognize problems either in vignettes or in situations drawn from their daily experiences. The next step is brainstorming — having the children enumerate all their alternatives in solving the problem. Early problem-

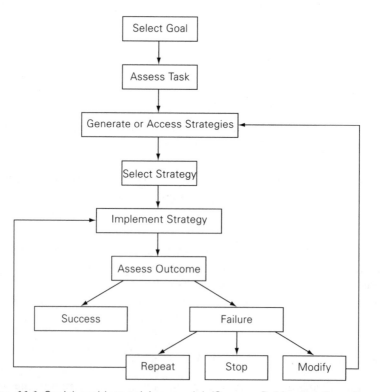

Figure 11.1 Social problem-solving model (Source: Rubin and Rose-Krasner, 1986)

solving programme manuals emphasized that the children's creativity should be stimulating by having them generate as many alternative solutions as possible (Spivack and Shure, 1974). For example, in dealing with a schoolmate who teases, the alternatives might be to walk away, tell the teacher, tease back, hit the child, ignore him or her totally, send him to the moon in a spaceship, or tell the child's mother. However, placing no limits on the alternatives can result in many anti-social solutions to the problem (Weissberg *et al.*, 1981) and many silly ones. Therefore, although the general practice is to praise the children for every solution offered, the leader sometimes is best to thank the child offering the solution for his or her contribution, but comment that he or she would not implement a particular solution because of the harm it might do, detailing the harm.

The next part of the programme is promoting consequential thinking — having the child recognize what would happen if each of the solutions contemplated is carried out. In guided discussions, the group learns to recognize that hitting the other child could result in injury and sanctions by the school authorities, walking away could either defuse the situation or lead to more teasing, etc. Once the children have learned to evaluate the alternatives in this way, they are then assisted in planning, step by step, how to go about implementing the solution that has the highest likelihood of leading to a satisfactory outcome. Needless to say, problem-solving interventions depend on the children's ability to use language to modulate their social behaviour, and, for that reason, cannot be effective with children who have some types of language or intellectual disabilities (Cartledge and Milburn, 1995).

Self-control interventions

Self-control interventions are another product of the 'cognitive revolution', one that reflects in particular the work of the Russian psychologists Luria and Vygotsky, who studied the ways in which language influences behaviour. Vygotsky demonstrated that the internalization of verbal commands is necessary in order to control one's behaviour (Kendall and Braswell, 1985). Self-control approaches are best known for their applications in helping children who display problems in controlling their impulsive reactions and anger. Like other forms of social skills training, self-control can be taught to whole classes (as in the classic 'Think Aloud' programme by Bash and Camp, 1985), in small groups (the usual format for anger-control interventions) or with individuals.

The crux of self-control therapy is getting impulsive children to 'stop and think' (Kendall and Braswell, 1982, p. 8). An important first step is to help the children become aware of the problem behaviours by teaching them to observe their own behaviour carefully and record it objectively. A variety of gimmicks have been used to help children slow down, observe, and reflect, rather than automatically revert to the familiar trigger reactions that have

led to difficulties in the past. For example, they can be taught to visualize a traffic 'Stop' sign, or to count backwards from 10 to 1. Once they are aware of the situations in which behavioural improvement is needed, the children can use language to re-direct their behaviour away from maladaptive behaviours that are all too familiar. They are taught to use self-statements whose content suggests self-control. Typically, the teacher or leader begins by providing a self-statement that the children can repeat out loud, such as 'I am being teased, but I can stay in charge of things.' Gradually, the self-statements are relegated to whispers, then to private speech. It is considered vital that the children monitor their use of the self-statements in their daily lives outside the training sessions, and learn to evaluate their own behaviour objectively (Ervin, Bankert and DuPaul, 1996).

Promoting generalization and maintenance: social-skills training travels uphill

It was probably naïve on the part of social skills trainers in the 1970s to expect that a brief, verbal intervention would permanently change the course of well-ingrained patterns of maladaptive social behaviour patterns that may be partly genetic in origin. Nevertheless, and perhaps paradoxically, these brief, focused interventions do have a track record of some degree of success.

As discussed in Chapter 1, scholars interested in children's peer relations have always been, and perhaps not entirely by coincidence, very active researchers or avid readers of the research literature. For that reason, the effects of children's social skills training have been studied very thoroughly. Research and practice related to children's peer relations are very closely linked. This is not the case for other modalities in the prevention and treatment of children's emotional and behavioural problems, such as child psychotherapy. Many clinicians practising child psychotherapy feel that much of the research on the techniques they use is irrelevant to their daily practice (Cohen, Sargent and Sechrest, 1986).

The 'commandments' of research methodology listed in Box 2 on p. 208 summarize the most important standards relevant to the evaluation of children's social skills training, or, indeed any other type of intervention with children. Virtually no studies of children's social skills training or any other intervention meet all of the standards, but several articles in the literature do come close. As evidenced in statistical summaries of the literature by Schneider (1992) and by Beelmann, Pfingsten and Loesel (1994), many but certainly not all of the published studies on children's social skills training demonstrate positive effects when effectiveness is measured immediately after treatment. Schneider (1992) found that, across studies, the best predictor of responsiveness to social skills training is the nature of the child's social behaviour before the treatment started. Aggressive young-

sters, in particular, are less responsive than others, though there have been some successes with that population.

As already mentioned, the long-term success of social skills training with children has been questioned very vehemently. Until recently, there were very few long-term follow-up studies. The results of follow-ups of children's studies are summarized in Table 11.1. Although it has been documented that the effects of social skills training are often ephemeral, the recent research displayed in Table 11.1 shows that there is evidence for long-term maintenance of the effects in some but by no means all studies. In reading Table 11.1, it is important not to overlook the fact that in the Coie and Krehbiel (1984) study, it is the academic intervention, and not the social skills intervention, that appeared effective at follow-up. Nevertheless, long-term effectiveness is evident in a substantial number, but by no means all or nearly all, of the other studies.

Nevertheless, what has been criticized as 'train and hope' (Stokes and Baer, 1977) social skills training no longer represents the state of the art. At the height of the cognitive revolution in psychology, Meichenbaum (1977), one of the revolutionaries, introduced the distinction between cognitive-behaviour modification and cognitive-HYPHEN-behaviour modification. Cognitive-behaviour modification means working on cognition with the intent of affecting behaviour via the route of cognitive change. Cognitive-HYPHEN-behaviour modification means intervening to correct maladaptive cognitive processes and also working on the behavioural level to help consolidate and promote the use of what is learned. Thus, only in cognitive-HYPEN-behaviour modification is any specific attempt made at facilitating the transfer between cognitive change during training and behaviour change in the trainee's natural environment. This transfer can be implemented in several ways, which are emphasized increasingly in recent social-skills-training manuals, as summarized by Cartledge and Milburn (1995).

Some of the ways of promoting generalization and maintenance involve making the training setting as similar as possible to the setting in which the skills are supposed to be used. If videotapes are used for modelling, the settings depicting in the videos might be several places within a typical school. The actors should resemble the trainees and the persons in their immediate social worlds, such as the teachers of the school. The groups themselves can be led by several different adults, so that the learning is not specific to a specific group leader. 'Homework' can be assigned, in which trainees are required to chart their use during the school week of the skills they have learned (e.g. Sasso, Melloy and Kavale, 1990).

Thus, some aspects of the training sessions can be adapted in order to promote generalization and maintenance of the skills. Evaluation data have yet to demonstrate conclusively the effectiveness of these 'bridges to generalization' (Schneider, 1992). By far the most promising means of

Table 11.1 Studies of the long-term effectiveness of social skills training with children and adolescents

Author	Population	Training technique	Design	Outcome measures	Short-term results	Follow-up results	Length of follow-up
Studies Conducted With Children With Typical Social Development							
Oden and Asher (1977) (USA)	8- and 9-year-old isolated children	Coaching	1 Treatment 2 Control 3 No-treatment control	1 Play observations 2 Best-friends test (children asked to name one, two or three of their best friends in the classroom) 3 Behavioural assessment	Coaching group increased on play rating and showed greater gain in friendship nominations.	Children in coaching group received similarly high results on play ratings at follow-up.	1 year
Rotheram (1982) (USA)	74 8- and 9-year-old children	Assertiveness Training by trainers with varying levels of assertiveness	Pre-treatment and post-treatment measures only	1 Assertion Quiz 2 Group Decision Task 3 Interpersonal Problem Solving	The assertiveness of children trained by highly assertive trainers increased. Children taught by less assertive trainers showed higher scores on interpersonal problem-solving test and Group Decision Task.	The higher assertiveness of children trained by highly assertive trainers was maintained at follow-up.	1 year
Rotheram, Armstrong and Booraem (1982) (USA)	343 Children ages 10 and 11	Assertiveness Training	1 Treatment 2 Control 3 No-treatment control	1 Assertion Quiz 2 Group Decision Task 3 Problem Solving 4 Self-esteem and peer popularity 5 Behavioural observations, teacher ratings and academic performance	Better comportment, higher achievement, and higher popularity among assertion groups.	School marks increased at follow-up for trainees.	1 year

Study	Intervention	Groups	Measures	Results	Follow-up	Follow-up period
Shure and Pivack (1982) (USA)	113 Black and low socio-economic status inner-city 4- and 5-year-olds	Interpersonal cognitive problem-solving	1 Twice-trained 2 Once-trained 3 Never-trained controls	Interpersonal problem-solving test	Trained children improved interpersonal problem solving.	Improvement maintained at follow-up, both at 6 months and 1 year.	6 months and 1 year
Coie and Krehbiel (1984) (USA)	40 Socially rejected, low-achieving 9-year-olds	Academic Skills Training (AS) Social Skills Training (SS)	1 AS 2 SS 3 AS & SS 4 No-treatment control	1 Sociometrics 2 Academic achievement tests	AS training produced significant improvement in reading, maths, and sociometrics	All increases except maths were evident at follow-up.	1 year

Studies Conducted With Children With Atypical Social Development

Study	Intervention	Groups	Measures	Results	Follow-up	Follow-up period
Kazdin, Esveldt-Dawson, French, and Unis (1987) (USA)	56 Psychiatric inpatient children, 11 girls and 45 boys	Cognitive-behavioural problem-solving skills training, and nondirective relationship therapy	1 Cognitive-Behavioural Problem-Solving 2 Nondirective Relationship Therapy 3 Placebo control	Parents' and teachers' ratings of child's behaviour	Cognitive-behavioural problem-solving led to decreases in aggressive behaviours, behavioural problems at home, and increases in overall adjustment.	These differences evident at one year follow-up.	1 year
Hundert, and Houghton (1992) (CAN)	14 children, ages 3 to 5 with moderate retardation, behaviour disorders, moderate hearing or vision impairment, or mild cerebral palsy	Teacher-led social skills programme	Pre-treatment and post-treatment measures only	Classroom behavioural observation	Social skills programme increased the positive play of children with disabilities to levels comparable to classmates without disabilities.	These findings were not maintained at follow-up.	6 months

Table 11.1 Continued

Author	Population	Training technique	Design	Outcome measures	Short-term results	Follow-up results	Length of follow-up
Lochman, Coie, Underwood, and Terry (1993) (USA)	52 Black aggressive rejected and non-aggressive rejected children	1 Social problem solving 2 Positive play training 3 Group-entry skill training 4 Lessons in dealing effectively with strong negative feelings	1 Treatment and 2 No-treatment control	1 Perceived Competence Scale for Children (self-report) 2 Sociometrics 3 Teacher Behaviour Checklist	Social relations interventions were shown (by teacher ratings and socio-metrics) to be effective only for aggressive rejected children.	These findings were maintained at follow-up.	1 year
Antia, and Kreimeyer (1997) (USA)	43 Young children deaf or hard of hearing	Teacher modeling and prompting	1 Treatment 2 Placebo control	Observation of indoor play behaviour	Children receiving the social skills inter-vention decreased their frequency of solitary and parallel play.	These changes were maintained at follow-up.	1 year
King, Specht, Warr-Leeper, Redekop and Risebrough (1997) (Canada)	21 Children with cerebral palsy or spina bifida, aged between 8 and 15	Social skills training programme called 'Joining In' containing elements of social learning and cognitive-behavioural methods	1 Treatment 2 Normative sample control	1 Self-Perception Profile for Children 2 Social Support Scale for Children 3 Loneliness Scale	Significant improvement in perceptions of their own social acceptance.	These findings were not maintained at follow-up.	6 months

promoting generalization and maintenance is enlisting the cooperation of other children, teachers, and parents to monitor, prompt, and reinforce the trainees' use of the skills learned in the training session outside the training sessions. This reality may come as something of a disappointment to some enthusiastic proponents of social skills training who expect the training by itself to be so effective that it changes the child's response repertoire completely enough for the responses to be evoked spontaneously by the child in his or her natural environment without any change on the part of the people in that environment. To no one is that disappointment more acute than to some 'reformed' behaviourists who fleetingly harboured the belief that they could permanently improve the peer relations of seriously maladjusted children by working only with the children. True to their earlier behavioural training, they discovered that the child's social environment has to be re-engineered for change, though perhaps not exactly in accordance with Skinner's *Walden Two* fantasy.

Harnessing the help of peers represents an important alternative to adults' training an individual child in social skills and relying on that child to implement what he or she has learned. Enhanced peer involvement probably represents the most viable way of increasing the effectiveness of current peer relations interventions. Cartledge and Milburn (1995, p. 324) maintain that peers have an enormous influence on each other's behaviour. That influence can undermine what adults try to teach, as when the peer group rewards the aggressive behaviours that adult social-skills trainers try to eliminate. Peers have participated in several ways. One of the ways, mentioned earlier, is by involving them in social skills training groups. By including pro-social peers, the groups are not dominated by anti-social children, which results in the mutual encouragement of aggression. Peers have also been taught to monitor each other's behaviour, and reinforce use of positive social skills (Fowler, 1988). Peers have been trained as mediators who help reduce conflict in schools by assisting other pupils in negotiating peaceful solutions to disagreements that could lead to violence (see review of research by Johnson and Johnson, 1996). Finally, in comprehensive anti-bullying campaigns, peers can be enlisted to provide support to victims or potential victims of bullies. This would help make bullying less rewarding to the bullies. It could also make victims less vulnerable. Under typical conditions, victims tend to be outsiders who do not really belong to any cohesive social group in the school (Salmivalli, Huttenen and Lagerspetz, 1997). If victims could be integrated into the peer network, bullies might be less prone to attack them, because the victims would have friends who might rally to their defence.

Social skills training as part of multi-modal interventions

The most current thinking in dealing with the problems of children who display the most serious and pervasive problems in their peer relations is to intervene simultaneously in a number of ways in several parts of the children's social worlds. Kazdin, Siegel and Bass (1992) conducted an influential study illustrating that, in work with children displaying behaviour problems severe enough to warrant clinic treatment, it might be best to provide both social skills training to the child and training to the parents in managing children's behaviour, rather than debate about which treatment route to choose. They assigned 97 children referred to a clinic because of severe behaviour problems to one of three conditions: social skills training only, parent-management training only, and both treatments simultaneously. The children in either of the two conditions involving only one form of treatment did improve somewhat. However, both at the end of treatment and at one-year follow-up, the children who had received the combined treatment improved much more.

The largest and best-known multi-pronged intervention in the peer relations field is known as Project FAST Track (FAST is an acronym for Families and Schools Together). An exhaustive effort is underway at four sites in the United States to determine whether intensive, simultaneous intervention in schools, homes, communities and families can prevent youngsters already showing signs of aggressive behaviour from following the familiar path to lives of school failure, violence and delinquency. Children and families participating in Project FAST Track receive individual social skills training and supervised play experiences in 'friendship groups' that meet on Saturday mornings when school is closed. Class-wide lessons on social skills are provided to their schools. Their parents receive intensive instruction in parenting skills. Assistance is provided in arranging summer camp and after-school recreational activities for the participating children. Transportation is offered to families who would not otherwise be able to bring their children to the activities of the programme (Bierman and Greenberg, 1996).

The evaluation of FAST Track is comprehensive. Initial findings after a few years of intervention do indicate some success. However, only long-term follow-up data will tell if the project achieves its goals. FAST Track is intended as a demonstration project. However, even if it is successful, it is doubtful that many communities that would like to repeat the experiment will have the resources to mount something similar. Nevertheless, the data from Project FAST Track are invaluable, because it is important to establish how successful intervention can be with children in high-risk situations given the best intervention attempt that current knowledge can offer.

Multi-pronged interventions have also become the norm in dealing with

the exasperating problem of bullying in schools. The best-known programme designed to reduce bullying in schools was implemented by
Olweus (1993) in Norway. The unifying thread of the programme is changing the opportunity and reward structures for bullying, that is, reducing the
opportunities for bullying to occur and making bullying a less rewarding
behaviour. The core components include a public campaign to sensitize
adults about the problem, better training of teachers in recognizing bullying as a serious problem, closer supervision of play periods, clear classroom
rules enforced consistently and without corporal punishment, and confer-
ences with the parents of bullies and victims. This 'restructuring of the
social environment' of bullying (Olweus, 1999, p. 41) has resulted in a very
marked drop in incidents of bullying in Norwegian schools.

Olweus' intervention was certainly facilitated by the Scandinavian traditions of strong national policies on social problems and of heavy investment
in matters of social well-being. However, similar interventions have been
successful in other countries as well. For example, in Sheffield, England,
Smith and Sharp (1994) adapted a multi-modal approach to the varying
resources, interests, and motivation in different schools. Some elements
were considered core components of the intervention to be implemented in
all schools: consciousness raising; consultation with teaching and non-
teaching staff, parents and pupils; and clear school policies about bullying,
in order to leave no doubt that pupils may communicate their concerns
about bullies and to provide guidelines for teachers, pupils and parents
regarding the handling of bullying incidents. Schools could choose from
among the optional components of the programme depending on their own
interests, needs, and resources. Those components included the incorpora-
tion of anti-bullying content in the school curriculum, using videos, books,
or drama; enhanced playground supervision; assertiveness training for victims, and counselling by peer helpers. Evaluations of the project clearly
indicate a reduction in incidents of bullying in the Sheffield schools.

Empathy training is an important component of multi-modal efforts to
reduce bullying. This is based on the assumption that bullies either fail to
recognize the suffering they cause, or are not concerned about others' suffering even though they are aware of it (Menesini, Berdondini, Ciucci and
Almeida, 1999). As an example of empathy training in the schools, a large-
scale intervention programme underway in Scotland features the introduction of lessons on perspective-taking in an effort to prevent and reduce
incidents of bullying, though, importantly, as part of a multifaceted intervention (Christie, Warden, Fitzpatrick and Reid 1999).

Student-mediated conflict resolution is gaining in popularity as an intervention that capitalizes on the peer perspective. As noted by Cunningham
et al. (1998), most conflicts at school occur in the playground, often outside of the awareness of adults. Therefore, sanctions by adults are often
ineffectual in dealing with bullying. Cunningham and his colleagues

provided 15 hours of training in conflict resolution to selected students at two Canadian primary schools, using a detailed training manual and providing ongoing teacher support and direction. At a school assembly, the trainees were introduced to their fellow students as mediators who could be approached to solve conflicts on the playground. Direct observations of recess play suggested that the programme resulted in a reduction in aggressive incidents by at least 50 per cent.

Interventions with a focus on friendship

Paralleling the recent increase in interest in studying children's relationships at the dyadic rather than the group level is the emergence of interventions designed specifically to foster children's friendships. Murphy and Schneider (1994) implemented an intervention focusing on friendship with 12-year-olds who were rejected by their classroom peers according to sociometric choice nominations. The researchers decided to concentrate on friendship based on their speculation that it might be easier to help rejected children find one close friend than to reverse the history of rejection by substantial numbers of their schoolmates. Murphy and Schneider conducted the intervention in a private, counselling format, for no more than ten sessions. The participants were asked to select a classmate with whom they wished to form or enhance a friendship. The adult counsellors guided the rejected children through a series of steps designed to indicate to the intended friend the friendly intentions of the child receiving counselling. The counsellors supported the children in case the overtures were rebuffed, and helped them direct friendly overtures to other potential friends where necessary. At the end of the intervention, both the children receiving counselling and the targeted friends indicated significantly greater liking for each other. There was no change in the friendship ratings given and received by children in the control group, who were on a waiting list to receive the counselling after the first experimental group had completed the study.

Pair therapy is a modality of intervention in which an adult therapist works to facilitate the relationship between two children who have the potential to become friends. The technique is the major method in current friendship research by Robert Selman and his colleagues at Harvard University (Selman, Watts and Schultz, 1997). In pair therapy, the children hopefully develop skills useful in close relationships in general, whether or not the two children who participate directly decide to become and stay friends. The children are brought together as pairs for a pre-specified reason that requires considerable forethought, and implies that the two members would benefit from a deeper understanding of each other. In some cases, it is a bully and a victim; in others, the pair consists of two aggressive children of different cultural or racial origins. Pair therapy is not as structured as such forms of social skills training as modelling, coaching, or problem solving. The children select a 'baseline activity' — something they would like to do together, but which does not totally absorb all of their attention, leaving some room for conversation and sharing. Often they decide to play chess or checkers or assemble a model. Inevitably, conflict arises. The task of the therapist is to help resolve the conflict, help the children understand each other's perspectives, and help them reflect on their friendships and the problems within it. Often, pair therapy continues for months and years. Observations of the interactions of the pairs and of their understanding of interpersonal relationships indicates the potential of this method (Selman, Watts, and Schultz, 1997). More systematic research, featuring long-term follow-up, is needed to confirm that pair therapy in fact achieves its aim of fostering friendship.

Conclusion

During the twentieth century, techniques for studying children's peer relations were devised and refined. These methods were used to chart the course of peer relations over the life course, identifying the patterns of peer relationships that predict problems later on. Despite dozens of longitudinal studies, the prediction remains far from perfect, even in the North American context where most of the research has been conducted. Methods were also devised to help improve the peer relations of children who seem headed towards a lifetime of problems in relating to others. Although these methods have a documented record of success, the extent to which it is possible to alter the maladaptive social-behaviour patterns of children at risk for maladjustment is not clear. Furthermore, it is not yet certain that these interventions can prevent the lifelong psychological difficulties that have been found to relate to early peer relations problems. Some recent research suggests that more intensive and more extensive interventions, involving families, schools, and communities may be needed to achieve long-term improvement for those children who need it most. Some scholars have taken up the task of devising such multi-component prevention programmes and studying their effectiveness over extended periods of people's lives. Other researchers continue to improve the assessment and training methods themselves, and study their applicability to populations that have previously been under-represented in peer relations research. Thus, despite their failure to agree on a common definition of social competence, despite the fact that different measures of peer relations often tell different tales about the social lives of individual children, and despite the fact that social skills interventions have not yet proved as successful as the need indicates, contemporary scholars studying children's peer relations have not totally abandoned Jacob Moreno's dream (see Chapter 1) of changing a troubled world by changing the interpersonal relationships in it one by one.

Box 2 Methodological standards for outcome studies

1. A treatment group must be compared with a control or comparison group.
2. The participants must be good representatives of the population the intervention is intended for.
3. Participants must be assigned randomly to treatment and control groups.
4. The sample size must be adequate to answer the questions asked.
5. Data must be collected before and after treatment
6. Follow-up data must be collected.
7. Multiple measures must be used.
8. Each measure must have demonstrated reliability and validity.
9. The intervention and the outcome measures must be administered by persons who have no bias in favour of the hypotheses under study.
10. There must be some systematic verification that the intervention was actually carried out the way the programme developer intended and the way it is described in the research report.
11. There must not be so many measures that some positive effects will probably be found just by chance.
12. The measures should represent dimensions of social behaviour that are important in the participants' lives.
13. Participant variables (e.g. age, gender, cultural origin, temperament, history of problem behaviour) should be analysed to establish whether the intervention is more or less effective for particular groups of children.

(Adapted from Peterson and Bell-Dolan's (1995) ten-plus commandments)

References

Aboud, F.E. 1993: The developmental psychology of racial prejudice. *Transcultural Psychiatric Research Review* **30**, 229–42.

Aboud, F.E. and Doyle, A. 1995: The development of in-group pride in Black Canadians. *Journal of Cross-Cultural Psychology* **26**, 243–54.

Abramovitch, R., Corter, C., Pepler, D.J. and Stanhope, L. 1986: Sibling and peer interaction: a final follow-up and a comparison. *Child Development* **57**, 217–29.

Achenbach, T.M. and Edelbrock, C.S. 1986: *Child behavior checklist and youth self-report.* Burlington, VT: University of Vermont Department of Psychiatry.

Adams, G.P. and Roopnarine, J.L. 1994: Physical attractiveness, social skills, and same-sex peer popularity. *Journal of Group Psychotherapy, Psychodrama and Sociometry* **47**, 15–35.

Adler, J.C., Mueller, R.J. and Ary, D. 1987: Non-gifted elementary and middle school childrens' sociometric choices of gifted versus non-gifted helpers. Paper presented at the annual meeting of the American Educational Research Association, Washington, DC, April.

Adler, P.A. and Adler, P. 1998: *Peer power: preadolescent culture and identity.* New Brunswick, NJ: Rutgers University Press.

Aho, J.S. 1994: *This thing of darkness: a sociology of the enemy.* Seattle: University of Washington Press.

Ainsworth, M.S., Blehar, M.C., Waters, E. and Wall, S. 1978: *Patterns of attachment: a psychological study of the strange situation.* Hillsdale, NJ: Erlbaum.

Ainsworth, M.S. and Marvin, R.S. 1995: On the shaping of attachment theory and research: an interview with Mary D. S. Ainsworth (Fall 1994, *Monographs of the Society for Research in Child Development* **60**, 3–21.

Ainsworth, M.S. and Whittig, B.A. 1969: Attachment and exploratory behaviour of one-year-olds in a strange situation. In Foss, B.M. (ed.), *Determinants of infant behaviour.* vol. 4. London: Methuen.

Albee, G.W. 1959: *Mental health manpower trends.* New York: Basic Books.

Albee, G.W. and Gullotta T.P. 1997: *Primary prevention works.* Thousand Oaks, CA: Sage.

Alexandrovna, D.N. 1999: Gender differences in aggression by young children. Paper presented at the 9th European Conference on Developmental Psychology Spetses, Greece, September.

Allport, G. W. 1954: *The nature of prejudice.* Cambridge, MA: Addison-Wesley.

Altman, I. and Taylor, D.A. 1973: *Social penetration: the development of interpersonal relationships.* New York: Holt, Rinehart and Winston.

American Psychiatric Association 1994: *Diagnostic and statistical manual of mental disorders.* 4th edn. Washington, DC: American Psychiatric Association.

Amir, Y. 1969: Contact hypothesis in ethnic relations. *Psychological Bulletin* **71**, 319–42.

Anderson, S. and Messick, S. 1974: Social competency in young children. *Developmental Psychology* **10**, 282–93.

Andreasen, N.C. and Canter, A. 1975: Genius and insanity revisted: psychiatric symptoms and family history in creative writers. In Wirt, R., Winokur, G. and Roff, M. (eds), *Life history research in psychopathology*. Minneapolis: University of Minnesota Press, 187–210.

Antia, S.D. and Kreimeyer, K.H. 1997: The generalization and maintenance of the peer social behaviours of young children who are deaf or hard of hearing. *Language, Speech and Hearing Services in the Schools* **28**, 59–69.

Argyle, M. 1983: *The psychology of interpersonal behaviour*. New York: Pergamon.

Argyle, M. 1991: *Cooperation: the basis of sociability*. London: Routledge.

Argyle, M. 1992: *The social psychology of everyday life*. London: Routledge.

Argyle, M., Furnham, A. and Graham, J.A. 1981: *Social situations*. Cambridge: Cambridge University Press.

Argyle, M., Henderson, M., Bond, M., Iizuka, Y. and Contarello, A. 1986: Cross-cultural variations in relationship rules. *International Journal of Psychology* **21**, 287–315.

Argyle, M. and Lu, L. 1990: Happiness and social skills. *Personality and Individual Differences* **11**, 1255–61.

Asendorpf, J.B. 1986: Shyness in middle and late childhood. In Jones, W.H., Cheek, J.M. and Briggs, S.R. (eds), *Shyness: perspectives on research and treatment*. New York: Plenum Press, 91–103.

Asendorpf, J.B. and van Aken, M.A.G. 1994: Traits and relationship status: stranger versus peer group inhibition and test intelligence versus peer group competence as early predictors of later self-esteem. *Child Development* **65**, 1786–98.

Asher, S. 1985: An evolving paradigm in social skills training research with children. In Schneider, B.H., Rubin, K.H. and Ledingham, J.E. (eds), *Children's peer relations: issues in assessment and intervention*. New York: Springer-Verlag, 151–71.

Asher, S.R. and Coie, J.D. (eds) 1990: *Peer rejection in childhood*. New York: Cambridge University Press.

Asher, S.R. and Dodge, K.A. 1986: Identifying children who are rejected by their peers. *Developmental Psychology* **22**, 444–9.

Asher, S.R. and Hymel, S. 1981: Children's social competence in peer relations: sociometric and behavioural assessment. In Wine, J.D. and Smye, M.D. (eds), *Social competence*. New York: Guilford Press, 52–77.

Asher, S.R., Hymel, S. and Renshaw, P. D. 1984: Loneliness in children. *Child Development* **55**, 1456–64.

Asher, S.R. and Taylor, A.R. 1981: Social outcomes of mainstreaming: Sociometric assessment and beyond. *Exceptional Education Quarterly* **1**, 13–30.

Asher, S.R. and Wheeler, V.A. 1985: Children's loneliness: a comparison of rejected and neglected peer status. *Journal of Consulting and Clinical Psychology* **53**, 500–5.

Ashman, A.F. and Gillies, R.M. 1997: Children's cooperative behaviour and interactions in trained and untrained workgroups in regular classrooms. *Journal of School Psychology* **35**, 261–79.

Attili, G., Vermigli, P. and Schneider, B.H. 1997: Peer acceptance and friendship patterns among Italian elementary-school children within a cross-cultural perspective. *International Journal of Behavioural Development* **21**, 277–98.

Auerbach-Major, S.T. 1997: Contributors to early childhood social competence: the direct and interactive effects of parent disciplinary style and child temperament [CD-ROM]. Abstract from: *ProQuest File: Dissertation Abstracts* Item: 9735204.

Austin, A.B. and Lindauer, S.K. 1990: Parent-child conversation of more-liked and less-liked children. *Journal of Genetic Psychology* **151**, 5–23.

Aviezer, O., van IJzendoorn, M. H., Sagi, A. and Schuengel, C. 1994: 'Children of the dream' revisited: 70 years of collective early child care in Israeli kibbutzim. *Psychological Bulletin* **116**, 99–116.

Ayer, M.E. and Bernreuter, R. 1936: A study of the relationship between discipline and personality traits in little children. *Journal of Genetic Psychology* **50**, 165–70.

Azmitia, M. 1988: Peer interaction and problem solving: when are two heads better than one? *Child Development* **59**, 87–96.

Azmitia, M. and Hesser, J. 1993: Why siblings are important agents of cognitive development: a comparison of siblings and peers. *Child Development* **64**, 430–44.

Azmitia, M. and Perlmutter, M. 1989: Social influences in children's social cognition. In Reese, H. (ed.), *Advances in child development and behaviour*. Vol. 22. New York: Academic Press, 89–144.

Bakeman, R.R. and Gottman, J.M. 1997: *Observing interaction: an introduction to sequential analysis*. New York: Cambridge University Press.

Baldwin, A.L. 1948: Socialization and the parent-child relationship. *Child Development* **19**, 127–36.

Ballard, M., Corman, L., Gottlieb, J. and Kaufman, M. J. 1977: Improving the social status of mainstreamed retarded children. *Journal of Educational Psychology* **69**, 605–11.

Bandura, A. 1978: The self-system in reciprocal determinism. *American Psychologist* **33**, 344–58.

Barnett, L.A. and Fiscella, J. 1985: A child by any other name . . . a comparison of the playfulness of gifted and non-gifted children. *Gifted Child Quarterly* **29**, 61–6.

Barr, D. 1997: Friendship and belonging. In Selman, R.S., Watts, C.L. and Schultz, L.H. (eds), *Fostering friendship for treatment and prevention*. New York: de Gruyter, 19–30.

Barton, E.J. and Ascione, F.R. 1984: Direct observation. In Ollendick, T.H. and Herson, M. (eds), *Child behavioural assessment: principles and procedures*. New York: Pergamon, 164–94.

Bash, M.A. and Camp, B.W. 1985: *Think aloud: increasing social and cognitive skills*. Champaign, IL: Research Press.

Baumrind, D. 1989: Rearing competent children. In Damon, W. (ed.), *Child development today and tomorrow*. San Francisco: Jossey-Bass, 349–78.

Baumrind, D. 1996: The discipline controversy revisited. Family relations. *Journal of Applied Family and Child Studies* **45**, 405–14.

Baumrind, D. and Black, A.E. 1967: Socialization practices associated with dimensions of competence in preschool boys and girls. *Child Development* **38**, 291–327.

Bear, G.G., Juvonen, J. and McInerney, F. 1993: Self-perceptions and peer relations of boys with and boys without learning disabilities in an integrated setting: a longitudinal study. *Learning Disability Quarterly* **16**, 127–36.

Bearison, D.J., Magzamen, S. and Filardo, E.K. 1986: Cognitive conflict and cognitive growth in young children. *Merrill-Palmer Quarterly* **32**, 51–72.

Becker, W.C., Peterson, D.R., Hellmer, L.A., Shoemaker, D.J. and Quay, H.S. 1959: Factors in parental behaviour and personality as related to problem behaviour in children. *Journal of Consulting Psychology* **23**, 107–18.

Becker, W.C., Peterson, D.R., Luria, Z., Shoemaker, D.J. and Hellmer, L.A. 1962: Relations of factors derived from parent-interview ratings to behaviour problems of five-year olds. *Child Development* **33**, 509–35.

Beelmann, A., Pfingsten, U. and Loesel, F. 1994: Effects of training social competence in children: a meta-analysis of recent evaluation studies. *Journal of Clinical Child Psychology* **23**, 260–71.

Bellack, A.S. and Hersen, M. 1979: *Behaviour modification: an introductory textbook.* Baltimore, MD: Williams and Wilkins.

Bell-Dolan, D.J., Foster, S.L. and Christopher, J.S. 1992: Children's reactions to participating in a peer relations study: an example of cost-effective assessment. *Child Study Journal* **22**, 137–55.

Bell-Dolan, D.J., Foster, S.L. and Sikora, D.M. 1989: Effects of sociometric testing on children's behaviour and loneliness in school. *Developmental Psychology* **25**, 306–11.

Bell-Dolan, D.J., Foster, S.L. and Tishelman, A.C. 1989: An alternative to negative nomination sociometric measures. *Journal of Clinical Child Psychology* **18**, 153–7.

Bell-Dolan, D.J. and Wessler, A.E. 1994: Ethical administration of sociometric measures: procedures in use and suggestions for improvement. *Professional Psychology: Research and Practice* **25**, 23–32.

Belsky, J. and Cassidy, J. 1995: Attachment theory and evidence. In Rutter, M. and Hay, D. (eds), *Development through life.* London: Blackwell, 373–402.

Bender, W.N., Wyne, M.D., Stuck, G.B. and Bailey, D.B., Jr. 1984: Relative peer status of learning disabled, educable mentally retarded, mentally handicapped, low achieving and normally achieving children. *Child Study Journal* **13**, 209–16.

Berndt, T.J. 1981: Age changes and changes over time in prosocial intentions and behaviour between friends. *Developmental Psychology* **17**, 408–16.

Berndt, T.J. 1982: The features and effects of friendship in early adolescence. *Child Development* **53**, 1447–60.

Berndt, T.J. 1996: Transitions in friendship and friends' influence. In Garber, J.A. and Brooks-Gunn, J. (eds), *Transitions through adolescence: interpersonal domains and context.* Mahwah, NJ: Lawrence Erlbaum Associates, 57–84.

Berndt, T.J. and Hanna, N.A. 1995: Intimacy and self-disclosure in friendships. In Rotenberg, K.J. (ed.), Disclosure processes in children and adolescents. *Cambridge studies in social and emotional development.* New York: Cambridge University Press, 57–77.

Berndt, T.J., Hawkins, J.A. and Hoyle, S.G. 1986: Changes in friendships during a school year: effects on children's and adolescents' impressions of friendships and sharing with friends. *Child Development* **57**, 1284–97.

Berndt, T.J., Hawkins, J.A. and Jiao, Z. 1999: Influences of friends and friendships on adjustment to Junior High School. *Merrill-Palmer Quarterly* **45**, 13–41.

Berndt, T.J. and Keefe, K. 1992: Friends' influence on adolescents' perceptions of themselves in school. In Schunk, D.H. and Meece, J.L. (eds), *Students' perceptions in the classroom.* Hillsdale, NJ: Erlbaum, 51–73.

Berndt, T.J. and Keefe, K. 1995: Friends' influence on adolescents' adjustment to school. *Child Development* **66**, 1312–29.

Berndt, T.J. and Perry, T.B. 1986: Children's perceptions of friendships as supportive relationships. *Developmental Psychology* **22**, 640–8.

Berndt, T.J., Perry, T.B. and Miller, K.E. 1988: Friends' and classmates' interactions on academic tasks. *Journal of Educational Psychology* **80**, 506–13.

Bernicot, J. and Mahrokhian, A. 1988: La production de demandes par les enfants: le rôle de la nature de la demande et du statut de l'interlocuteur [Production of requests by children: the effects of the nature of the request and the status of the interlocutor]. *Revue Internationale de Psychologie Sociale* **1**, 389–407.

Berscheid, E. and Walster, E.H. 1978: *Interpersonal attraction.* 2nd edn. Reading, MA: Addison-Wesley.

Bierman, K.L. and Furman, W. 1984: The effects of social skills training and peer involvement in the social adjustment of preadolescents. *Child Development* 57, 230–40.

Bierman, K.L. and Greenberg, M.T. 1996: Social skills training in the Fast Track Program. In Peters, R.D. and McMahon, R.J. (eds) *Preventing childhood disorders, substance abuse, and delinquency.* Thousand Oaks, CA: Sage, 65–89.

Bigelow, B.J. 1977: Children's friendship expectations: a cognitive-developmental study. *Child Development* 48, 246–53.

Bigelow, B.J. and La Gaipa, J.J. 1975: Children's written descriptions of friendship: a multidimensional analysis. *Developmental Psychology* 11, 857–8.

Björkqvist, K., Lagerspetz, K.M.J. and Osterman, K. 1992: *The direct and indirect aggression scales.* Vasa, Finland: Abo Akademi University, Department of Social Sciences.

Björkqvist, K. and Osterman, K. 1999: Finland. In Smith, P. K., Morita, Y., Junger-Tas, J., Olweus, D., Catalano, R. and Slee, P. (eds), *The nature of school bullying: a cross-national perspective.* London: Routledge, 56–67.

Björkqvist, K., Osterman, K. and Kaukiainen, A. 1992: The development of direct and indirect aggressive strategies in males and females. In Björkqvist, K. and Niemela, P. (eds), *Of mice and women: aspects of female aggression.* San Diego, CA: Academic Press, 125–57.

Black, B. and Logan, A. 1995: Links between communication patterns in mother–child, father–child, and child–peer interactions and children's social status. *Child Development* 66, 255–71.

Blatz, W.E. 1944: *Understanding the young child.* Toronto: Clarke, Irwin and Company.

Bloom, B.S. 1977: Affective outcomes of school learning. *Phi Delta Kappan* 59, 193–8.

Blos, P. 1967: The second individuation process of adolescence: *Psychoanalytic study of the child.* Vol. 22. New York: International Universities Press.

Boivin, M. and Begin, G. 1989: Peer status and self-perception among early elementary school children: the case of the rejected children. *Child Development* 60, 591–6.

Boivin, M., Vitaro, F., Hodges, E. 1998: Proactive and reactive aggression among preadolescent boys: the cumulative experience of affiliating with other aggressive boys and the moderating role of negative peer status. Poster session presented at the biennial meeting of the International Society for the Study of Behavioural Development, Berne, Switzerland, July.

Bonn, M. and Kruger, P. 1996: Popularity and rejection in children's peer groups: a South African perspective. *Early Child Development and Care* 125, 1–14.

Boulton, M.J. and Smith, P. K. 1994: Bully/victim problems among middle school children. *British Journal of Developmental Psychology* 12, 315–29.

Bowlby, J. 1969: *Attachment and loss.* New York: Basic Books.

Bowlby, J. 1978: *Attachement et perte* (Attachment and loss). Paris: Presses Universitaires de France.

Bowlby, J. 1980: *Attachment and loss.* vol. 3. New York: Basic Books.

Bowlby, J. 1990: The study and reduction of group tensions in the family. In Trist, E. and Murray, H. (eds), *The social engagement of social science: a Tavistock anthology,* Vol. I: *The socio-psychological perspective.* Philadelphia, PA: University of Pennsylvania Press, 291–8.

Boyum, L.A. and Parke, R.D. 1995: The role of emotional expressiveness in the development of children's social competence. *Journal of Marriage and the Family* 57, 593–608.

Braha, V. and Rutter, D.R. 1980: Friendship choice in a mixed-race primary school. *Educational Studies* **6**, 217–23.

Brand, J.L. 1966: The United States: a historical perspective. In Williams, R.H. and Ozarin, L.D. (eds), *Community mental health*. San Francisco: Jossey-Bass, 18–43.

Bronfenbrenner, U., Kessel, F., Kessen, W. and White, S. 1986: Toward a critical social history of developmental psychology. *American Psychologist* **41**, 1218–30.

Brook, J.S., Whiteman, M.M. and Finch, S. 1992: Childhood aggression, adolescent delinquency, and drug use: a longitudinal study. *Journal of Genetic Psychology* **153**, 369–83.

Brook, J.S., Whiteman, M., Finch, S. and Cohen, P. 1995: Aggression, intrapsychic distress, and drug use: antecedent and intervening processes. *Journal of the American Academy of Child and Adolescent Psychiatry* **34**, 1076–84.

Brook, J.S., Whiteman, M.M., Finch, S.J. and Cohen, P. 1996: Young adult drug use and delinquency: childhood antecedents and adolescent mediators. *Journal of the American Academy of Child and Adolescent Psychiatry* **35**, 1584–92.

Brownell, C.A. and Brown, E. 1992: Peers and play in infants and toddlers. In Van Hasselt, V.B. and Hersen, M. (eds), *Handbook of social development: a lifespan perspective*. New York: Plenum Press, 183–200.

Brownell, C.A. and Carriger, M.S. 1990: Changes in cooperation and self-other differentiation during the second year. *Child Development* **61**, 1164–74.

Buchanan, H.T., Blankenbaker, J. and Cotton, D. 1976: Academic and athletic ability as popularity factors in elementary school children. *Research Quarterly* **47**, 320–5.

Buhrmester, D. 1996: Need fulfillment, interpersonal competence, and the developmental contexts of early adolescent friendship. In Bukowski, W.M., Newcomb, A.F. and Hartup, W.W. (eds), *The company they keep: friendship in childhood and adolescence*. New York: Cambridge University Press, 158–85.

Bukowski, W.M., Boivin, M. and Hoza, B. 1994: Measuring friendship quality during pre- and early adolescence: the development and psychometric properties of the Friendship Qualities Scale. *Journal of Social and Personal Relationships* **11**, 471–84.

Bukowski, W.M., Gauze, C., Hoza, B. and Newcomb, A. F. 1993: Differences and consistency between same-sex and other-sex peer relationships during early adolescence. *Developmental Psychology* **29**, 255–63.

Bukowski, W.M. and Hoza, B. 1989: Popularity and friendships: issues in theory, measurement, and outcome. In Berndt, T.J and Ladds, G.W. (eds), *Peer relations in child development*. New York: Wiley, 15–45.

Bukowski, W.M. and Kramer, T.L. 1986: Judgements of the features of friendship among early adolescent boys and girls. *Journal of Early Adolescence* **6**, 331–8.

Bukowski, W.M. and Newcomb, A.F. 1984: Stability and determinants of sociometric status and friendship choice: a longitudinal perspective. *Developmental Psychology* **20**, 941–52.

Bukowski, W.M., Newcomb, A.F. and Hoza, B. 1987: Friendship conceptions among early adolescents: a longitudinal study of stability and change. *Journal of Early Adolescence* **7**, 143–52.

Bukowski, W.M., Sippola, L., Gauze, C., Hoza, B. and Newcomb, A.F. 1993: Differences in the processes, properties, and perceptions of friendship among boys and girls. Paper presented at the Society for Research in Child Development New Orleans, LA, March.

Burack, J. 1997: The study of atypical and typical populations in developmental psychology: the quest for a common science. In Luthar, S.S., Burack, J.A., Cicchetti, D. and Weisz, J.R. (eds), *Developmental psychology: perspectives on adjustment, risk, and disorder*. Cambridge: Cambridge University Press, 136–65.

Burks, V.S., Dodge, K.A. and Price, J.M. 1995: Models of internalizing outcomes of early rejection. *Development and Psychopathology* 7, 683–96.

Burleson, B.R., Applegate, J.L., Burke, J.A., Clark, R.A., Delia, J.G. and Kline, S.L. 1986: Communicative correlates of peer acceptance in childhood. *Communicative Education* 35, 349–61.

Burleson, B.R., Delia, J.G. and Applegate, J.L. 1992: Effects of maternal communication and children's social-cognitive and communication skills on children's acceptance by the peer group. *Family Relations* 41, 264–72.

Burlingham, D. and Freud, A. 1942: *Young children in wartime in a residential nursery school*. London: Allen and Unwin.

Bursuck, W.D. 1983: Sociometric status, behaviour ratings and social knowledge of learning disabled and low achieving students. *Learning Disability Quarterly* 6, 329–38.

Bursuck, W.D. 1989: A comparison of students with learning disabilities to low achieving and higher achieving students on 3 dimensions of social competence. *Journal of Learning Disabilities* 22, 188–94.

Buss, A.H. 1985: Two kinds of shyness. In Schwarzer, R. (ed.), *Self-related cognitions in anxiety and motivation*. Hillsdale, NJ: Erlbaum, 65–75.

Buss, A.H. and Plomin, R. 1975: *A temperament theory of personality development*. New York: Wiley-interscience.

Buss, A.H. and Plomin, R. 1984: *Temperament: early developing personality traits*. Hillsdale, NJ: Erlbaum.

Buzzelli, C.A. 1988: The development of trust in children's relations with peers. *Child Study Journal* 18, 22–46.

Byrne, B. and Schneider, B.H. 1986: Student-teacher concordance on dimensions of student social competence: a multitrait-multimethod analysis. *Journal of Psychopathology and Behavioural Assessment* 8, 263–79.

Cairns, R.B. and Cairns, B.D. 1994: *Lifelines and risks: pathways of youth in our time*. Cambridge: Cambridge University Press.

Cairns, R.B., Cairns, B.D., Neckerman, H.J., Gest, S.D. and Gariépy, N. 1988: Social networks and aggressive behaviour: peer support or peer rejection? *Developmental Psychology* 24, 815–23.

Campbell, P. T. and Fiske, D.W. 1959: Convergent and discriminant validation by the multitrait-multimethod matrix. *Psychological Bulletin* 56, 81–105.

Cantor, N. and Harlow, R.E. 1994: Social intelligence and personality: flexible life task pursuit. In Sternberg, R.J. and Ruzgis, P. (eds), *Personality and intelligence*. New York: Cambridge University Press.

Cantrell, V.L. and Prinz, R.J. 1985: Multiple perspectives of rejected, neglected, and accepted children: relation between sociometric status and behavioural characteristics. *Journal of Consulting and Clinical Psychology* 53, 884–9.

Carlson, C.L., Lahey, B.B. and Neeper, R. 1984: Peer assessment of the social behaviour of accepted, rejected, and neglected children. *Journal of Abnormal Child Psychology* 12, 187–98.

Carter, K.A. and Kuechenmeister, M.A. 1986: Evaluating the consequences of participating in a gifted pull-out program. *Journal for the Education of the Gifted* 9, 265–75.

Cartledge, G.C. and Milburn, J.F. 1995: *Teaching social skills to children and youth: innovative approaches*. 3rd edn. Needham Heights, MA: Allyn and Bacon.

Casiglia, A.C., LoCoco, A. and Zappulla, C. 1998: Aspects of social reputation and peer relationships in Italian children: a cross-cultural perspective. *Developmental Psychology* 34, 723–30.

Caspi, A. 1998: Personality development across the life course. In Damon, W.

(series ed.) and Eisenberg, N. (vol. ed.), *Handbook of child psychology:* Vol. 3. *Social, emotional, and personality development.* 5th edn. New York: Wiley, 311–88.

Caspi, A., Elder, G.H., Jr. and Bem, D. J. 1988: Moving away from the world: life-course patterns of shy children. *Developmental Psychology* 24, 824–31.

Cha, J.H. 1994: Aspects of individualism and collectivism in Korea. In Kim, U., Triandis, H.C., Kagitcibasi, C., Choi, S. and Yoon, G. (eds), *Individualism and collectivism: theory, methods, and applications.* Thousand Oaks, CA: Sage, 157–74.

Chao, P. 1983: *Chinese kinship.* London: Kegan Paul.

Chen, X., Hastings, P. D., Rubin, K.H., Chen, H., Cen, G. and Stewart, S.L. 1998: Child-rearing attitudes and behavioural inhibition in Chinese and Canadian toddlers: a cross-cultural study. *Developmental Psychology* 34, 667–86.

Chen, X., Rubin, K.H. and Li, B. 1995: Social and school adjustment of shy and aggressive children in China. *Developmental Psychopathology* 7, 337–49.

Chen, X., Rubin, K.H., Li, B. and Li, D. 1999: Adolescent outcomes and social functioning in Chinese children. *International Journal of Behavioural Developmental* 23, 199–223.

Chen, X., Rubin, K.H. and Li, D. 1997: Relation between academic achievement and social adjustment: evidence from Chinese children. *Developmental Psychology* 33, 518–25.

Chen, X., Rubin, K.H. and Li, Z.Y. 1994: Social functioning and adjustment in Chinese Children: a longitudinal study. Paper presented at the meeting of the International Society for the Study of Behavioural Development, Amsterdam, The Netherlands, July.

Chen, X., Rubin, K.H. and Sun, Y. 1992: Social reputation and peer relationships in Chinese and Canadian children: a cross-cultural study. *Child Development* 63, 1336–43.

Chess, S. and Thomas, A. 1996: *Temperament: theory and practice.* vol. 12. New York: Brunner-Mazel.

Chiu, C.Y., Tsang, S.C. and Yang, C.F. 1988: The role of face situation and attitudinal antecedents in Chinese consumer complaint behaviour. *The Journal of Social Psychology* 128, 173–80.

Christie, D., Warden, D., Fitzpatrick, H. and Reid, K. 1999: Assessing and promoting children's social competence. Paper presented at the 9th European Conference on Developmental Psychology, Spetses, Greece, September.

Chu, L. 1979: The sensitivity of Chinese and American children to social influences. *The Journal of Social Psychology* 109, 175–86.

Cillessen, A.N.H., van IJzendoorn, H.W., van Lieshout, C.F.M. and Hartup, W.W. 1992: Heterogeneity among peer-rejected boys: subtypes and stabilities. *Child Development* 63, 893–905.

Clark, M.L. and Ayers, M. 1992: Friendship similarity during early adolescence: gender and racial patterns. *Journal of Psychology* 126, 393–405.

Clark, M.L. and Drewry, D.L. 1985: Similarity and reciprocity in the friendships of elementary school children. *Child Study Journal* 15, 251–64.

Cloke, K. 1987: Politics and values in mediation: the Chinese experience. *Mediation Quarterly* 17, 69–82.

Cohen, L.H., Sargent, M.M. and Sechrest, L.B. 1986: Use of psychotherapy research by professional psychologists. *American Psychologists* 41, 198–206.

Cohen, R., Duncan, M. and Cohen, S. 1994: Classroom peer relations of children participating in a pull-out enrichment program. *Gifted Child Quarterly* 38, 33–7.

Cohen, Y.A. 1966: Forms of friendship. In Cohen, Y.A. (ed.), *Social structure and personality.* New York: Holt, Rinehart and Winston, 351–86.

Coie, J.D. and Dodge, K.A. 1988: Multiple sources of data on social behaviour and social status in the school: a cross-age comparison. *Child Development* **59**, 815–29.

Coie, J.D., Dodge, K.A. and Coppotelli, H. 1982: Dimensions and types of social status: a five-year longitudinal study. *Developmental Psychology* **18**, 557–70.

Coie, J.D., Dodge, K.A. and Kupersmidt, J. 1990: Peer group behaviour and social status. In Asher, S.R. and Coie, J.D. (eds), *Peer rejection in childhood*. Cambridge: Cambridge University Press, 17–59.

Coie, J.D., and Krehbiel, G. 1984: Effects of academic tutoring on the social status of low-achieving, socially rejected children. *Child Development* **55**, 1465–78.

Coie, J.D. and Kupersmidt, J.B. 1983: A behavioural analysis of emerging social status in boys' groups. *Child Development* **54**, 1400–16.

Coie, J.D., Terry, R., Lenox, K., Lochman, J. and Hyman, C. 1995: Childhood peer rejection and aggression as predictors of stable patterns of adolescent disorder. *Development and Psychopathology* **7**, 697–714.

Coie, J.D., Terry, R., Zabriski, A. and Lochman, J. 1995: Early adolescent social influences on delinquent behaviour. In McCord, J. (ed.), *Coercion and punishment in long-term perspective*. New York: Cambridge University Press, 229–44.

Cole, D.A. and Carpentieri, S. 1990: Social status and the comorbidity of child depression and conduct disorder. *Journal of Consulting and Clinical Psychology* **58**, 748–57.

Coleman, J.S. 1961: *The adolescent society*. New York: Free Press of Glencoe.

Committee for Economic Development 1994: *Putting learning first: governing and managing the schools for high achievement*. New York: Committee for Economic Development.

Conrad, M. and Hammen, C. 1993: Protective and resource factors in high-risk and low-risk children: a comparison of children with unipolar, bipolar medically ill, and normal mothers. *Development and Psychopathology* **5**, 593–607.

Contarello, A. and Volpata, C. 1991: Images of friendship: literary depictions through the ages. *Journal of Social and Personal Relationship* **8**, 49–75.

Cook, H. 1992: Matrilocality and female aggression in Margeriteno society. In Björkqvist, K. and Nimela, P. (eds), *Of mice and women: aspects of female aggression*. San Diego, CA: Academic Press, 149–62.

Cooper, C.R., Marquis, A. and Edward, D. 1986) Four perspectives on peer learning among elementary school children. In Mueller, E.C. and Cooper, C.R. (eds), *Process and outcome in peer relations*. New York: Academic Press, 269–99.

Cooper, J.E., Brooks, A.J., LeCroy, C.W. and Ashford, J.B. 1994: Adolescent friendship patterns: mediators of risky behaviours. Paper presented at the Society for Research in Adolescence, San Diego, California, February.

Coplan, R.J., Rubin, K.H., Fox, N.A., Calkins, S.D. and Stewart, S.L. 1994: Being alone, playing alone, and acting alone: distinguishing among reticence, and passive, and active solitude in young children. *Child Development* **65**, 129–37.

Corsaro, W.A. 1981: Friendship in the nursery school: social organization in a peer environment. In Asher, R. and Gottman, J.M. (eds), *The development of children's friendships*. New York: Cambridge University Press.

Corsaro, W.A. 1985: *Friendship and peer culture in the early years*. Norwood, NJ: Ablex.

Corsaro, W.A. 1988: Routines in the peer culture of American and Italian nursery school children. *Sociology of Education* **61**, 1–14.

Cowen, E.L., Pedersen, A., Babigian, H., Izzo, L.D. and Trost, M.A. 1973: Long term follow-up of early-detected vulnerable children. *Journal of Consulting and Clinical Psychology* **41**, 438–46.

Craig, W.M. and Pepler, D.J. 1997: Observations of bullying and victimization in the school yard. *Canadian Journal of School Psychology* 13, 41–57.

Craik, K. 1943: *The nature of explanation.* Cambridge: Cambridge University Press.

Crick, N.R., Bigbee, M.A. and Howes, C. 1996: Gender differences in children's normative beliefs about aggression: how do I hurt thee? Let me count the ways. *Child Development* 67, 1003–14.

Crick, N.R., Casas, J.F. and Mosher, M. 1997: Relational and overt aggression in preschool. *Developmental Psychology* 33, 579–88.

Crick, N.R. and Dodge, K.A. 1994: A review and reformulation of social informa-tion-processing mechanisms in children's social adjustment. *Psychological Bulletin* 115, 74–101.

Crick, N.R. and Dodge, K.A. 1996: Social information-processing mechanisms in reactive and proactive aggression. *Child Development* 67, 993–1002.

Crick, N.R. and Dodge, K.A 1999: Superiority is in the eye of the beholder: a com-ment on Sutton, Smith and Swettenham. *Social Development* 8, 128–31.

Crick, N.R. and Grotpeter, J.K. 1995: Relational aggression, gender, and social-psychological adjustment. *Child Development* 66, 710–22.

Cryderman, B.K. 1992: Chinese. In Cryderman, B.K. and Fleras, A. (eds), *Police, race, and ethnicity: a guide for police services.* Toronto: Butterworths, 191–208.

Crystal, D.S., Watanabe, H. and Chen, R. 1999: Children's reactions to physical dis-ability: a cross-national and developmental study. *International Journal of Behav-ioural Development* 23, 91–111.

Csikzmentmihalyi, M. and Larson, R. 1987: The experience sampling method. *Journal of Nervous and Mental Disease* 175, 537–44.

Cuksts, B. 1988: Peer acceptance, friendships, and attitudes towards academically integrated physically disabled adolescents. Unpublished master's thesis, Ontario Institute for Studies in Education, Ontario, Canada.

Cunningham, C.E., Cunningham, L.J., Martorelli, V., Tran, A., Young, J. and Zacharias, R. 1998: The effects of primary division, student-mediated conflict resolution programs on playground aggression. *Journal of Child Psychology and Psychiatry and Allied Disciplines* 39, 653–62.

Damico, S.B. and Sparks, C. 1986: Cross-group contact opportunities: impact on interpersonal relationship in desegregated middle schools. *Sociology of Education* 59, 113–23.

Daniels-Beirness, T. M. and Leshono, S. 1988: Children's social relationships out-side of school. Paper presented at the NATO Advanced Study Institute: Social competence in Developmental Perspective, Savoy, France, July.

DeFries, J.C., Plomin, R. and Fulker, D.W. (eds) 1994: *Nature and nurture during middle childhood.* Oxford: Blackwell.

Dekovic, M. and Gerris, J.R.M. 1994: Developmental analysis of social cognitive and behavioural differences between popular and rejected children. *Journal of Applied Developmental Psychology* 15, 367–86.

Dekovic, M. and Janssens, J.M. 1992: Parents' child-rearing style and child's socio-metric status. *Developmental Psychology* 28, 925–32.

Denscombe, M. 1983: Ethnic group and friendship choice in the primary school. *Educational Research* 25, 184–90.

Denscombe, M., Szulc, H., Patrick, C. and Wood, A. 1986: Ethnicity and friend-ship: the contrast between sociometric research and fieldwork observation in pri-mary school classrooms. *British Educational Research Journal* 12, 221–35.

DeRosier, M. 1989: Costa Rican children's perceptions of their social networks. Paper presented at the biennial meeting of the Society for Research in Child Development, Kansas City, MO., April.

DeRosier, M., Kupersmidt, J. and Patterson, C. 1994: Children's academic and behavioural adjustment as a function of the chronicity and proximity of peer rejection. *Child Development* **65**, 1799–813.

Dewey, J. 1900: *The school and society*. Chicago: University of Chicago Press.

Diehl, D.S., Lemerise, E.A., Caverly, S.L., Ramsay, S. and Roberts, J. 1998: Peer relations and school adjustment in ungraded primary children. *Journal of Educational Psychology* **90**, 506–15.

Dion, K.K. and Berscheid, E. 1974: Physical attractiveness and peer perception among children. *Sociometry* **37**, 1–12.

Dishion, T., McCord, J. and Poulin, F. 1999: When interventions harm: peer groups and problem behaviour. *American Psychologist* **54**, 755–64.

Dishion, T.J. 1990: The ecology of boys' peer relations in middle childhood. *Child Development* **61**, 874–92.

Dishion, T.J., Andrews, D.W. and Crosby, L. 1995: Antisocial boys and their friends in early adolescence: relationship characteristics, quality, and interactional process. *Child Development* **65**, 139–51.

Dishion, T.J., Eddy, M., Haas, E., Li, F. and Spracklen, S. 1997: Friendships and violent behaviour during adolescence. *Social Development* **6**, 207–23.

Dodge, K.A. 1983: Behavioural antecedents of peer social status. *Child Development* **54**, 1386–99.

Dodge, K.A. 1985: Attributional bias in aggressive children. In Phillips, P. C. (ed.), *Advances in cognitive-behavioural research and therapy*. Vol. 4: *Advances in cognitive-behavioural research and therapy*. Orlando, FL: Academic Press, 73–110.

Dodge, K.A. and Coie, J.D. 1987: Social-information-processing factors in reactive and proactive aggression in children's peer groups. *Journal of Personality and Social Psychology*, **53**, 1146–58.

Dodge, K A., Coie, J.D. and Brakke, N.P. 1982: Behaviour patterns of socially rejected and neglected preadolescents: the roles of social approach and aggression. *Journal of Abnormal Child Psychology* **10**, 389–410.

Dodge, K.A., Coie, J.D., Pettit, G.S. and Price, J.M. 1990: Peer status and aggression in boys' groups: developmental and contextual analyses. *Child Development* **55**, 163–73.

Dodge, K.A. and Frame, C.L. 1982: Social cognitive biases and deficits in aggressive boys. *Child Development* **53**, 620–35.

Dodge, K.A., Schlundt, D..C., Schocken, I. and Delugach, J.D. 1983: Social competence and children's sociometric status: the role of peer group entry strategies. *Merrill-Palmer Quarterly* **29**, 309–36.

Dodge, K.A. and Tomlin, A.M. 1987: Utilization of self-schemas as a mechanism of interpretational bias in aggressive children. *Social Cognition* **5**, 280–300.

Doise, W. and Mugny, G. 1984: *The social development of the intellect*. Oxford: Pergamon.

Doise, W., Mugny, G. and Perret-Clermont, A. 1975: Social interaction and the development of cognitive operations. *European Journal of Social Psychology* **5**, 367–83.

Dong, Q., Yang, B. and Ollendick, T.I. 1994: Fears in Chinese children and adolescents and their relations to anxiety and depression. *Journal of Child Psychology and Psychiatry* **35**, 351–63.

Donnelly, M. 1992: *The politics of mental health in Italy*. New York: Tavistock/Routledge.

Dosen, A. 1994: The European scene. In Bourras, N. (ed.), *Mental health in mental retardation*. Cambridge: Cambridge University Press, 375–8.

Doyle, A.B. and Aboud, F.E. 1995: A longitudinal study of White children's racial prejudice as a social-cognitive development. *Merrill-Palmer Quarterly* **41**, 209–28.

Dubow, E.F. and Cappas, C.L. 1988: Peer social status and reports of children's adjustment by their teachers, by their peers, and by their self-ratings. *Journal of School Psychology* **26**, 69–75.

Duck, S. 1991: Diaries and logs. In Montgomery, B.M. and Duck, S. (eds), *Studying interpersonal interaction*. New York: Plenum Press, 141–61.

Duck, S.W., Miell, D.K. and Gaebler, H.C. 1980: Attraction and communication in children's interactions. In Foot, H.C., Chapman, A.J. and Smith, R.J. (eds), *Friendship and social relations in children*. New York: Wiley, 89–115.

Dumas, J.E. and LaFrenière, P. J. 1993: Mother-child relationships as sources of support or stress: a comparison of competent, average, aggressive, and anxious dyads. *Child Development* **64**, 1732–54.

Dunn, J. 1993: *Young children's close relationships: beyond attachment*. London: Sage.

East, P. L. and Rook, K.S. 1992: Compensatory patterns of support among children's peer relationships: a test using school friends, nonschool friends, and siblings. *Developmental Psychology* **28**, 163–72.

Eccles, A.L. and Bauman, E. and Rotenberg, K.J. 1989: Peer acceptance and self-esteem in gifted children. *Journal of Social Behaviour and Personality* **4**, 401–9.

Edelstein, L.N. 1983) Maternal bereavement: coping with the unexpected death of a child. *Dissertation Abstracts International*, **43**(10–b), 3356–7.

Eder, D. and Hallinan, M.T. 1978: Sex differences in children's friendships. *American Sociological Review* **43**, 237–50.

Ederer, E. 1990: Peer relations and depressed mood in children and early adolescents: a critical review of recent reviews. In Zapatoczeky, H.G. and Wenzel, T. (eds), The scientific dialogue: from basic research to clinical intervention. *Annual series on European research in behaviour therapy*: Vol. 5. Amsterdam: Swets and Zeitlinger, 55–63.

Edwards, C.P. 1986: *Promoting social and moral development in young children: creative approaches for the classroom*. New York: Teachers College Press.

Eisenberg, L. 1958: School phobia: a study in the communication of anxiety. *American Journal of Psychiatry* **114**, 712–18.

Eisenberg, N., Fabes, R.A. and Murphy, B. 1996: Parents' reactions to children's negative emotions: relations to children's social competence and comforting behaviour. *Child Development* **67**, 2227–47.

Elias, M.J., Zins, J.E., Weissberg, R.P. , Frey, K.S., Greenberg, M.T., Haynes, M.M., Norris, M.K., Kessler, R., Schwab-Stone, M.E. and Shriver, T.P. 1997: *Promoting social and emotional learning: guidelines for educators*. Virginia: Association for Supervision and Curriculum Development.

Engfer, A. 1993: Antecedents and consequences of shyness in boys and girls: a 6–year longitudinal study. In Rubin, K.H. and Asendorf, J.B. (eds), *Social withdrawal, inhibition, and shyness in childhood*. Hillsdale, NJ: Lawrence Erlbaum Associates, 49–79.

Enright, D.J. and Rawlinson, D. (eds) 1992: *The Oxford Book of Friendship*. Oxford: Oxford University Press.

Entralgo, P.L. 1985: *Sobre la amistad* [About friendship]. Madrid: Austral.

Epstein, J.L. 1989: The selection of friends: changes across the grades and in different classroom environments. In Berndt, T.J. and Ladd, G.W. (eds), *Peer relationships in child development*. New York: Wiley, 158–87.

Erdley, C.A., Nangle, D.W., Carpenter, M.E., Grover, R. and Newman, J.E. 1999: Children's friendship experiences as buffers to loneliness and depression. Paper presented at the Biennial Meeting of the Society for Research in Child Development Albuquerque, New Mexico, April.

Erdley, C.A., Nangle, D.W. and Gold, J.A. 1998: Operationalizing the construct of friendship among children: a psychometric comparison of sociometric-based definitional methodologies. *Social Development* 7, 62–71.

Eron, L.D. and Huesmann, L.R. 1987: The stability of aggressive behaviour in cross-national comparison. In Kagitcibasi, C. (ed.), *In growth and progress in cross-cultural psychology.* Lisse, Netherlands: Swets, 207–17.

Eron, L.D., Walder, L.O., Toigo, R. and Lefkowitz, M.M. 1963: Social class, parental punishment for aggression, and child aggression. *Child Development* 34, 849–67.

Ervin, R.A., Bankert, C.L. and DuPaul, G.J. 1996: Treatment of attention-deficit/hyperactivity disorder. In Reinecke, M.A. Dattilio, F.M. and Freeman, A. (eds), *Cognitive therapy with children and adolescents.* New York: Guilford, 38–61.

Erwin, P. G. 1985: Similarity of attitudes and constructs in children's friendships. *Journal of Experimental Child Psychology* 40, 470–85.

Erwin, P. G. 1994: Social problem solving, social behaviour, and children's peer popularity. *The Journal of Psychology* 128, 299–306.

Farmer, T.W. and Farmer, E.M.Z. 1996: Social relationships of students with exceptionalities in mainstream classrooms: social networks and homophily. *Exceptional Children* 62, 431–50.

Farver, J.M. 1996: Aggressive behaviour in preschoolers' social networks: do birds of a feather flock together? *Early Childhood Research Quarterly* 11, 333–50.

Farver, J.M., Welles-Nyström, B., Frosch, D.L., Wibarti, S. and Hoppe-Graff, S. 1997: Toy stories: aggression in children's narratives in the United States, Sweden, Germany and Indonesia. *Journal of Cross-Cultural Psychology* 28, 393–420.

Fehr, B. 1996: *Adult friendships.* Thousand Oaks, CA: Sage.

Feldman, E. and Dodge, K.A. 1987: Social information processing and sociometric status: Sex, age, and situational effects. *Journal of Abnormal Child Psychology* 15, 211–27.

Feldman, S.S., Rubenstein, J.L. and Rubin, C. 1988: Depressive affect and restraint in early adolescents: relationships with family structure, family process and friendship support. *Journal of Early Adolescence* 8, 279–26.

Feldman, S.S. and Wentzel, K.R. 1990: The relationship between parenting styles, sons' self-restraint, and peer relations in early adolescence. *Journal of Applied Developmental Psychology* 12, 205–18.

Felson, R.B. and Russo, N. 1988: Parental punishment and sibling aggression. *Social Psychology Quarterly* 51, 11–18.

Fenzel, M.L. and Blyth, D.A. 1986: Individual adjustment to school transition: An exploration of the role of supportive peer relations. *Journal of Early Adolescence* 6, 315–29.

Finnie, V. and Russell, A. 1988: Preschool children's social status and their mothers' behaviour and knowledge in the supervisory role. *Developmental Psychology* 24, 789–801.

Flicek, M. and Landau, S. 1985: Social status problems of learning disabled and hyperactive/learning disabled boys. *Journal of Clinical Child Psychology* 14, 340–4.

Fonzi, A., Tomada, G. and Ciucci, E. 1994: Uso di indici informativi nell'interazione tra bambini del nido [Use of informative indexes in the interaction among creche children]. *Eta evolutiva* 47, 5–13.

Fonzi, A.F., Genta, M.L., Menesini, E., Bacchini, D., Bonino, S. and Costabile, A. 1999: Italy. In Smith, P. K., Morita, Y. Junger-Tas, J., Olweus, D., Catalano, R.

and Slee, P. (eds), *The nature of school bullying: a cross-national perspective*. New York: Routledge, 140–56.

Fonzi, A.F., Schneider, B.H., Tani, F. and Tomada, G. 1997: Predicting the continuation of children's friendship from their behaviour in structured situations of potential conflict. *Child Development* **68**, 496–506.

Ford, M.E. 1982: Social cognition and social competence in adolescence. *Developmental Psychology* **18**, 323–40.

Forgatch, M S. and Patterson, G.R. 1998: Behavioural family therapy. In Dattilio, F.M. (ed.), Case studies in couple and family therapy: systemic and cognitive perspectives. *The Guilford family therapy series*. New York: The Guilford Press, 85–107.

Fornari, G. 1966: *Psicanalisi della guerra* (Psychoanalysis of war), Milan: Feltrinelli.

Foster, S.L., Bell-Dolan, D. and Berler, E.S. 1986: Methodological issues in the use of sociometrics for selecting children for social skills training. *Advances in the Behavioural Assessment of Children and Families* **2**, 227–48.

Foster, S.L. and Ritchey, W. 1979: Issues in the assessment of social competence in children. *Journal of Applied Behaviour Analysis* **12**, 625–38.

Fowler, S. 1988: The effects of peer-mediated interventions on establishing, maintaining, and generalizing children's behaviour changes. In Horner, R., Dunlop, G. and Koegel, R. (eds), *Generalization and maintenance*. Baltimore: Paul H. Brookes, 143–70.

Franz, D.Z. and Gross, A.M. 1996: Parental correlates of socially neglected, rejected and average children: a laboratory study. *Behavior Modification* **20**, 170–82.

Frazee, H.E. 1953: Children who later became schizophrenic. *Smith College Studies in Social Work* **23**, 125–49.

Frederickson, N.L. and Furnham, A.F. 1998: Sociometric classification methods in school peer groups: a comparative investigation. *Journal of Child Psychology and Psychiatry and Allied Disciplines* **39**, 921–33.

French, D.C. 1988: Heterogeneity of peer-rejected boys: aggressive and nonaggressive subtypes. *Child Development* **59**, 976–85.

French, D.C. 1990: Heterogeneity of peer-rejected girls. *Child Development* **61**, 2028–31.

French, D.C., Setiono, K. and Eddy, J.M. 1999: Bootstrapping through the cultural comparison minefield: childhood social status and friendship in the United States and Indonesia. In Collins, W.A. and Laursen, B. (eds), *Relationships as developmental contexts. The Minnesota symposia on child psychology.* vol. 30. Mahwah, NJ: Lawrence Erlbaum Associates, 109–31.

Frones, I. 1995: *Among peers: on the meaning of peers in the process of socialization.* Cambridge, MA: Scandinavian Universities Press.

Frude, N. 1993: Hatred between children. In Varma, V. (ed.), *How and why children hate*. London: Kingsley, 72–93.

Fry, D.P. 1988: Intercommunity differences in aggression among Zapotec children. *Child Development* **59**, 1008–19.

Furfey, P. H. 1928: *The gang age: a study of the preadolescent boy and his recreational needs.* New York: The Macmillan Company.

Furman, W. 1996: The measurement of friendship perceptions: Conceptual and methodological issues. In Bukowski, W.M., Newcomb, A.F. and Hartup, W.W. (eds) *The company they keep: friendship in childhood and adolescence.* Cambridge: Cambridge University Press, 41–65.

Furman, W. and Bierman, K.L. 1983: Developmental changes in young children's conceptions of friendship. *Child Development* **54**, 549–56.

Furman, W. and Buhrmester, D. 1985: Children's perceptions of the personal relationships in their social networks. *Developmental Psychology* 21, 1016–24.

Furnam, W. and Robbins, P. 1985: What's the point? Issues in the selection of treatment objectives. In Schneider B.H., Rubin, K. and Ledingham, J.E. (eds), *Children's peer relations: issues in assessment and intervention.* New York: Springer-Verlag, 141–54.

Galdston, I. 1965: Community psychiatry: its social and historic derivations. *Journal of the Canadian Psychiatric Association* 10, 461–73.

Galloway, B. and Porath, M. 1997: Parent and teacher views of gifted childrens' social abilities. *Roeper Review* 20, 118–21.

Garmezy, N. 1989: The role of competence in the study of children and adolescents under stress. In Schneider, B. H., Attili, G., Nadel, J. and Weissberg, R.D. (eds), *Social competence in developmental perspective.* NATO Science Institutes series. Series D: Behavioural and social sciences, Vol. 51. Dordrecht, Netherlands: Kluwer Academic Publishers, 25–39.

Garret, M.K. and Crump, W.D. 1980: Peer acceptance, teacher preference and self-appraisal of social status among learning disabled students. *Learning Disability Quarterly* 3, 42–8.

Gelb, R. and Jacobson, J.L. 1988: Popular and unpopular children's interactions during cooperative and competitive peer group activities. *Journal of Abnormal Child Psychology* 16, 247–61.

Genta, M.L., Menesini, E., Fonzi, A., Constable, A. and Smith, P. K. 1996: Bullies and victims in schools in central and southern Italy. *European Journal of Psychology of Education* 11, 97–110.

Georgas, J., Christakopoulou, S., Poortinga, Y.H., Angleitner, A., Goodwin, R. and Charalambous, N. 1997: The relationship of family bonds to family structure and function across cultures. *Journal of Cross-Cultural Psychology* 28, 303–20.

Gesell, A. and Ilg, F. L. 1943: *Infant and child in the culture of today.* New York: Harper.

Gest, S.D. 1997: Behavioural inhibitions: stability and associations with adaptation from childhood to early adulthood. *Journal of Personality and Social Psychology* 72, 467–75.

Ginsberg, D., Gottman, J. M. and Parker, J. G. 1986: The importance of friendship. In Gottman, J.M. and Parker, J.G. (eds), Conversations of friends: speculations on affective development. *Studies in emotion and social interaction.* Cambridge: Cambridge University Press, 3–48.

Ginter, E.J., Lufi, D., Trotzky, A.S. and Richmond, B.O. 1989: Anxiety among children in Israel. *Psychological Reports* 65, 803–9.

Goldbeck, L. 1998: Die familiäre Bewältigung einer Krebserkrankung im Kindes- und Jugendalter. Möglichkeiten der standardisierten Erfassung mit Selbstbeurteilungsverfahren: Ergebnisse einer empirischen Vorstudie [Families coping with cancer during childhood and adolescence: practicability of standardized self-assessment methods]. *Praxis der Kinderpsychologie und Kinderpsychiatrie* 47, 552–73.

Goldstein, A. 1999: *The PREPARE curriculum.* Champaign, IL: Research Press.

Goodlad, S. and Hirst, B. (eds) 1990: *Explorations in peer tutoring.* Oxford: Blackwell.

Goodwin, S. 1990: *Community care and the future of mental-health service provision.* Aldershot: Avebury.

Gordon, J.E. and Smith, E. 1965: Children's aggression, parental attitudes, and the effects of an affiliation-arousing story. *Journal of Personality and Social Psychology* 1, 654–9.

Gottlieb, B.W., Gottlieb, J., Berkell, D. and Levy, L. 1986: Sociometric status and solitary play of learning disabled boys and girls. *Journal of Learning Disabilities* **19**, 619–22.

Gottlieb, J., Semmel, M.I. and Veldman, D. J. 1978: Correlates of social status among mainstreamed mentally retarded children. *Journal of Educational Psychology* **70**, 396–405.

Gottman, J. M. 1983: How children become friends. *Monographs of the Society for Research in Child Development* **48** (3, Serial No. 201).

Goudena, P. and Sánchez, J. A. 1996: Peer interaction in Andalusia and Holland: a comparative study. *Infancia y Aprentizaje* **75**, 49–58.

Green, K.D.,Vosk, B. and Beck, S. 1981: An examination of differences among psychometrically identified accepted, rejected, and neglected children. *Child Study Journal* **11**, 117–24.

Greenspan, S. 1981: Defining childhood social competence: a proposed working model. *Advances in Special Education* **3**, 1–39.

Greenwood, C., Carta, J. and Kamps, D. 1990: Teacher-mediated versus peer-mediated instruction: a review of educational advantages and disadvantages. In Foot, H.C., Morgan, M/.J. and Shute, R.H. (eds), *Children helping children*. New York: John Wiley and Sons, 177–205.

Gresham, F.M 1981: Assessment of children's social skills. *Journal of School Psychology* **19**, 120–33.

Gresham, F.M. 1982: Misguided mainstreaming: the case for social skills training with handicapped children. *Exceptional Children* **48**, 422–33.

Gresham, F.M. 1986: Conceptual and definitional issues in the assessment of children's social skills: Implications for classification and training. *Journal of Clinical Child Psychology* **15**, 3–15.

Gresham, F.M. and Elliott, S.N. 1990: *The social skills rating system*. Circle Pines, Minnesota: American Guidance Service.

Gresham, F.M. and Reschly, D.J. 1986: Social skills deficits and low peer acceptance of mainstreamed learning disabled children. *Learning Disability Quarterly* **9**, 23–32.

Gresham, F.M. and Reschly, D.J. 1987: Differences between mildly handicapped and nonhandicapped black and white children. *Journal of Educational Psychology* **79**, 195–7.

Grotpeter, J.K. and Crick, N.R. 1996: Relational aggression, overt aggression, and friendship. *Child Development* **67**, 2328–38.

Grusec, J.E. and Lytton, H. 1988: *Social development: history, theory, and research*. New York: Springer-Verlag.

Guerra, N.C. and Slaby, R.C. 1989: Evaluative factors in problem solving by aggressive boys. *Journal of Abnormal Child Psychology*, **17**, 277–89.

Gumpel,T. and Frank, R. 1999: An expansion of the peer paradigm: cross-age peer tutoring of social skills among socially rejected boys. *Journal of Applied Behaviour Analysis* **32**, 115–18.

Gundykunst, W.B. and Ting-Toomey, S. 1988: *Culture and interpersonal communication*. Newbury Park, CA: Sage.

Hagekull, B. and Bohlin, G. 1998: Preschool temperament and environmental factors related to the five-factor model of personality in middle childhood. *Merrill-Palmer Quarterly* **44**, 194–215.

Hall, E.T. 1976: *Beyond culture*. New York: Doubleday.

Hallinan, M.T. and Smith, S.S. 1985: The effects of classroom racial composition on students' interracial friendliness. *Social Psychology Quarterly* **48**, 3–16.

Hallinan, M.T. and Teixeira, R.A. 1987a: Students' interracial friendships:

individual characteristics, structural effects, and racial differences. *American Journal of Education* **95**, 563–83.

Hallinan, M.T. and Teixeira, R.A. 1987b: Opportunities and constraints: Black-White differences in the formation of interracial friendships. *Child Development* **58**, 1358–71.

Hallinan, M.T. and Williams, R.A. 1987: The stability of students' interracial friendships. *American Sociological Review* **52**, 653–64.

Hare, A P. and Hare, J.R. 1996: *J. L. Moreno*. London: Sage Publications.

Hareven, T.K. 1989: Historical changes in children's networks in the family and community. In Belle, D. (ed.), *Children's social networks and social supports.* New York: Wiley, 15–36.

Hargie, O. 1986: Communication as skilled behaviour. In Hargie, O. (ed.), *A handbook of communication skills.* London: Croom Helm, 7–21.

Hargreaves, D. 1967: *Social relations in a secondary school.* London: Routledge.

Harralson, T.L. and Lawler, K.A. 1992: The relationship of parenting styles and social competency to Type A behaviour in children. *Journal of Psychosomatic Research* **36**, 625–34.

Harris, J.R. 1998: *The nurture assumption: why children turn out the way they do.* New York: Free Press.

Harrist, A.W. 1992: Synchronous and nonsynchronous parent-child interaction: relations with children's later competence with peers [CD-ROM]. Abstract from: *ProQuest File: Dissertation Abstracts. Item:* 9212750.

Hart, C., Robinson, C.C., Nelson, D.A., Porter, C. and Nelson, L.J. 1998: Subtypes of aggression and victimization in Russian preschoolers: Linkages with parenting and family processes. Paper presented at the International Society for the Study of Behavioural Development, Berne, Switzerland, July.

Hart, C.H., DeWolf, D.M., Wozniak, P. and Burts, D.C. 1992: Maternal and paternal disciplinary styles: Relations with preschoolers' playground behavioural orientations and peer status. *Child Development* **63**, 872–92.

Hart, C.H., DeWolf, M. and Burts, D.C. 1993: Parental disciplinary strategies and preschoolers' play behaviour in playground settings. In Hart, C.H. (ed.), *Children on playgrounds: research perspectives and applications.* Albany, NY: State University of New York Press, 271–313.

Hart, C.H., Ladd, G.W. and Burleson, B.R. 1990: Children's expectations of the outcomes of social strategies: relations with sociometric status and maternal disciplinary styles. *Child Development* **61**, 127–37.

Hart, C.H., Nelson, D.A., Robinson, C.C., Olsen, S.F. and McNeilly-Choque, M.K. 1998: Overt and relational aggression in Russian nursery-school-age children: parenting style and marital linkages. *Developmental Psychology* **34**, 687–97.

Hart, C.H., Young, C., Nelson, D.A., Jin, S., Bazarskaya, N., Nelson, L., Wu, X. and Wu, P. 1999: Peer contact patterns, parenting practices, and preschoolers' social competence in China, Russia, and the United States. In Slee, P. T. and Rigby, K. (eds), *Children's peer relations.* London: Routledge, 3–30.

Hartshorne, H. and May, M. 1928: *Studies in deceit.* New York: Macmillan.

Hartup, W.W. 1989: Behavioural manifestations of children's friendships. In Berndt, T.J. and Ladd, G.W. (eds), *Peer relationships in child development.* New York: Wiley.

Hartup, W.W. 1992: Conflict and friendship relations. In Shantz, C.U. and Hartup, W.W. 1992: *Conflict in child and adolescent development: Cambridge studies in social and emotional development.* New York: Cambridge University Press, 186–215.

Hartup, W.W. 1995: The three faces of friendship. *Journal of Social and Personal Relationships* **12**, 569–74.

Hartup, W.W. 1996: The company they keep: friendships and their developmental significance. *Child Development* **67**, 1–13.

Hartup, W.W., French, D.C., Laursen, B., Johnston, M.K. and Ogawa, J.R. 1993: Conflict and friendship relations in a closed-field situation. *Child Development* **64**, 445–54.

Hartup, W.W. and Stevens, N. 1997: Friendships and adaptation in the life course. *Psychological Bulletin* **121**, 355–70.

Hatfield, E., Utne, M.K. and Traupmann, J. 1979: Equity theory and intimate relationships. In Burgess, R.L. and Huston, T.L. (eds), *Social exchange in developing relationships*. New York: Academic Press, 99–133.

Hayes, D.S., Gershman, E. and Bolin, L. J. 1980: Friends and enemies: cognitive bases for preschool children's unilateral and reciprocal relationships. *Child Development* **51**, 1276–9.

Hayes, D.S., Gershman, E.S. and Halteman, W. 1996: Enmity in males at four developmental levels: cognitive bases for disliking peers. *Journal of Genetic Psychology*, **157**, 153–60.

Hayvren, M. and Hymel, S. 1984: Ethical issues in sociometric testing: impact of sociometric measures on interaction behaviour. *Developmental Psychology* **20**, 844–9.

Heflin, A.H. 1989: An exploration of links between parental nurturance and control and children's sociometric status [CD-ROM]. Abstract from: *ProQuest File: Dissertation Abstracts* Item: 8823429.

Henggeler, S.W., Edwards, J.J., Cohen, R. and Summerville, M.B. 1991: Predicting changes in children's popularity: the role of family relations. *Journal of Applied Developmental Psychology* **12**, 205–18.

Hertz-Lazarowitz, R. 1995: Understanding interactive behaviours: looking at six mirrors of the classroom. In Hertz-Lazarovitz, R. and Miller, N. (eds), *Interaction in cooperative groups: the theoretical anatomy of group learning*. New York: Cambridge University Press, 71–101.

Hertz-Lazarowitz, R., Fuchs, I., Sharabany, R. and Eisenberg, N. 1989: Students' interactive and noninteractive behaviours in the classroom: a comparison between two types of classrooms in the city and the kibbutz in Israel. *Contemporary Educational Psychology* **14**, 22–32.

Hewitt, J.P. 1998: *The myth of self-esteem*. New York: St. Martin's Press.

Hewstone, M., Bond, M.H. and Wan, K. 1983: Social facts and social attributions: the explanation of intergroup differences in Hong Kong. *Social Cognition* **2**, 142–57.

Hinde, R.A. 1979: *Towards understanding relationships*. London: Academic Press.

Hinde, R.A. 1988: Continuities and discontinuities: conceptual issues and methodological considerations. In Rutter, M. (ed.), *Studies of psychosocial risk: the power of longitudinal data*. Cambridge: Cambridge University Press, 367–83.

Hirshfeld, D.R., Rosenbaum, J.F., Biederman, J., Bolduc, E.A., Faraone, S.V., Snidman, N., Reznick, J.S. and Kagan, J. 1992: Stable behavioural inhibition and its association with anxiety disorder. *Journal of American Academic Child Adolescent Psychiatry* **31**, 103–11.

Hodge, R.L. 1989: *A myriad of values: a brief history*. (ERIC Document Reproduction Service No. ED 307 218).

Hodgens, J.B. and McCoy, J.F. 1989: Distinctions among rejected children on the basis of peer-nominated aggression. *Journal of Clinical Child Psychology* **18**, 121–8.

Hofman, P. 1985: Aperçus de la prise en charge educative [General survey on educational handling]. *Neuropsychiatrie de l'Enfance et de l'Adolescence* **33**, 37–42.

Hofstede, G. 1979: Value systems in forty countries. In Eckensberger, L., Lonner, W. and Poortinga, Y. (eds), *Cross-cultural contributions to psychology.* Lisse, The Netherlands: Swets and Zeitlinger.

Hofstede, G. 1980: *Culture's consequences: international differences in work-related values.* Beverly-Hills, CA: Sage.

Hofstede, G. 1983: Dimensions of national cultures in fifty countries and three regions. In Deregowski, J., Dzuirawiec, S. and Annis, R. (eds), *Explications in cross-cultural psychology.* Lisse, The Netherlands: Swets and Zeitlinger, 335–55.

Hofstede, G. 1984: The cultural relativity of the quality of life concept. *Academy of Management Review* **9**, 389–98.

Hofstede, G. 1991: *Cultures and organization: software on the mind.* London: McGraw-Hill.

Hogan, S. and Prater, M.A. 1998: The effects of peer tutoring and self-management on on-task, academic, and disruptive behaviours. *Behavioural Disorders* **18**, 118–28.

Hollander, E. 1958: Conformity, status, and idiosyncrasy credit. *Psychological Review* **65**, 117–27.

Hops, H., Davis, B. and Longoria, N. 1995: Methodological issues in direct observation: Illustrations with the living in familial environments (LIFE) coding system. *Journal of Clinical Child Psychology* **24**, 193–203.

Hops, H. and Finch, M. 1985: Social competence and skill: a reassessment. In Schneider, B.H., Rubin, K.H. and Ledingham, J.E. (eds), *Children's peer relations: issues in assessment and intervention.* New York: Springer-Verlag, 23–39.

Horowitz, E.C. 1981: Popularity, decentering ability and role-taking skills in learning disabled and normal children. *Learning Disability Quarterly* **4**, 23–30.

Hortacsu, N. 1994: Parents' education level, popularity, individual cognitions, and academic performance: an investigation with Turkish children. *Journal of Genetic Psychology* **155**, 179–89.

Howes, C. 1983: Patterns of friendship. *Child Development* **54**, 1041–53.

Howes, C. 1988: *Peer interaction of young children.* Monographs of the Society for Research in Young Children, 53 (Serial No. 217).

Howes, C. 1996: The earliest friendships. In Bukowski, W.M., Newcomb, A.F. and Hartup, W.W. (eds), *The company they keep: friendship in childhood and adolescence.* New York: Cambridge University Press, 66–86.

Howes, C. and Farver, J. 1987: Toddlers' responses to the distress of their peers. *Journal of Applied Developmental Psychology* **8**, 441–52.

Howes, C. and Phillipsen, L.C. 1992: Gender and friendship: relations within peer groups of young children. *Social Development* **1**, 231–42.

Howes, C. and Wu, F. 1990: Peer interactions and friendships in an ethnically diverse school setting. *Child Development* **61**, 537–41.

Hoyle, S.G. and Serafica, F.C. 1988: Peer status of children with and without learning disabilities: a multimethod study. *Learning Disability Quarterly* **11**, 322–32.

Hoza, B., Molina, B.S.G., Bukowski, W.M. and Sippola, L.K. 1995: Peer variables as predictors of later childhood adjustment. *Development and Psychopathology* **7**, 787–802.

Huesmann, L.R., Eron, L.D. and Warnick Yarmel, P. 1987: Intellectual functioning and aggression. *Journal of Personality and Social Psychology* **53**, 232–40.

Huesmann, L.R. and Guerra, N.G. 1997: Children's normative beliefs about aggression and aggressive behaviour. *Journal of Personality and Social Psychology* **72**, 408–19.

Huesmann, L.R., Lagerspetz, K. and Eron, L.D. 1984: Intervening variables in the

TV violence-aggression relation: evidence from two countries. *Developmental Psychology* **20**, 746–75.

Hundert, J. and Houghton, A. 1992: Promoting social interaction of children with disabilities in integrated preschools: a failure to generalize. *Exceptional Children* **58**, 311–20.

Hymel, S. and Rubin, K.H. 1985: Children with peer relationship and social skills problems: Conceptual, methodological, and developmental issues. In Whitehurst, G.J. (ed.), *Annals of child development*. Vol. 2. Greenwich, CT: JAI Press, 254–97.

Hymel, S., Rubin, K.H., Rowden, L. and LeMare, L. 1990: Children's peer relationships: longitudinal predictions of internalizing and externalizing problems from middle to late childhood. *Child Development* **61**, 2004–21.

Hymel, S., Wagner, E. and Butler, L. 1990: Reputational bias: view from the peer group. In Asher, S.R. and Coie, J. (eds), *Peer rejection in childhood*. Cambridge: Cambridge University Press, 156–86.

Isaacs, S. 1933: *Social development in young children: a study of beginnings*. London: Routledge.

Isherwood, G.B. and Ahola, J.A. 1981: School life: a conceptual model, or where you stand depends on where you sit. In Epstein, J.L. (ed.) *The quality of school life*. Lexington, MA: Lexington Books, 173–7.

Jack, L.M. 1934: *An experimental study of ascendant behaviour in pre-school children*. Des Moines, Iowa: University of Iowa Press.

Jelinek, M.M. and Brittan, E.M. 1975: Multiracial education: I. Inter-ethnic friendship patterns. *Educational Research* **18**, 44–53.

Johnson, D.W. and Johnson, R. 1989: *Co-operation and competition: theory and research*. Edina, MN: Interaction.

Johnson, D.W. and Johnson, R.T. 1996: Conflict resolution and peer mediation programs in elementary and secondary schools: a review of the research. *Review of Educational Research*, **66**, 459–506.

Johnson, R. 1989: Thatcherism and English education: breaking the mould, or confirming the pattern? *History of Education* **18**, 91–121.

Johnson, R.T. and Johnson, D.W. 1983: Effects of co-operative, competitive and individualistic learning experiences on social development. *Exceptional Children*, **49**, 323–30.

Johnstone, B., Frame, C. and Bouman, D. 1992: Physical attractiveness and athletic and academic ability in controversial-aggressive and rejected-aggressive children. *Journal of Social and Clinical Psychology* **11**, 71–9.

Jones, D.C. 1985: Persuasive appeals and responses to appeals among friends and acquaintances. *Child Development* **56**, 757–63.

Jordan, D.W. and Le Métais, J. 1997: Social skills through co-operative learning. *Educational Research* **39**, 3–21.

Juvonen, J. and Bear, G. 1992: Social adjustment of children with and without learning disabilities in integrated classrooms. *Journal of Educational Psychology* **84**, 322–30.

Kagan, J. 1998: The nature of nurture: parents or peers? Interview with Microsoft Network Slate, 21 November 1998.

Kagan, S. and Madsen, M.C. 1971: Co-operation and competition of Mexican, Mexican-American, and Anglo-American children of two ages under four instructional sets. *Developmental Psychology* **5**, 32–9.

Kagan, S. and Madsen, M.C. 1972: Experimental analysis of cooperation and competition of Anglo-American and Mexican children. *Developmental Psychology* **6**, 49–59.

Kazdin, A.E., Esveldt-Dawson, K., French, N.K. and Unis, A.S. 1987: Effects of parent management training and problem-solving skills training combined in the treatment of antisocial child behaviour. *Journal of the American Academy of Child and Adolescent Psychiatry* **26**, 416–24.

Kazdin, A.E., Siegel, T.C., Bass, D. 1992: Cognitive problem-solving skills training and parent management training in the treatment of antisocial behaviour in children. *Journal of Consulting and Clinical Psychology* **60**, 733–47.

Keller, M. and Edelstein, W. 1990: The emergence of morality in personal relationships. In Wren, T. (ed.), *The moral domain.* Cambridge, MA: MIT Press, 255–82.

Kendall, P. C. and Braswell, L. 1982: Cognitive-behavioural self-control therapy for children: a components analysis. *Journal of Consulting and Clinical Psychology* **50**, 672–89.

Kendall, P. C. and Braswell, L. 1985: *Cognitive-behavioural therapy for impulsive children.* New York: Guilford.

Kennedy, J.H. 1992: Relationship of maternal beliefs and childbearing strategies to social competence in preschool children. *Child Study Journal* **22**, 39–60.

Kennedy, M. 1990: Controlled evaluation of peer tutoring on the tutors: Are the 'learning by teaching' theories viable? In Goodlad, S. and Hirst, B. (eds), *Explorations in peer tutoring.* Oxford: Blackwell, 58–72.

Kerns, K.A. 1996: Individual differences in friendship quality: links to child-mother attachment. In Bukowski, W.M., Newcomb, A.F. and Hartup, W.W. (eds), *The company they keep: friendship in childhood and adolescence.* New York: Cambridge University Press, 137–57.

Kerns, K.A., Klepac, L. and Cole, A. 1996: Peer relationship and preadolescents' perceptions of security in the mother-child relationship. *Developmental Psychology* **32**, 457–66.

Kerr, M., Lambert, W.W. and Bem, D.J. 1996: Life course sequelae of childhood shyness in Sweden: comparison with the United States. *Developmental Psychology* **32**, 1100–5.

Kidd, J.W. 1951: An analysis of social rejection in a college men's residence hall. *Sociometry* **14**, 226–34.

King, G.A., Specht, J.A., Schultz, I., Warr-Leeper, G., Redekop, L. and Risebrough, C. 1997: Social skills training for withdrawn unpopular children with physical disabilities: a preliminary evaluation. *Rehabilitation Psychology* **42**, 47–60.

Kirchler, E., Pombeni, M. L. and Palmonari, A. 1991: Sweet sixteen: adolescents' problems and the peer group as social support. *European Journal of the Psychology of Education* **6**, 393–410.

Kistner, J.A. and Gatlin, D. 1989: Correlates of peer rejection among children with learning disabilities. *Learning Disability Quarterly* **12**, 133–40.

Klindová, L. 1985: Longitudinale sledovanie niektorych ukazovatel'ov socialnej akitivity y predskolson veku [Longitudinal investigation of some indicators of social activity in preschoolers]. *Psychologia a Patopsychologia Dietata*, **20**, 483–96.

Klinger, J.K. and Vaughn, S. 1996: Reciprocal teaching of reading comprehension strategies for students with learning disabilities who use English as a second language. *The Elementary School Journal* **96**, 275–93.

Klinger, J.K., Vaughn, S. and Schumm, J.S. 1998: Collaborative strategic reading during social studies and heterogeneous fourth-grade classrooms. *The Elementary School Journal* **99**, 3–22.

Koentjaraningrat, R.M. 1985: *Javanese culture.* New York: Oxford University Press.

Kohlberg, L., LaCrosse, J. and Ricks, D. 1972: The predictability of adult mental health from childhood behaviour. In Wolman, B.B. (ed.), *Manual of child psychopathology.* New York: McGraw-Hill, 1217–84.

Kong, S.L. 1985: Counselling Chinese immigrants: issues and answers. In Samnite,

R.J. and Wolfgang, A. (eds), *Intercultural counselling and assessment: global perspectives*, Lewiston: C. J. Hogrefe, 181–9.

Kovacs, M. 1981: Rating scales to assess depression in school-aged children. *Acta Paedopsychiatrica* **46**, 305–15.

Kovacs, D.M., Parker, J.G. and Hoffman, L. W. 1996: Behavioural, affective, and social correlates of involvement in cross-sex friendship in elementary school. *Child Development* **67**, 2269–86.

Krantz, M. 1987: Physical attractiveness and popularity: a predictive study. *Psychological Reports* **60**, 723–6.

Krappmann, L. 1989: Family relationships and peer relationships in middle childhood: an exploratory study of the associations between children's integration into the social network of peers and family development. In Kreppner, K. and Lerner, R.M. (eds) *Family systems and life-span development.* Hillsdale, NJ: Erlbaum, 93–104.

Krappmann, L. 1996: Amicitia, drujba, shin-yu, philia, freundschaft, friendship: on the diversity of a human relationship. In Bukowski, W.M., Newcomb, A.F. and Hartup, W.W. (eds), *The company they keep: friendship in childhood and adolescence.* Cambridge: Cambridge University Press, 19–40.

Krappmann, L., Uhlendorff, H. and Oswald, H. 1995: Existence and effects of close relationships in childhood and preadolescence. Paper presented at the meeting of the European Conference of Developmental Psychology, Krakow, Poland, August.

Kundrátová, B. 1995: Socialno-psychologicke charakteristiky postavenia romskych deti v etnicky zmiesanych triedach ZS [The socio-psychological characteristics of gypsy children in ethnically mixed primary school classes]. *Psychologia a Patopsychologia Dietata* **30**, 215–26.

Kupersmidt, J.B. and Coie, J.D. 1990: Preadolescent peer status, aggression and school adjustment as predictors of externalizing problems in adolescence. *Child Development* **61**, 1350–62.

Kupersmidt, J.B., DeRosier, M.E. and Patterson, C.P. 1995: Similarity as the basis for children's friendships: the roles of sociometric status, aggressive and withdrawn behaviour, academic achievement and demographic characteristics. *Journal of Social and Personal Relationships* **12**, 439–52.

Kupersmidt, J.B. and Patterson, C.J. 1991: Childhood peer rejection, aggression, withdrawal, and perceived competence as predictors of self-reported behaviour problems in preadolescence. *Journal of Abnormal Child Psychology* **19**, 427–49.

Kupersmidt, J.B. and Trejos, L. 1987: Behavioural correlates of sociometric status among Costa Rican children. Paper presented at the biennial meeting of the Society for Research in Child Development Baltimore, MD, April.

Ladd, G., Kochenderfer, B.J. and Coleman, C.C. 1996: Friendship quality as a predictor of young children's early school adjustment. *Child Development* **67**, 1103–18.

Ladd, G.W. 1981: Effectiveness of a social learning method for enhancing children's social interactions and peer acceptance. *Child Development* **52**, 171–8.

Ladd, G.W. 1983: Social network of popular, average and rejected children in school settings. *Merrill-Palmer Quarterly* **29**, 283–307.

Ladd, G.W. 1990: Having friends, keeping friends, making friends, and being liked by peers in the classroom: predictors of children's early school adjustment? *Child Development* **61**, 1081–100.

Ladd, G.W. and Emerson, E.S. 1984: Shared knowledge in children's friendships. *Developmental Psychology* **20**, 932–40.

Ladd, G.W. and Golter, B.S. 1988: Parents' management of preschooler's peer relations: is it related to children's social competence? *Developmental Psychology* **24**, 109–17.

Ladd, G.W. and Hart, C.H. 1992: Creating informal play opportunities: are parents' and preschoolers' initiations related to children's competence with peers? *Developmental Psychology* **28**, 1179–87.

Ladd, G.W., Hart, C.H., Wadsworth, E.M. and Golter, B.S. 1988: Preschoolers' peer networks in nonschool settings: relationship to family characteristics and school adjustment. In Salzinger, S., Antrobus, J. and Hammer, M. (eds), *Social networks of children, adolescents and college students*. Hillsdale, NJ: Erlbaum, 61–92.

Ladd, G.W., Kochenderfer, B.J. and Coleman, C.C. 1996: Friendship quality as a predictor of young children's early school adjustment. *Child Development* **67**, 1103–118.

Ladd, G.W. and Price, J.M. 1987: Predicting children's social and school adjustment following the transition from preschool to kindergarten. *Child Development* **58**, 1168–89.

Lagerspetz, K.M., Björkqvist, K. and Peltonen, T. 1988: Is indirect aggression typical of females? Gender differences in aggressiveness in 11– to 12–year-old children. *Aggressive Behaviour* **14**, 403–14.

Laird, R.D., Pettit, G.S., Mize, J., Brown, E.G. and Lindsey, E. 1994: Mother–child conversations about peers: contributions to competence. *Family Relations* **43**, 425–32.

Landau, S. and Moore, L.A. 1991: Social skill deficits in children with attention deficit- hyperactivity. *School Psychology Review* **20**, 235–51.

Larzelere, R.E. 1986: Moderate spanking: model or deterrent of children's aggression in the family? *Journal of Family Violence* **1**, 27–36.

Ledingham, J.E. 1999: Children and adolescents with oppositional defiant disorder and conduct disorder in the community: Experiences at school and with peers. In Quay, H.C. and Hogan, A.E. (eds), *Handbook of disruptive behaviour disorders*. New York: Kluwer-Plenum, 353–70.

Ledingham, J.E. and Schwartzman, A.E. 1984: A 3–year follow-up of aggressive and withdrawn behaviour in childhood: preliminary findings. *Journal of Abnormal Child Psychology* **12**, 157–68.

Lerner, R. M. and Lerner, J.V. 1977: Effects of age, sex, and physical attractiveness on child–peer relations, academic performance, and elementary school adjustment. *Developmental Psychology* **13**, 585–90.

Lesser, G.R. 1957: The relationship between overt and fantasy aggression as a function of maternal response to aggression. *Journal of Abnormal and Social Psychology* **55**, 218–21.

Leung, K. 1987: Some determinants of reactions to procedural models for conflict resolution: A cross-national study. *Journal of Personality and Social Psychology* **53**, 898–908.

Leve, L.D., Winebarger, A.A., Fagot, B.I., Reid, J.B. and Goldsmith, H.H. 1998: Environmental and genetic variance in children's observed and reported maladaptive behaviour. *Child Development* **69**, 1286–98.

Levine, F.M., Fasnacht, G., Funabiki, D. and Burkart, M.R. 1979: Methodological considerations regarding the evaluation of maintenance of gains due to token programs. *Psychology in the Schools* **16**, 568–75.

Levinger, G. 1980: Toward the analysis of close relationships. *Journal of Experimental Social Psychology* **16**, 510–44.

Levy, D.M. 1966: *Maternal overprotection*. New York: Norton.

Levy, L. and Gottlieb, J. 1984: Learning disabled and non-learning disabled children at play. *Remedial and Special Education* 5, 43–50.

Levy-Shiff, R. and Hoffman, M.A. 1985: Social behaviour of urban and kibbutz preschool children in Israel. *Developmental Psychology* 21, 1204–05.

Lewis, M. and Feiring, C. 1989: Infant, mother, and mother-infant interaction behaviour and subsequent attachment. *Child Development* 60, 831–7.

Libet, J. M. and Lewinsohn, P. M. 1973: Concept of social skills with special reference to the behaviour of depressed persons. *Journal of Consulting and Clinical Psychology* 40, 304–12.

Light, P. and Glachan, M. 1985: Facilitation of individual problem solving through peer interaction. *Educational Psychology* 5, 217–25.

Lindsey, E.W., Mize, J. and Pettit, G.S. 1997: Mutuality in parent-child play: consequences for children's peer competence. *Journal of Social and Personal Relationships* 14, 523–38.

Little, T.D., Brendgen, M., Wanner, B. and Krappmann, L. 1999: Children's reciprocal perceptions of friendship quality in the sociocultural contexts of East and West Berlin. *International Journal of Behavioural Development* 23, 63–89.

Litwinski, L. 1950: Constitutional shyness: its active and passive forms. *Journal of General Psychology* 42, 299–311.

Lloyd, J.W., Crowley, E.P. , Kohler, F.W. and Strain, P. S. 1988: Redefining the applied research agenda: Co-operative learning, preferral, teacher consultation, and peer-mediated interventions. *Journal of Learning Disabilities* 21, 43–52.

Lochman, J.E., Coie, J.D., Underwood, M.K. and Terry, R. 1993: Effectiveness of a social relations intervention program for aggressive and nonaggressive, rejected children. *Journal of Consulting and Clinical Psychology* 61, 1053–8.

Lochman, J.E. and Dodge, K.A. 1994: Social-cognitive processes of severely violent, moderately aggressive and nonaggressive boys. *Journal of Consulting and Clinical Psychology* 62, 366–74.

Loeber, R., Green, S.M., Keenan, K. and Lahey, B.B. 1995: Which boys will fare worse? Early predictors of the onset of conduct disorder in a six-year longitudinal study. *Journal of the American Academy of Child and Adolescent Psychiatry* 34, 499–509.

Loehlin, J.C. 1989: Models of behaviour and the behaviour of models. *International Journal of Behavioural Development* 12, 403–6.

Lopata, H.Z. 1981: Friendship: historical and theoretical introduction. *Research in the Interweave of Social Roles* 2, 1–19.

Lorion, R.P. , Cowen, E.L., Kraus, R.M. and Milling, L.S. 1977: Family background characteristics and school adjustment problems. *Journal of Community Psychology* 5, 142–8.

Luftig, R.L. and Nichols, M.L. 1991: An assessment of the social status and perceived personality and school traits of gifted students by nongifted peers. *Roeper Review* 13, 148–53.

Lundberg, G.A. and Dickson, L. 1952: Selective association among ethnic groups in a high school population. *American Sociological Review* 17, 23–35.

Lupkowski, A.E. 1989: Social behaviours of gifted and typical preschool children in laboratory school programs. *Roeper Review* 11, 124–7.

Maccoby, E. 1988: Gender as a social category. *Developmental Psychology* 24, 755–65.

Maccoby, E. 1990: Gender and relationships: a developmental account. *American Psychologist* 45, 513–20.

MacDonald, K. 1987: Parent-child physical play with rejected, neglected, and popular boys. *Developmental Psychology* 23, 705–11.

MacDonald, K. and Parke, R D. 1984: Bridging the gap: parent-child play interaction and peer interactive competence. *Child Development* 55, 1265–77.

MacDonald, M.A. and Sherman, P. D. 1987: Stuck for words: combining social skills training with a token economy system for adolescents. *Journal of Child Care* 3, 51–8.

MacMillan, D.L. and Morrison, G.M. 1980: Correlates of social status among mildly handicapped learners in self-contained special cases. *Journal of Educational Psychology* 72, 437–44.

Maddux, C.D., Scheiber, L.M. and Bass, J. 1982: Self-concept and social distance in gifted children. *Gifted Child Quarterly* 26, 77–81.

Madsen, M.C. 1971: Developmental and cross-cultural differences in the co-operative and competitive behaviour of young children. *Journal of Cross-Cultural Psychology* 2, 365–71.

Madsen, M.C. and Shapira, A. 1970: Co-operative and competitive behaviour of urban Afro-American, Anglo-American, Mexican-American, and Mexican village children. *Developmental Psychology* 3, 16–20.

Manetti, M., Schneider, B.H. and Siperstein, G. (2000): Social acceptance on developmentally challenged children: Testing the contact hypothesis with an Italian sample. *International Journal of Behavioural Development.*

Mannarino, A.P. 1978: The interactional process in preadolescent friendships. *Psychiatry* 41, 308–12.

Manning, B.H. 1990: A categorical analysis of children's self-talk during independent school assignments. *Journal of Instructional Psychology* 17, 208–17.

Maraspini, A.J. 1968: *The study of an Italian village.* Paris: Mouton.

Margalit, M. 1998: Loneliness and coherence among preschool children with learning disabilities. *Journal of Learning Disabilities* 31, 173–80.

Marlowe, M. 1979: The games analysis intervention: a procedure to increase the peer acceptance and social adjustment of a retarded child. *Education and Training of the Mentally Retarded* 14, 262–8.

Marotz Ray, B. 1985: Measuring the social position of the mainstreamed handicapped child. *Exceptional Children* 52, 57–62.

Masten, A.S., Morrison, P. and Pellegrini, D.S. 1985: A revised class play method of peer assessment. *Developmental Psychology* 21, 523–33.

McCord, W., McCord, J. and Howard, A. 1961: Familial correlates of aggression in nondelinquent male children. *Journal of Abnormal and Social Psychology* 62, 79–93.

McDougall, P. and Hymel, S. 1998: Moving into middle school: individual differences in the transition experience. *Canadian Journal of Behavioural Science* 30, 108–20.

McFall, R. M. 1982: A review and reformulation of the concept of social skills. *Behavioural Assessment* 4, 1–33.

McGuire, K.D. and Weisz, J.R. 1982: Social cognition and behaviour correlates of preadolescent chumship. *Child Development* 53, 1478–84.

McGuire, W.J., McGuire, C.V., Child, P. and Fujioka, T. 1978: Salience of ethnicity in the spontaneous self-concept as a function of one's ethnic distinctiveness in the social environment. *Journal of Personality and Social Psychology* 36, 511–20.

McMichael, P. 1980: Reading difficulties, behaviour and social status. *Journal of Educational Psychology* 72, 76–86.

Meichenbaum, D. 1975: Enhancing creativity by modifying what subjects say to themselves. *American Educational Research Journal* 12, 129–45.

Meichenbaum, D. 1977: *Cognitive-behaviour modification: an integrative approach.* New York: Plenum Press.

Mendelson, M.J., Aboud, F.E. and Lanthier, R.P. 1994: Personality predictors of friendship and popularity in kindergarten. *Journal of Applied Developmental Psychology* **15**, 413–35.

Menesini, E., Berdondini, L., Ciucci, E. and Almeida, A. 1999: Emotion attributions and feelings in bully/victim relationships. Paper presented at the IXth European conference on Developmental Psychology, Spetses, Greece, September.

Merrell, K.W. and Gimpel, G.A. 1998: *Social skills of children and adolescents: conceptualization, assessment, and treatment.* Mahwah, NJ: Erlbaum.

Mills, R.S.L. and Rubin, K.H. 1993: Socialization factors in the development of social withdrawal. In Rubin, K.H. and Asendorf, J.B. (eds), *Social withdrawal, inhibition, and shyness in childhood.* Hillsdale, NJ: Lawrence Erlbaum Associates, Inc., 117–48.

Mischel, W. 1983: Alternatives in the pursuit of the predictability and consistency of persons: stable data that yield unstable interpretations. *Journal of Personality* **51**, 578–604.

Mize, J. and Pettit, G.S. 1997: Mother's social coaching, mother-child relationship style, and children's peer competence: Is the medium the message? *Child Development* **68**, 312–32.

Moreno, J.L. 1953: *Who shall survive? Foundations of sociometry, group psychotherapy and sociodrama.* Beacon, NY: Beacon House.

Moreno, J.L. (ed.) 1960: *The sociometry reader.* Glencoe, IL: Free Press.

Moreno, J.L. 1972: *Psychological drama.* Vol. 1. Beacon, NY: Beacon House.

Morgan, W.R. and Sawyer, J. 1967: Bargaining, expectations, and the preference for equality over equity. *Journal of Personality and Social Psychology* **6**, 139–49.

Morrison, G.M., Forness, S.R. and MacMillan, D.L. 1983: Influences on the sociometric ratings of mildly handicapped children: a path analysis. *Journal of Educational Psychology* **75**, 63–74.

Moskowitz, D.S. and Schwartzman, A.E. 1989: Painting group portraits: studying life outcomes for aggressive and withdrawn children. *Journal of Personality* **57**, 723–46.

Mugny, G., Giroud, J. and Doise, W. 1979: Conflict of centration and cognitive progress: II. new experimental illustrations. *Bulletin de Psychologie* **32**, 979–85.

Murphy, K. and Schneider, B.H. 1994: Coaching socially rejected early adolescents regarding behaviours used by peers to infer liking: a dyad-specific intervention. *Journal of Early Adolescence* **14**, 83–95.

Murray, B. 1999: Boys to men: emotional miseducation. *APA Monitor* July/August, pp. 1–39.

Nabuzoka, D. and Ronning, J.A. 1997: Social acceptance of children with intellectual disabilities in an integrated school setting in Zambia: a pilot study. *International Journal of Disability, Development and Education* **44**, 105–15.

Nabuzoka, D. and Smith, P. K. 1993: Sociometric status and social behaviour of children with and without learning difficulties. *Journal of Child Psychology and Psychiatry and Allied Disciplines* **34**, 1435–48.

Nadel, J. and Butterworth, G. 1999: *Imitation in infancy.* New York: Cambridge University Press.

Nadel, J. and Tremblay-Leveau, H. 1999: Dyadic and triadic paradigms: early perception of social contingencies and interpersonal intentionality. In Rochat, P. (ed.), *Early social cognition understanding others in the first months of life.* Mahwah, NJ: Erlbaum, 189–212.

Neel, R.S., Cheney, D., Meadows, N.B. and Gelhar, S. 1992: *Interviewing middle school students to determine problematic social tasks in school settings.* [Monograph in behavioural disorders:] *Severe behaviour disorders of children and youth.* Reston, VA: Council for Children with Behaviour Disorders.

Neiderheiser, J.N. and McGuire, S. 1994: Competence during middle childhood. In DeFries, J.C., Plomin. R. and Fulker, D.W. (eds), *Nature and nurture during middle childhood.* Oxford: Blackwell, 141–51.

Nelson, J. and Aboud, F.E. 1985: The resolution of social conflict between friends. *Child Development* **56**, 1009–17.

Newcomb, A.F. and Bagwell, C.L. 1996: The developmental significance of children's friendship relations. In Bukowski, W.M., Newcomb. A.F. and Hartup, W.W. (eds), *The company they keep: friendship in childhood and adolescence.* New York: Cambridge University Press, 289–321.

Newcomb, A.F. and Brady, J.E. 1982: Mutuality in boys' friendship relations. *Child Development* **53**, 392–5.

Newcomb, A.F., Brady, J.E. and Hartup, W. 1979: Friendship and incentive condition as determinants of children's task-oriented social behaviour. *Child Development* **50**, 878–81.

Newcomb, A.F. and Bukowski, W.M. 1983: Social impact and social preference as determinants of children's peer group status. *Developmental Psychology* **19**, 856–67.

Nietzel, M.T., Guthrie, P.R. and Susman, D.T. 1991: Utilization of community and social support resources. In Kanfer, F.H. and Goldstein, A.P. (eds), *Helping people change: a textbook of methods.* 4th edn. New York: Pergamon, 396–421.

Noesjirwan, J, 1978: A rule-based analysis of cultural differences in social behaviour: Indonesia and Australia. *International Journal of Psychology* **13**, 305–16.

Northway, M. 1952: *A primer of sociometry.* Toronto: University of Toronto Press.

Northway, M. 1956: *Well children: a progress report.* Toronto: University of Toronto Press.

Northway, M. 1967: *A primer of sociometry.* 2nd edn.. Toronto: University of Toronto Press.

Nowicki, S. and Duke, M.P. 1992: The association of children's nonverbal decoding abilities with their popularity, locus of control, and academic achievement. *Journal of Genetic Psychology* **153**, 385–93.

Ochoa, S.H. and Palmer, D.J. 1991: A sociometric analysis of between-group differences and within group status variability of Hispanic learning disabled and non-handicapped pupils in academic and play contexts. *Learning Disability Quarterly* **14**, 208–18.

Oden, S. and Asher, S. R. 1977: Coaching children in social skills for friendship making. *Child Development* **48**, 495–506.

Ogbu, J.U. 1981: *Origins of human competence: a cultural-ecological perspective.* Child Development **52**, 413–29.

O'Keefe, P. J., Saxon, S.E. and Siperstein, G.N. 1991: Relationship between social status and peer assessment of social behaviour among mentally retarded and non-retarded children. Paper presented at the biennial meeting of the Society for Research in Child Development, Seattle, Washington.

Oldenburg, C.M. and Kerns, K.A. 1997: Associations between peer relationships and depressive symptoms: testing moderator effects of gender and age. *Journal of Early Adolescence* **17**, 319–37.

Olweus, D. 1980: Familial and temperamental determinants of aggressive behaviour in adolescent boys: a causal analysis. *Developmental Psychology* **16**, 644–60.

Olweus, D. 1993: *Bullying at school: what we know and what we can do.* Oxford: Blackwell.

Olweus, D. 1999: Norway. In Smith, P. K., Morita, Y., Junger-Tas, J., Olweus, D., Catalono, R. and Slee, P. (eds), *The nature of school bullying*. London: Blackwell, 28–48.

Oppenheim, D., Sagi, A. and Lamb, M.E. 1988: Infant-adult attachments on the kibbutz and their relation to socioemotional development four years later. *Developmental Psychology* **24**, 427–33.

Orlick, T., Zhou, Q.Y. and Partington, J. 1990: Co-operation and conflict within Chinese and Canadian kindergarten settings. *Canadian Journal of Behavioural Science* **22**, 20–5.

Osguthorpe, R. T. and Scruggs, T. E. 1990: Special education students as tutors: review and analysis. In Goodlad. S. and Hirst, B. (eds), *Explorations in peer tutoring*. Oxford: Blackwell, 76–93.

Osman, B.B. 1982: *No-one to play with: te social life of learning disabilities*. New York: Warner Books.

Osterman, K., Björkqvist, K., Lagerspetz, K.M.J., Kaukiainen, A., Huesmann, L.R. and Fraczek, A. 1994: Peer and self-estimated aggression and victimization in 8–year-old children from 5 ethnic groups. *Aggressive Behaviour* **20**, 411–28.

Oswald, H. and Krappmann, L. 1995: Social life of children in a former bipartite city. In Noack, P. , Hofer, M. and Youniss, J. (eds), *Psychological responses to social change: human development in changing environments*. Berlin: de Gruyter, 163–85.

Pakaslahti, L., Spoof, I., Asplund-Peltola, R. and Keltikangas-Jaevinen, L. 1998: Parents' social problem-solving strategies in families with aggressive and non-aggressive girls. *Aggressive Behaviour* **24**, 37–51.

Palinscar, A.S. and Brown, A.L. 1984: The reciprocal teaching of comprehension-fostering and comprehension-monitoring activities. *Cognition and Instruction* **1**, 117–75.

Parens, H. 1979: *The development of aggression in early childhood*. London: Jason Aronson.

Parke, R.D., O'Neil, R., Spitzer, S., Isley, S., Welsh, M., Wang, S., Lee, J., Strand, C. and Cupp, R. 1997: A longitudinal assessment of sociometric stability and the behavioural correlates of children's social acceptance. *Merrill-Palmer Quarterly* **43**, 635–62.

Parker, J.G. 1986: Becoming friends: conversation skills for friendship formation in young children. In Gottman, J.M. and Parker, J.G. (eds), *Conversations of friends: speculations on affective development*. Cambridge: Cambridge University Press, 103–38.

Parker, J.G. and Asher, S.R. 1987: Peer acceptance and later personal adjustment: are low-accepted children at risk? *Psychological Bulletin* **102**, 357–89.

Parker, J.G. and Asher, S.R. 1993a: friendship and friendship quality in middle childhood: links with peer group acceptance and feelings of loneliness and social dissatisfaction. *Developmental Psychology* **29**, 611–21.

Parker, J.G. and Asher, S.R. 1993b: Beyond group acceptance: Friendship and friendship quality as distinct dimensions of children's peer adjustment. In Perlman, D. and Jones, W. (eds), *Advances in personal relationships*. vol. 4. London: Kingsley, 261–94.

Parker, J.G. and Gottman, J.M. 1989: Social and emotional development in a relational context: Friendship interaction from early childhood to adolescence. In Berndt, T.J. and Ladd, G.W. (eds), *Peer relationships in child development*. New York: John Wiley, 95–131.

Parkhurst, J.T. and Asher, S.R. 1992: Peer rejection in middle school: Subgroup differences in behaviour, loneliness and interpersonal concerns. *Developmental Psychology* **28**, 231–41.

Parks, M.R. 1985: Interpersonal communication and the quest for personal competence. In Knapp, M.L. and Miller, G.R. (eds), *Handbook of interpersonal communication*, Beverly Hills, CA: Sage 171–201.

Parten, M.B. 1932: Social participation among preschool children. *Journal of Abnormal Psychology* **27**, 243–69.

Patterson, C.J., Kupersmidt, J.B. and Griseler, P. C. 1990: Children's perceptions of self and of relationships with others as a function of sociometric status. *Child Development* **61**, 1335–49.

Patterson, G.R. 1982: *A social learning approach.* vol. 3. *Coercive family processes.* Eugene, OR: Castalia.

Patterson, G.R. and Cobb, J.A. 1971: A dyadic analysis of 'aggressive' behaviours. In Hill, J.P. (ed.), *Minnesota symposia on child psychology.* vol. 5. Minneapolis, MN: University of Minnesota Press, 74–102.

Pearl, R., Farmer, T.W., van Acker, R., Rodkin, P. C., Bost, K., Coe, M. and Henley, W. 1998: The social integration of students with disabilities in general education classrooms: peer group membership and peer-assessed social behaviour. *The Elementary School Journal* **99**, 167–85.

Peery, J.C. 1979: Popular, amiable, isolated, rejected: a reconceptualization of sociometric status in preschool children. *Child Development* **50**, 1231–34.

Peery, J.C., Jensen, L. and Adams, G.R. 1985: The relationship between parents' attitudes toward child rearing and the sociometric status of their preschool children. *Journal of Psychology* **119**, 567–74.

Pepler, D.J. and Craig, W.M. 1995: A peek behind the fence: naturalistic observations of aggressive children with remote audiovisual recording. *Developmental Psychology* **31**, 548–53.

Peres, Y. and Pasternack, R. 1991: To what extent can the school reduce the gaps between children raised by divorced and intact families? *Journal of Divorce and Remarriage* **15**, 143–58.

Perry, H.S. 1982: *Psychiatrist of America: the life of Harry Stack Sullivan.* Cambridge, MA: Harvard University Press.

Peterson, L. and Bell-Dolan, D. 1995: Treatment outcome in child psychology: realistic coping with the 'Ten commandments of methodology'. *Journal of Clinical Child Psychology* **24**, 149–62.

Pettit, G.S., Brown, E.G., Mize, J. and Lindsey, E. 1998: Mothers' and fathers' socializing behaviours in three contexts: links with children's peer competence. *Merrill-Palmer Quarterly* **44**, 173–93.

Pettit, G.S., Dodge, K.A. and Brown, M.M. 1988: Early family experience, social problem solving patterns, and children's social competence. *Child Development* **59**, 107–20.

Pettit, G.S, Harrist, A.W., Bates, J.E. and Dodge, K.A. 1991: Family interaction, social cognition and children's subsequent relations with peers and kindergarten. *Journal of Social and Personal Relationships* **8**, 383–402.

Philipsen, G. 1987: The prospect for cultural communication. In Kincaid, D. (ed.), *Communication theory: Eastern and Western perspectives.* New York: Academic Press, 245–54.

Phillips, E.L. 1979: *The social skills basis of psychopathology.* New York: Grune and Stratton.

Piaget, J. 1932: *The language and thought of the child.* New York: Harcourt Brace and Company.

Pinto, G., Bombi, A. S. and Cordioli, A. 1997: Similarity of friends in three countries: a study of children's drawings. *International Journal of Behavioural Development* **20**, 453–69.

Plomin, R. 1990: The role of inheritance in behaviour. *Science* **248**, 183–8.

Plomin, R., Foch, T.T. and Rowe, D.C. 1981: Bobo clown aggression in childhood: Environment, not genes. *Journal of Research in Personality* **15**, 331–42.

Plomin, R., Pedersen, J.R., McClearn, N.L., Nesselroade, J.R. and Bergeman, C.S. 1988: Genetic influence on child family environment perceived retroactively from the last half of the life span. *Developmental Psychology* **24**, 738–45.

Plomin, R. and Rowe, D.C. 1979: Genetic and environmental etiology of social behaviour in infancy. *Developmental Psychology* **15**, 62–72.

Polloway, E.A., Patton, J. R., Smith, T.E.C. and Buck, G.H. 1997: Mental retardation and learning disabilities: conceptual and applied issues. *Journal of Learning Disabilities* **30**, 297–308.

Poulin, F., Cillessen, A.H.N., Hubbard, J.A., Coie, J.D., Dodge, K.A. and Schwartz, D. 1997: Children's friends and behavioural similarity in two social contexts. *Social Development* **6**, 224–36.

Poulin, F., Dishion, T.J. and Medici, N. 1998: Antisocial behaviour and stability of friendship networks: network structure, behavioural confluence, and relationship satisfaction. Poster session presented at the biennial meeting of the International Society for the Study of Behavioural Development, Berne, Switzerland, July.

Prillaman, D. 1981: Acceptance of learning disabled students in the mainstream environment: a failure to replicate. *Journal of Learning Disabilities* **14**, 344–6.

Pryor-Brown, L. and Cowen, E.L. 1989: Stressful life events, support, and children's school adjustment. *Journal of Clinical Child Psychology* **18**, 214–20.

Pulkinnen, L. 1999: Social-emotional behaviour in childhood as a predictor of adult outcomes: Gender differences. Paper presented at the 9th European Conference on Developmental Psychology, Spetses, Greece, September.

Putallaz, M. 1983: Predicting children's sociometric status from their behaviour. *Child Development* **54**, 1417–26.

Putallaz, M., 1987: Maternal behaviour and children's sociometric status. *Child Development* **58**, 324–40.

Putnam, J., Markovchick, K., Johnson, D.W. and Johnson, R.T. 1996: Co-operative learning and peer acceptance of students with learning disabilities. *The Journal of Social Psychology* **136**, 741–52.

Qvotrop, J. 1990: *Childhood as a social phenomenon*. Vienna: European Centre for Social Welfare Policy and Research.

Rackham, H. 1945: *Aristotle's ethics for English readers*. Oxford: Blackwell.

Ray, G.E. and Cohen, R. 1997: Children's evaluations of provocation between peers. *Aggressive Behaviour* **23**, 417–41.

Ray, G.E., Cohen, R., Secrist, M.E. and Duncan, M.K. 1997: Relating aggressive and victimization behaviours to children's sociometric status and friendships. *Journal of Social and Personal Relationships* **14**, 95–108.

Reese-Dukes, J.L. and Stokes, E.H. 1978: Social acceptance of elementary EMR pupils in the regular classroom. *Education and Training of the Mentally Retarded* **13**, 356–61.

Renshaw, P. D. 1981: The roots of current peer interaction research: a historical analysis of the 1930s. In Asher, S.R. and Gottman, J.M. (eds), *The development of children's friendships*. Cambridge: Cambridge University Press.

Renshaw, P. D. and Asher, S.R. 1983: Children's goals and strategies for social interaction. *Merrill-Palmer Quarterly* **29**, 353–74.

Renshaw, P. D. and Brown, P. J. 1993: Loneliness in middle childhood: concurrent and longitudinal predictors. *Child Development* **64**, 1271–84.

Renshaw, P. D. and Parke, R.D. 1992: Family and peer relationships in historical perspective. In R. D. Parke and G. W. Ladd (eds), *Family-peer relationships: modes of linkage*. Hillsdale, NJ: Erlbaum Associates Inc., 35–74.

Research and Policy Committee of the Committee for Economic Development. 1994: *Putting learning first: governing and managing the schools for high achievement*. New York: Research and Policy Committee of the Committee for Economic Development.

Rican, P. 1996: Sociometric status of Gypsy children in ethnically mixed classes. *Studia Psychologica* **38**, 177–84.

Richard, B.A. and Dodge, K.A. 1982: Social maladjustment and problem solving in school-aged children. *Journal of Consulting and Clinical Psychology* **50**, 226–33.

Rizzo, T. A. 1992: The role of conflict in children's friendship development. In Corsaro, W.A. and Miller, P. J. (eds), *Interpretive approaches to children's socialization*. San Francisco: Jossey-Bass, 93–112.

Roazzi, A. and Bryant, P. 1998: The effects of symmetrical and asymmetrical social interaction on children's logical inferences. *British Journal of Developmental Psychology* **16**, 175–81.

Roberts, W.L. and Strayer, J. 1987: Parents' responses to the emotional distress of their children: relations with children's competence. *Developmental Psychology* **23**, 415–22.

Roff, J.D. 1992: Childhood aggression, peer status, and social class as predictors of delinquency. *Psychological Reports* **70**, 31–4.

Roff, J.D. and Wirt, R.D. 1984: Childhood aggression and social adjustment as antecedents of delinquency. *Journal of Abnormal Child Psychology* **12**, 111–26.

Roff, M., Sells, B.B. and Golden, M.M. 1972: *Social adjustment and personality development*. Minneapolis: University of Minnesota Press.

Rogoff, B. 1991: Children's guided participation in planning imaginary errands with skilled adult or peer partners. *Developmental Psychology* **27**, 381–9.

Roopnarine, J.L. and Adams, G.R. 1987: The interactional teaching patterns of mothers and fathers with their popular, moderately popular, or unpopular children. *Journal of Abnormal Child Psychology* **15**, 125–36.

Rose, A. J. and Asher, S. R. 1999: Children's goals and strategies in response to conflicts within a friendship. *Developmental Psychology* **35**, 69–79.

Rosenthal, M.J., Ni, E., Finkelstein, M. and Berkowitz, G.K. 1962: Father–child relationships and children's problems. *Archives of General Psychiatry* **7**, 360–73.

Rotenberg, K.J. and Mann, L. 1986: The development of the norm of reciprocity of self-disclosure and its functions in children's attraction to peers. *Child Development* **57**, 1349–57.

Rotenberg, K.J. and Pilipenko, T.A. 1983: Mutuality, temporal consistency, and helpfulness in children's trust in peers. *Social Cognition* **2**, 235–55.

Rotenberg, K.J. and Sliz, D. 1988: Children's restrictive disclosure to friends. *Merrill-Palmer Quarterly* **34**, 203–15.

Rotheram, M.J. 1982: Social skills training with underachievers, disruptive, and exceptional children. *Psychology in the Schools* **19**, 532–39.

Rotheram, M.J., Armstrong, M. and Booraem, C. 1982: Assertiveness training in fourth and fifth-grade children. *American Journal of Community Psychology* **10**, 567–82.

Rowe, D.C. 1994: *The limits of family influence: genes, experience, and behaviour.* New York: Guilford.

Rubin, K.H. 1993: The Waterloo Longitudinal Project: correlates and consequences of social withdrawal from childhood to adolescence. In Rubin, K.H. and Asendorpf, J.B. (eds), *Social withdrawal, inhibition and shyness in childhood*. Hillsdale, NJ: Erlbaum, 291–314.

Rubin, K.H. 1998: Social and emotional development from a cross-cultural perspective. *Developmental Psychology* **34**, 611–15.

Rubin, K.H., Bukowski, W. and Parker, J.G. 1998: Peer interactions, relationships, and groups. In Damon, W. (series ed.) and Eisenberg, N. (vol. ed.), *Handbook of child development.* vol. 3. *Social, emotional, and personality development.* 5th edn. New York: Wiley, 619–700.

Rubin, K.H., Chen, X. and Hymel, S. 1993: Sociometric characteristics of withdrawn and aggressive children. *Merrill-Palmer Quarterly* **39**, 518–34.

Rubin, K.H., Chen, X., McDougall, P. , Bowker, A., McKinnon 1995: The Waterloo Longitudinal Project: predicting internalizing and externalizing problems in adolescence. *Development and Psychopathology* 7, 751–64.

Rubin, K.H., Daniels-Beirness, T. and Hayvren, M. 1982: Social and social-cognitive correlates of sociometric status in preschool and kindergarten children. *Canadian Journal of Behavioural Science* **14**, 338–49.

Rubin, K.H., Hymel, S., Lemare, L. and Rowden, L. 1989: Children experiencing social difficulties: sociometric neglect reconsidered. *Canadian Journal of Behavioural Science* **21**, 94–111.

Rubin, K.H., Hymel, S. and Mills, R.S.L. 1989: Sociability and social withdrawal in childhood: stability and outcomes. *Journal of Personality* 5b7, 237–55.

Rubin, K.H. and Rose-Krasnor, L. 1986: Social-cognitive and social behaviour perspectives on problem-solving. In Perlmutter, M. (ed.), *Minnesota Symposium on child psychology* **18**, 1–68. Hillsdale, N. J: Erlbaum.

Rubin, K.H. and Mills, R. S. L. 1988: The many faces of social isolation in childhood. *Journal of Consulting and Clinical Psychology* **56**, 916–24.

Rubin, K.H., Stewart, K.H. and Chen, X. 1995: Parents of aggressive and withdrawn children. In Bornstein, M.H. (ed.), *Handbook of parenting.* vol. 1. Mahwah, NJ: Erlbaum, 255–84.

Rubin, Z. and Sloman, J. 1984: How parents influence their children's friendships. In Lewis, M. (ed.), *Beyond the dyad.* New York: Plenum Press, 223–50.

Rutter, M. 1979: Maternal deprivation, 1972–1978: new findings, new concepts, new approaches. *Child Development* **50**, 283–305.

Ryan, A.S. 1985: Cultural factors in casework with Chinese-Americans: social casework. *The Journal of Contemporary Social Work*, **66**, 333–40.

Rys, G.S., and Bear, G.G. 1997: Relational aggression and peer relations: gender and developmental issues. *Merrill-Palmer Quarterly* **43**, 87–106.

Sagi, A., Lamb, M.E., Estes, D., Shoham, R., Lewkowitz, K. and Dvir, R. 1982: Security of infant-adult attachment among kibbutz-reared infants. Paper presented at the meeting of the International Conference on Infant Studies, Austin, TX, April.

Sagi, A., van Ijzendoorn, M.H., Aviezer, O., Donnell, F. and Mayseless, O. 1994: Sleeping out of home in a kibbutz communal arrangement: it makes a difference for infant-mother attachment. *Child Development* **65**, 992–1004.

Sainato, D.M., Zigmond, N. and Strain, P. S. 1983: Social status and initiations of interaction by learning disabled students in a regular education setting. *Analysis and Intervention in Developmental Disabilities,* **3**, 71–87.

Sale, P. and Carey, D.M. 1995: The sociometric status of students with disabilities in a full-inclusion program. *Exceptional Children* **62**, 6–19.

Salisch, M. von and Uhlendorff, H. 1998: Peer rejection and angry, aggressive behavior in open-field situations and scorn during a cooperative task. Unpublished manuscript, Free University of Berlin.

Salmivalli, C., Huttunen, A. and Lagerspetz, K.M.J. 1997: Peer networks and bullying in schools. *Scandinavian Journal of Psychology* **38**, 305–12.

San Miguel, S.K., Forness, S.R. and Kavale, K. 1996: Social skills deficits in learning disabilities: The psychiatric comorbidity hypothesis. *Learning Disability Quarterly* **19**, 252–61.

Sasso, G., Melloy, K.G. and Kavale, K. 1990: Generalization, maintenance, and covariation associated with social skills training through social learning. *Behaviour Disorders* **16**, 9–22.

Scarr, S. 1992: Developmental theories for the 1990s: developmental and individual differences. *Child Development* **63**, 1–19.

Schaughency, E.A., Vannatta, K., Langhinrichsen, J., Lally, C. and Seeley, J. 1992: Correlates of sociometric status in school children in Buenos Aires. *Journal of Abnormal Child Psychology* **20**, 317–26.

Schmitz, S. 1994: Personality and temperament. In DeFries, J.C., Plomin, R. and Fulker, D.W. (eds), *Nature and nurture during middle childhood*. Oxford: Blackwell, 120–40.

Schmitz, S., Cherny, S.S., Fulker, D.W. and Mrazek, D. 1994: Genetic and environmental influences on early childhood behaviour. *Behaviour Genetics* **24**, 25–34.

Schmitz, S., Saudino, K.J., Plomin, R., Fulkner, D. and DeFries, J.C. 1996: Genetic and environmental influences on temperament in middle childhood: analysis of teacher and tester ratings. *Child Development* **67**, 409–22.

Schneider, B.H. 1987: *The gifted child in peer group perspective*. New York: Springer-Verlag.

Schneider, B.H. 1992: Didactic methods for enhancing children's peer relations. *Clinical Psychology Review* **12**, 363–82.

Schneider, B.H. 1993: *Children's social competence in context: the contributions of family, school and culture*. Oxford: Pergamon.

Schneider, B.H., Attili, G., Vermigli, P. and Younger, A. 1997: A comparison of middle class English-Canadian and Italian mothers' beliefs about children's peer-directed aggression and social withdrawal. *International Journal of Behavioural Development* **21**, 133–54.

Schneider, B.H. and Byrne, B.M. 1987: Individualizing social skills training for behaviour-disordered children. *Journal of Consulting and Clinical Psychology* **55**, 444–5.

Schneider, B.H., Clegg, M.R., Byrne, B.M., Ledingham, J.E. and Crombie, G. 1989: Social relations of gifted children as a function of age and school program. *Journal of Educational Psychology*, **81**, 48–56.

Schneider, B.H. and Daniels, T. 1992: Peer acceptance and social play of gifted kindergarten children. *Exceptionality* **3**, 17–29.

Schneider, B.H., Fonzi, A., Tomada, G. and Tani, F. 2000: A cross-national comparison of children's behaviour with their friends in situations of potential conflict. *Journal of Cross-Cultural Psychology* **31**, 259–66.

Schneider, B.H., Fonzi, A., Tani, F. and Tomada, G. 1997: A cross-cultural exploration of the stability of children's friendships and predictors of their continuation. *Social Development* **6**, 322–39.

Schneider B.H., Richard, J.F., Younger, A.J. and Freeman, P. 2000: A longitudinal exploration of the continuity of children's social participation and social withdrawal across socioeconomic status levels and social settings. *European Journal of Social Psychology*.

Schneider, J. 1971: On vigilance and virgins: honour, shame, and access to resources in Mediterranean societies. *Ethnology* **10**, 1–23.

Schofield, J.W. 1995: Promoting positive intergroup relations in school settings. In Hawley, W.D. and Jackson, A.W. (eds), *Toward a common destiny: improving race and ethnic relations in America*. San Francisco, CA: Jossey-Bass, 257–89.

Schwartz, C.E., Snidman, N. and Kagan, J. 1996: Early childhood temperament as a determinant of externalizing behaviour in adolescence. *Development and Psychopathology* **8**, 527–37.

Schwartz, D., McFayden-Ketchem, S., Dodge, K.A., Pettit, G.S. and Bates, J.E. 1999: Early behaviour problems as a predictor of later peer group victimization: moderators and mediators in the pathways of social risk. *Journal of Abnormal Child Psychology* **27**, 19–201.

Schwartz, J.C. 1972: Effects of peer familiarity on the behaviour of preschoolers in a novel situation. *Journal of Personality and Social Psychology* **24**, 276–84.

Schwartz, S.H. and Ros, M. 1995: Value priorities in West European nations: a cross-cultural perspective. In Ben-Shakar, G. and Lieblich, A. (eds), *Studies in psychology in honor of Solomon Kugelmass*. Jerusalem: Magnes Press, 322–47

Sears, R.R. 1961: Relation of early socialization experiences to aggression in middle childhood. *Journal of Abnormal and Social Psychology* **63**, 466–92.

Sears, R.R., Maccoby, E.E. and Levin, H. 1957: *Patterns of child rearing.* Evenston, IL: Row-Peterson.

Sears, R.R., Whiting, J.W.M., Nowlis, V. and Sears, P. S. 1953: Some child rearing antecedents of aggression and dependency in. *Genetic Psychology Monographs* **47**, 135–234.

Seligman, M.E. 1999: The president's address. *American Psychologist* **54**, 559–62.

Selman, R. and Schultz, L.H. 1990: *Making a friend in youth.* Chicago: University of Chicago Press.

Selman, R.L. 1980: *The growth of interpersonal understanding: developmental and clinical understandings.* New York: Academic Press.

Selman, R.L. and Schultz, L.H. 1989: Children's strategies for interpersonal negotiation with peers: An interpretative/empirical approach to the study of social development. In Berndt, T.J. and Ladd, G.W. (eds), *Peer relationships in child development.* Wiley series on personality processes. New York: John Wiley and Sons, 371–406.

Selman, R.L., Watts, C.L. and Schultz, L.H. (eds): 1997: *Fostering friendship: pair therapy for treatment and prevention.* New York: Aldine De Gruyter.

Selman, R.S., Levitt, M.Z. and Schultz, L.H. 1997: The friendship framework: tools for the assessment of psychosocial development. In Selman, R.S. Watts, C.L. and Schultz, L.H. (eds), *Fostering friendship for treatment and prevention.* New York: de Gruyter, 31–53.

Serbin, L.A., Peters, P. L., McAffer, V.J. and Schwartzman, A.E. 1991: Childhood aggression and withdrawal as predictors of adolescent pregnancy, early parenthood, and environmental risk for the next generation. *Canadian Journal of Behavioural Sciences* **23**, 318–31.

Shannon, K. and Kafer, N.F. 1984: Reciprocity, trust, and vulnerability in neglected and rejected children. *Journal of Psychology* **117**, 65–70.

Shantz, C. 1985: *Children's peer relations: sociometric status, dyads and triads.* Washington, DC: National Science Foundation.

Shapira, A. and Madsen, M.C. 1974: Between and within-group co-operation and competition among kibbutz and nonkibbutz children. *Developmental Psychology* **10**, 140–5.

Sharabany, R. 1982: Comradeship: peer group relations among preadolescents in kibbutz versus city. *Personality and Social Psychology Bulletin* **8**, 302–9.

Sharabany, R. 1994: Continuities in the development of intimate friendships: object relations, interpersonal, and attachment perspectives. In Erber, R. and Gilmour, R. (eds), *Theoretical frameworks for personal relationships.* Hillsdale, NJ: Erlbaum, 157–78.

Shenkar, O. and Ronen, S. 1987: The cultural context negotiations: the implications of Chinese interpersonal norms. *The Journal of Applied Behavioural Science* **23**, 263–75.

Shure, M. B. and Spivak, G. 1982: Interpersonal problem-solving in young children: a cognitive approach to prevention. *American Journal of Community Psychology* **10**, 341–56.

Siegelman, M. 1966: Loving and punishing parental behaviour and introversion tendencies in sons. *Child Development* **37**, 985–92.

Sillars, A. L. 1991: Behavioural observation. In Montgomery, B.M. and Duck, S. (eds), *Studying interpersonal interaction*. New York: Guilford, 197–218.

Silver, J.M. and Yudofsky, S.C. 1991: The Overt Aggression Scale: overview and guiding principles. *Journal of Neuropsychiatry and Clinical Neurosciences* **3**, 522–9.

Sinha, J.B.P. and Tripathi, R.C. 1994: Individualism in a collectivistic culture: a case of coexistence of opposites. In Kim, U., Triandis, H.C., Kagitcibasi, C., Choi, S.C. and Yoon, G. (eds), *Individualism and collectivism: theory, methods, and applications*. Thousand Oaks, CA: Sage, 123–36.

Siperstein, G.N., Leffert, J.S. and Widaman, K. 1996: Social behaviour and the social acceptance and rejection of children with mental retardation. *Education and Training in Mental Retardation and Development* **31**, 271–81.

Skinner, B.F. 1948: *Walden Two*. New York: Machultan.

Slanina, A.M. 1996: Factors that impact transitions between a regular-educational program and a gifted program: the perceptions of four African-American males. *Journal for the Education of the Gifted* **20**, 54–83.

Slavin, R.E. 1979: Effects of biracial learning teams on cross-racial friendships. *Journal of Educational Psychology* **71**, 381–7.

Slavin, R.E. 1987: Developmental and motivational perspectives on co-operative learning: a reconciliation. *Child Development* **58**, 1161–7.

Slavin, R.E. 1991: Co-operative learning and group contingencies. *Journal of Behavioural Education* **1**, 105–15.

Slee, P. T. 1999: Bullying amongst Australian primary school students: some barriers to help-seeking and links with sociometric status. In Slee, P. T. and Rigby, K. (eds), *Children's peer relations*. London: Routledge, 205–14.

Smith, L. 1996: The social construction of rational understanding. In Tryphon, A. and Voneche, J. (eds), *Piaget-Vygotsky: the social genesis of thought*. Psychology Press. 107–22.

Smith, M.C., Winningham, V. and Haro, L. 1999: Social and emotional competencies: Contributions to young African-American children's peer acceptance. Paper presented at the Society for Research and Development in Child Psychology, Albuquerque, NM, April.

Smith, P. K. 1989: The role of rough and tumble play in the development of social competence: theoretical perspectives and empirical evidence. In Schneider, B.H., Attili, G., Nadel, J. and Weissberg, R.P. (eds), *Social competence in developmental perspectives*. Dordrecht: Kluwer, 239–55.

Smith, P. K. 1999: Introduction. In Smith, P. K., Morita, Y., Junger-Tas, J., Olweus, D., Catalono, R. and Slee, P. (eds) *The nature of school bullying: a cross-national perspective*. London: Routledge, 1–4.

Smith, P. K., Morita, Y., Junger-Tas, J., Olweus, D., Catalano, R.F. and Slee, P. 1999: *The nature of school bullying: a cross-national perspective*. New York: Routledge.

Smith, P. K. and Sharp, S. (eds) 1994: *School bullying insights and perspectives*. London: Routledge.

Solano, C.H. 1976: Teacher and pupil stereotypes of gifted boys and girls. Paper presented at the annual conference of the American Psychological Association, Washington, DC, September.

Spence, S.H. 1987: The relationship between social-cognitive skills and peer sociometric status. *British Journal of Developmental Psychology* **5**, 347–56.

Spieker, S.J. and Booth, C.L. 1988: Maternal antecedents of attachment quality. In Belsky, J. and Nezworski, T. (eds), *Clinical implications of attachment*. Hillsdale, NJ: Erlbaum. 95–135.

Spiel, C., Weixelbaum, E. and Spiel, C. 1999: The impact of dropouts in a longitudinal study of children at risk. Paper presented at the 9th European Conference on Developmental Psychology, Spetses, Greece, September.

Spivack, G. and Shure, M. B. 1974: *Social adjustment of young children*. San Francisco: Jossey-Bass.

Spurgeon, P. , Hicks, C. and Terry, R. 1983: A preliminary investigation into sex differences in reported friendship determinants amongst a group of early adolescents. *British Journal of Social Psychology* **22**, 63–4.

Stanton, M.E. 1995: Patterns of kinship and residence. In Ingoldsby, B.B and Smith, S. (eds), *Families in multicultural perspective: perspectives on marriage and the family*. New York: Guilford, 97–116.

Stattin, H. and Magnusson, D. 1989: The role of early aggressive behaviour in the frequency, seriousness and types of later crime. *Journal of Consulting and Clinical Psychology* **57**, 710–18.

Stephens, T.M. 1976: *Directive teaching of children with learning and behavioral handicaps*. Columbus, OH: Merrill.

Stephens, T.S. 1992: *Social skills in the classroom*. 2nd edn. Odessa, FL: Psychological Assessment Resources.

Stevahn, L., Johnson. D.W., Johnson, R.T. and Real, D. 1996: The impact of a cooperative or individualistic context on the effectiveness of conflict resolution training. *American Educational Research Journal* **33**, 801–23.

Stocker, C.M. 1994: Children's perceptions of relationships with siblings, friends, and mothers: Compensatory processes and links with adjustment. *Journal of Child Psychology and Psychiatry* **35**, 1447–59.

Stokes, T.E. and Baer, D.M. 1977: An implicit technology of generalization. *Journal of Applied Behaviour Analysis* **10**, 349–67.

Stone, W.L. and La Greca, A.M. 1990: The social status of children with learning disabilities: A re-examination. *Journal of Learning Disabilities* **23**, 32–7.

Stoneman, Z., Brody, G. H. and MacKinnon, C. 1984: Naturalistic observations of children's activities and roles while playing with their siblings and friends. *Child Development* **55**, 617–27.

Stormshak, E.A., Bierman, K.L., Bruschi, C., Dodge, K.A. and Coie, J.D. 1999: The relation between behaviour problems and peer preference in different classroom contexts. *Child Development* **70**, 169–82.

Storr, A. 1968: *Human aggression*. London: Penguin Press.

Strassberg, Z., Dodge, K.A., Bates, J.E. and Pettit, G.S. 1992: The longitudinal relation between parental conflict strategies and children's sociometric standing in kindergarten. *Merrill-Palmer Quarterly* **38**, 477–93.

Strassberg, Z., Dodge, K.A., Pettit, G.S. and Bates, J.E. 1994: Spanking in the home and children's subsequent aggression toward kindergarten peers. *Development and Psychopathology* **6**, 445–61.

Strayer, F.F. 1989: Co-adaptation within the early peer group: a psychobiological study of social competence. In Schneider, B.H., Attili, G., Nadel, J. and Weissberg, R.D. (eds), *Social competence in developmental perspective*. NATO Science Institutes series. Series D: Behavioural and social sciences. vol. 51. Dordrecht: Kluwer Academic Publishers, 145–74.

Strichart, S.S. and Gottlieb, J. 1975: Imitation of retarded children by their non-retarded peers. *American Journal of Mental Deficiency* **179**, 506–12.

Sullivan, H.S. 1953: *The interpersonal theory of psychiatry.* New York: Norton.

Sutton, J., Smith, P. K. and Swettenham, J. 1999: Social cognition and bullying: social inadequacy or skilled manipulation? *British Journal of Developmental Psychology* **17**, 435–50.

Sutton-Smith, B. 1982: A performance theory for peer relations. In Borman, K. (ed.), *The social life of children in a changing society.* Hillsdale, NJ: Erlbaum, 65–77.

Symonds, P. M. 1939: *The psychology of the parent-child relationship.* New York: Appleton-Century.

Tarabulsy, G.M., Avgoustis, E., Phillips, J., Pederson, D. and Moran, G. 1997: Similarities and differences in mothers' and observers' descriptions of attachment behaviours. *International Journal of Behaviour Development* **21**, 599–619.

Tassi, F. and Schneider, B.H. 1997: Task-oriented versus other-referenced competition: differential implications for children's peer relations. *Journal of Applied Social Psychology* **27**, 1557–80.

Taylor, A.R., Asher, S.R. and Williams, G.A. 1987: The social adaptation of mainstreamed mildly retarded children. *Child Development* **58**, 1321–34.

Taylor, A.R. and Machida, S. 1994: The contribution of parent and peer support to Head Start children early school adjustment. *Early Childhood Research Quarterly* **9**, 387–405.

Terman, L.M. and Oden, M. 1959: *The gifted group at mid-life: thirty-five years' follow-up of the superior child.* Stanford, CA: Stanford University Press.

Terry, R. and Coie, J.D. 1991: A comparison of methods for defining sociometric status among children. *Developmental Psychology* **27**, 867–80.

Tesser, A., Campbell, J. and Smith, M. 1984: Friendship choice and performance: self- evaluation maintenance in children. *Journal of Personality and Social Psychology* **46**, 561–74.

Tessier, O., Tremblay, R.E. and Bukowski, W.M. 1994: Friendship, friendship quality and delinquency in an 'at risk' sample of boys between the ages of 10 and 15. Poster session presented at the biennial meeting of the International Society of Behavioural Development, Amsterdam, June.

Thrasher, F.M. 1927: *The gang: a study of 1,313 street gangs in Chicago.* Chicago: University of Chicago Press.

Tomada, G and Schneider, B.H. 1997: Relational aggression, gender, and peer acceptance: Invariance across culture, stability over time, and concordance among informants. *Developmental Psychology* **33**, 601–9.

Toupin, E.S.W.A. 1980: Counselling Asians: psychotherapy in the context of racism and Asian-American history. *American Journal of Orthopsychiatry* **50**, 76–86.

Triandis, H.C. 1990: Cross-cultural studies of individualism and collectivism. In Dienstbier, R.A. (series ed.) and Berman, J.J. (vol. ed.), *Nebraska symposium on motivation* 1989: vol. 37. Lincoln: University of Nebraska Press, 41–133.

Triandis, H.C., Bontempo, R., Villareal, M.J., Asai, M. and Lucca, N. 1988: Individualism and collectivism: cross-cultural perspectives on self-ingroup relationships. *Journal of Personality and Social Psychology* **52**, 323–38.

Trower, P. , Bryant, B. and Argyle, M. 1978: *Social skills and mental health.* Pittsburgh: University of Pittsburgh Press.

Tsui, P. and Schultz, G. L. 1988: Ethnic factors in group process: cultural dynamics in multi-ethnic therapy groups. *American Journal of Orthopsychiatry* **58**, 136–42.

Tuddenham, R.D. 1951: Studies in Reputation III: correlates of popularity among elementary-school children. *The Journal of Educational Psychology* **25**, 257–76.

Udvari, S.J. and Rubin, K.H. 1996: Gifted and non-selected children's perceptions of academic achievement, academic effort and athleticism. *Gifted Child Quarterly* **40**, 211–19.

van Aken, M.A.G. and Asendorpf, J.B. 1997: Support by parents, classmates, friends and siblings in preadolescence: covariation and compensation across relationships. *Journal of Social and Personal Relationships* **14**, 79–93.

Vandell, D.L. and Hembree, S.E. 1994: Peer social status and friendship: Independent contributors to children's social and academic adjustment. *Merrill-Palmer Quarterly* **40**, 461–77.

van IJzendoorn, M.H. and Kroonenberg, P. M. 1988: Cross-cultural patterns of attachment: a meta-analysis of the Strange Situation. *Child Development* **59**, 147–56.

Vaughn, B.E. and Langlois, J.H. 1983: Physical attractiveness as a correlate of peer status and social competence in preschool children. *Developmental Psychology* **19**, 561–7.

Vaughn, S. and Haager, D. 1994: Social competence as a multifaceted construct: how do students with learning disabilities fare? *Learning Disability Quarterly* **71**, 253–66.

Vaughn, S., Haager, D., Hogan, A. and Kouzekanani, K. 1992: Self-concept and peer acceptance in students with learning disabilities: a four-to-five year prospective study. *Journal of Educational Psychology* **84**, 43–50.

Vaughn, S., Hogan, A., Kouzekanani, K. and Shapiro, S. 1990: Peer acceptance, self-perception and social skills of learning disabled students prior to identification. *Journal of Educational Psychology* **82**, 101–6.

Vaughn, S., McIntosh, R., Schumm, J.S., Haager, D. and Callwood, D. 1993: Social status, peer status and reciprocal friendships revisited. *Learning Disabilities Research and Practice* **8**, 82–8.

Vitaro, F., Gagnon, C. and Tremblay, R.E. 1990: Predicting stable peer rejection from kindergarten to Grade One. *Journal of Clinical Child Psychology* **19**, 257–64.

Vitaro, F., Gendreau, P. L., Tremblay, R.E. and Oligny, P. 1998: Reactive and proactive aggression differentially predict later conduct problems. *Journal of Child Psychology and Psychiatry and Allied Disciplines* **39**, 377–85.

Volkan, V.D. 1988: *The need to have enemies and allies*. London: Jason Aronson, Inc.

Volling, B.L., Youngblade, L.M. and Belsky, J. 1997: Young children's social relationships with siblings and friends. *American Journal of Orthopsychiatry* **67**, 102–11.

Vosk, B., Forehand, R., Parker, J. B. and Rickard, K. 1982: A multimethod comparison of popular and unpopular children. *Developmental Psychology* **18**, 571–5.

Vygotsky, L.S. 1962: *Thought and language*. Cambridge, MA: Massachusetts Institute of Technology.

Walcott, E. 1932: Daydreamers: a study of their adjustment in adolescence. *Smith College Studies in Social Work* **2**, 283–335.

Waldrop, M.F. and Halverson, C.F.Jr. 1975: Intensive and extensive peer behavior: longitudinal and cross-sectional analyses. *Child Development* **46**, 19–26.

Walker, H.M. and Lamon, W.E. 1987: Social behaviour standards and expectations of Australian and U. S. teacher groups. *Journal of Special Education* **21**, 56–82.

Walker, H.M. and Rankin, R. 1983: Assessing the behavioural expectations and the demands of less restrictive settings. *School Psychology Review* **12**, 274–84.

Wallerstein, R.S. 1989: The psychotherapy research project of the Menninger

Foundation: an overview. *Journal of Consulting and Clinical Psychology* **55**, 195–205.

Wasserstein, S.B. and LaGreca, A. 1996: Can peer support buffer against behavioural consequences of parental discord? *Journal of Clinical Child Psychology* **25**, 177–82.

Waters, E. and Deane, K. 1985: Defining and assessing individual differences in attachment relationships: Q-methodology and the organization of behaviour in infancy and early childhood. In Bretherton, I. and Waters, E. (eds), *Growing points of attachment theory and research*, Monographs of the Society for Research in Child Development 50 (Serial No. 209).

Waters, E. and Sroufe, L.A. 1983: Social competence as a developmental construct. *Developmental Review* **3**, 79–97.

Watson, G. 1957: Some personality differences in children related to strict or permissive parental discipline. *Journal of Psychology* **44**, 227–49.

Weiss, B., Dodge, K.A., Bates, J.E. and Pettit, G.S. 1992: Some consequences of early harsh discipline: child aggression and maladaptive social information processing study. *Child Development* **63**, 1321–35.

Weissberg, R.P. 1981: Evaluation of a social-problem-solving skills training: a competence-building intervention with second- to fourth-grade children. *Journal of Consulting and Clinical Psychology* **49**, 251–61.

Weissberg, R.P. , Gesten, E., Carnrike, C., Toro, P. , Rapkin, B., Davidson, E. and Cowen, E.L. 1981: Social problem-solving training: a competence building intervention with second-to-fourth-grade children. *American Journal of Community Psychology* **9**, 411–23.

Weisz, J.R., Suwanlert, S., Chaiyasit and Weiss, B. 1988: Thai and American perspectives on over and undercontrolled child behaviour problems: exploring the threshold model among parents, teachers, and psychologists. *Journal of Consulting and Clinical Psychology* **56**, 601–9.

Weller, M.P. I. 1993: Where we come from: recent history of community provision. In Weller, M.P. I. and Muijen, M. (eds), *Dimensions of community mental health care*. London: Saunders, 1–19.

Wentzel, K. 1991: Relations between social competence and academic achievement in early adolescence. *Child Development* **62**, 1066–78.

Wentzel, K.R. and Asher, S.R. 1995: The academic lives of neglected, rejected, popular, and controversial children. *Child Development* **66**, 754–63.

Werebe, M.J. and Baudonniere, P. M. 1991: Social pretend play among friends and familiar peers. *International Journal of Behavioural Development*, **14**, 411–28.

Westen, J.H.A. 1995: Interpersonal relationship networks of Canadian children of East Indian origin. Unpublished master's thesis, University of Toronto, Toronto, Canada.

Westman, A. S. 1990: Do people's presence more than their presents makes children happy? *Perceptual and Motor Skills*, **71**, 674.

White, K. J. and Kistner, J. 1992: The influence of teacher feedback on young children's peer preferences and perceptions. *Developmental Psychology* **28**, 933–40.

Whiting, B.B. and Edwards, C.P. 1988: *Children of different worlds: the formation of social behaviour*. Cambridge, MA: Harvard University Press.

Whiting, B.B. and Whiting, J.W.M. 1975: *Children of six cultures: a psychocultural analysis*. Cambridge, MA: Harvard University Press.

Wiener, J. 1987: Peer status of learning disabled children and adolescents: a review of the literature. *Learning Disabilities Research*, **2**, 62–79.

Windle, M. 1994: A study of friendship characteristics and problem behaviours among middle adolescents. *Child Development* **65**, 1764–77.

Wiseman, J.P. and Duck, S. 1995: Having and managing enemies: a very challenging relationship. In Duck, S. and Wood, J.T. (eds), *Confronting relationship challenges*. Thousand Oaks, CA: Sage, 43–72.

Wolfensberger, W. 1972: *The principle of normalization in human services*. Toronto: National Institute on Mental Retardation.

Wolfensberger, W. and Tullman, S. 1982: A brief outline of the principle of normalization. *Rehabilitation Psychology* **27**, 131–45.

Wolman, B.B. 1973: *Dictionary of behavioural science*. New York: Van Nostrand Reinhold.

Wright, J.C., Giammarino, M. and Parad, H.W. 1986: Social status in small groups: individual-group similarity and the social 'misfit'. *Journal of Personality and Social Psychology* **50**, 523–36.

Yang, K.S. 1981: Social orientation and individual modernity among Chinese students in Taiwan. *Journal of Social Psychology* **113**, 159–70.

Young, M.R.R. and Bradley, M.T. 1998: Social withdrawal: self-efficacy, happiness, and popularity in introverted and extroverted adolescents. *Canadian Journal of School Psychology* **14**, 21–35.

Younger, A., Gentile, C. and Burgess, K. 1993: Children's perceptions of social withdrawal: changes across age. In Rubin, K.H. and Asendorpf, J.B. (eds), *Social withdrawal, inhibition, and shyness in childhood*. Hillsdale, NJ: Erlbaum, 215–35.

Zahn-Waxler, C., Schmitz, S., Fulker, D. and Robinson, J. 1996: Behaviour problems in 5–year-old monozygotic and dizygotic twins: genetic and environmental influences, patterns of regulation, and internalization of control. *Development and Psychopathology* **8**, 103–22.

Zigler, S. 1981: The effectiveness of cooperative learning teams for increasing cross-ethnic friendship: additional evidence. *Human Organization* **40**, 264–68.

Zigler, S. and Trickett, P. K. 1978: IQ, social competence and evaluation of early childhood intervention programs. *American Psychology* **33**, 789–98.

Index

academic achievement,
  aggression and, 75
  social competence and, 74
  social mediation of learning, 75
  peer acceptance and, 75
adolescent–parent relationships, 11
adult maladjustment, prediction of, 18
adoption studies, 41
aggression,
  and peer rejection, 99
  as a predictor of delinquency, 104
  as social incompetence, 99
  cultural differences in, 105
  gender differences in, 105
  overt and relational aggression, 105
aggressive peer group,
  antisocial attitude transmission
    amongst, 145
  formation of, 144
assessment of social competence see
    attachment; sociometrics
attachment,
  advantages of secure attachment, 44
  and friendship theory, 45
  and psychoanalysis, 11
  attachment styles,
    anxious-ambivalent attachment
      style, 44
    anxious-avoidant attachment style,
      44
  internal working models, 42
  longitudinal studies, 44
  methods of studying,
    Q-sort technique, 43
    Strange Situation technique, 43
  theoretical challenges to, 43

Baumrind, Diana, 47
bullying, 105, 106

Child Behaviour Checklist, 125
childhood,
  and happiness, 33
  as permanent feature in society, 17
  inherent nature of children, 6
  'incomplete adults', 17
  reasons for studying, 17
childhood maladjustment,
  causal and incidental models, 34
Chinese culture,
  Buddhism, 168
  Chinese society and verbal aggres-
    sion, 168
  Confucianism, 168
  individualism/collectivism in Chinese
    children, 167
  notion of 'face', 168
  peer relations in Chinese children,
    168–9
  shyness and sensitivity in Chinese
    and Canadian children, 169
  similarities between Chinese and
    Western children's peer
    relations, 169
  Taoism, 168
chumships, 21, 29
Civil Rights Movement, 14
cognitive growth,
  friendship and, 76
  peer interaction and, 80,81
  siblings and, 80
  socio-cognitive conflict and, 76
Committee for Economic Develop-
    ment,
  mission of, 88
companionship, 131
competitive learning,
  Collaborative Strategic Reading, 85
  conflict resolution skills and, 86

competitive learning (*cont.*)
  peer acceptance and, 86
  prosocial peer interactions and, 86
  reading comprehension and, 85
  'Six Mirrors' of, 84–5
competence, general,
  adaptive behaviour, 92
  as adaptive flexibility, 92
  as encompassing social skills, 108
conflict and conflict resolution, 135
contact hypothesis, 13
  cultural diversity, 14
  children with disabilities, 14
cooperation,
  age of emergence, 1
  and biological preparedness, 1
cross-cultural comparisons, 163
  and origins of social competence, 163
  between two separate societies, 163
  cross-cultural contact in schools, 187
  developmental and cultural
    differences, 166
  differences in tolerance for atypical
    behaviour, 179
  differences between East and West
    Berlin in socialization, 185
  East Asian children, 167
  friendship differences,
    in children from East and West
      Berlin, 185
    actual vs abstract notions of
      friendship in German children,
      186
    in Italian and Canadian children,
      185
  high-context cultures, 165
  low-context cultures, 165
  low-tolerance cultures, 166
  multicultural societies and individual
    identity, 165
  multi-ethnicity and tolerance levels,
    186
  power distance, 166
  rules, 166–7
  scripts, 163
  tolerance for over- and under-
    controlled behaviour, 180
  tolerance of ambiguity and diversity,
    166
  within one society, 164
cultural dimensions of childhood
  aggression, 175

Afro-American children, 178
challenges in cross-cultural research,
  181–2
context dependent, 176
Indonesian children, 178
negative sociometric status, 181
segregated schooling and aggression,
  178
school behaviour thresholds, 181
Six Culture Project, 177
sociometric acceptance and reciprocal friendships, 181
Zapotec communities, 175

de-institutionalization,
  and friendship, 12
  and mental health, 12
democracy,
  and child-rearing, 9
  and relationship choice, 9
development,
  family vs peer influences, 2
  learning through play, 3
  typical and atypical, 4–5

education,
  academic vs social development
    orientation to, 73
  'back to basics' motto, 73
    expressive socialization , 74
    instrumental socialization, 74
    social and emotional learning, 73
enemies,
  areas for future research, 148
  characteristics of, 145–6
  communication between, 147
  enemyship, 145
  group solidarity and, 147
  intensity of dislike, 145
  purpose of having, 146
  reasons for dislike, 146
  vigilance and, 147
experience sampling method, 126

families,
  and the industrial revolution, 2–3
FAST Track (Families and Schools
    Together), 204
friendship,
  Cross-age, 143
  aggressive children, amongst, 144
  and school transition, 82

and well-being, 29, 30
as a buffer against bullying, 30
as a protective environment, 187
assessment of, 130, 138
definition of, 129
characteristics of, 129
cross-gender, 142
cross-racial and cross-ethnic friend-
    ship selection,
    cooperative learning groups and,
        189
    ethnic homogeneity in Czech
        society, 190
    future directions in cross-cultural
        comparisons of children, 190
    normalcy of ethnocentrism in
        children's friendships, 189
    selection of Black or White friends
        in a competitive context, 189
duration of, 130
extended families and, 184
gender differences in, 141–2
life cycle of, 137
pictorial representations of similarity
    in friendship, 186
preschool children and, 130
primary school children and, 136
proximity in, 132
quality of, 139
race and ethnicity in friendship
    selection, 188
shared activity in, 132
similarity in, 132
societal influences on, 142
stability of, 131, 137
stage models of, 137
universally defined, 183
voluntary nature of, 184
friendship assessment methodology
direct observation, 138, 140
essay techniques, 138
Friendship Quality Questionnaire,
    140
laboratory observation, 141
reciprocal sociometric choice, 138
self-report, 139
with aggressive children, 143
future perspectives, 15

genetics, 37, 42,
gifted children,
    and boredom, 155

and creative suffering, 159
biographical study of, 159
defined by creativity, 159
defined by IQ and academic
    achievement, 155
issues in defining gifted, 155
'Terman myth', 155

Harris, Judith Rich, 2–3, 45, 71
heredity, 37
homophily, 144

individualism/collectivism,
    and friendships in a multi-ethnic
        study, 187
    collectivistic cultures, 164
        and children's friendships, 183
        and restraints on children's
            friendships, 184
    effect on friendships with disabled
        children, 151
    interplay of individualistic and
        collectivistic forces, 165
instrumental assistance, 133
intimacy, 134
Israel *see* kibbutzim
Italy,
    aggressive/disruptive behaviour and
        peer rejection, 176
    gender differences in aggression, 177
    parental attributions of children's
        behaviour, 179–80
    relational and overt aggression,
        176–7

kibbutzim,
    age differences and cooperation, 174
    and cooperation, 173
    and emotional detachment, 173
    and free play, 173
    communal sleeping arrangements,
        174
        and mother–child attachment, 174
    metaplot, attachment to, 175

Latin America, 170
    collectivism in Latin American
        cultures, 170
    comparison of Andalucian, Spanish
        and Dutch children, 172
    competition, 172
    cooperation, 172

Latin America (*cont.*)
   Costa Rican children, popularity and
      rejection, 170
   intimate relationships with family,
      171
learning,
   competitive,
      other-referenced, 84
      task oriented, 84
   cooperative, 84–6, 88
   individualistic, 84
longitudinal studies,
   attrition, 18
   follow-back studies, 19–20
   selecting target behaviours, 19

mainstreaming, 13
measurement *see* attachment; socio-
      metrics; self-report; observa-
      tional methods; friendship
      assessment methodology;
      research on peer relations;
      reports from third parties
Meichenbaum, Donald,
   cognitive – HYPHEN – behaviour
      modification, 199
methods of attaining leadership,
   direct, 9
   indirect, 9
models of development of social
      competence, 38
   contemporary indirect model, 38
   direct genetic model, 38
   group socialization model, 38
   indirect genetic model, 38
   parent socialization model, 38
Montessori schooling, 80
Moreno, Jacob, 3, 109, 110

observational methods,
   as participant, 118
   behaviourism and, 119
   contrived play groups, 122
   history of, 118
   inter-rater reliability, 120
   limitations of, 122–3
   Parten system, 119–20
   reactivity to the observer and, 122
   remote observation of distant events,
      126–7
   structured vs unstructured, 119
   time sampling, 120

pair therapy, 206–7
Panduit, 141
parenting,
   and cultural values, 46
   Baumrind's classification system of
      parenting practices, 47
   child-rearing styles, 45
   nurture assumption challenged, 45
   parental and educational fit to
      children's temperament, 46
   parenting styles,
      authoritarian parental style, 47
      authoritative parental style, 47
      permissive parental style, 47
   parent socialization model, 38
   parent training, 46
parents as initiators of peer contact, 69
   age differences, 69
   cross cultural differences, 69
peer relations,
   and birth rate, 15
   and happiness, 15
   and psychoanalysis, 3
   and working mothers, 15
   as early predictors of adult
      adjustment, 10
   as social instinct, 2
   atheoretical orientation in studying, 6
   atypical patterns, 150
   de-institutionalization, 10
   disabilities,
      differential treatment hypothesis,
        154
      discrepancy hypothesis, 154
      future directions: overcoming
        obstacles of dissimilarity, 162
      perspective-taking, 151
      psychological comorbidity
        hypothesis, 154
      psychological processing deficit,
        154
      socially competent behaviour, 154
      strategic deficit hypothesis, 154
      unequal rewards in friendships,
        151
   equity theory, 150
   leadership and social and political
      implications, 9
   longitudinal studies, 10
   normal development, 5
   practical applications of, 8
   theories of atypical development, 149

analogies drawn from the physical
sciences, 149
peer tutoring,
benefits of, 87
characteristics of effective peer
tutoring, 87
theories of, 87
person-group similarity model, 95
Phillips, E. Lakin, 192
post-war focus on the prevention of
mental illness, 12
prejudice,
own-group preference in children's
friendships, 188
social reflection theories and, 187
prevention of mental illness, 12
psychoanalysis,
as suppressor of objective research, 5
role enactment and stress reduction,
7
transference and community intervention, 11
counter-revolution against, 3
psychiatric problems as natural phenomena, 4
psychodrama, 7–8

reciprocity, 135
remote observation of distant events,
126–7
reports from third parties,
gender and, 125
parents, 124
peers, 124
teachers, 124
research on peer relations,
data sources, 110
measurement of, 110
methodology selection, 110
methods,
adoption studies, 41
Twin Studies, 39
multi-method approach, 111
rote memorization, 7

school adjustment,
classroom composition and, 82
frequency of peer contact, 83
friendship and, 81
gender differences, 83
important peer relationships and, 83
nature of friendships and, 82

peer attachment in novel situations,
81
scripted play sequences, 131
self-report, 123
diaries as, 126
problems with, 123
uses of, 123
youth self report form, 125
separating students according to
academic ability, 188
shyness, 106
and adolescent ostracism, 108
fearful, 107
longitudinal correlates of, 107
self-conscious, 107
social competence,
as appropriate to developmental
stage, 94
as goal satisfaction, 91
as knowledge, 93
as normative, 92
as outcome, 93
as process, 93
as relational competence, 94
molecular models of, 91
of groups, 94
situation specific, 91
trait, 90, 91
socialization by peers,
agricultural societies, 70
birth position and, 72
Harris' group socialization theory, 71
older siblings as social skill coaches,
71
similarities between siblings and
peers, 71
the effect of organized child-care and
recreational activities, 70
social role theory of personality, 4
social skills,
as determining social success, 90
as etiquette, 89
Social Skills Rating system, 125
social skills training,
as a nexus between individual and
environment, 192
assessment of success, 193
Bandura's reciprocal determinism,
193
and observational learning, 193
and cognitive abilities and beliefs,
193

social skills training (*cont.*)
  behaviour modification, 192
    Skinner's *Walden Two*, 192
    token economies, 192
  behaviourist movement and, 191
  by cooperation between teachers and
    caregivers, 203
  cognitive-HYPHEN-behaviour
    modification, 199
  cost effectiveness, 194
  early efforts, 191
  focused on friendship, 206
    pair therapy, 206
    pair therapy, future directions, 207
    success of pair therapy with
      rejected children, 206
  follow-up studies, 199
  generalization and maintenance, 199
  methods of modelling skills, 195
  multi-modal interventions,
    core components and optional
      components, 205
    empathy training in, 205
    Olweus' programme for reducing
      bullying in schools, 205
    Project FAST Track (Families and
      Schools Together), 204
    evaluation, 204
  peers in social skills training, 203
    as support for victims or potential
      victims of bullies, 203
  predictors of responsiveness, 198
  primary prevention, 194
  secondary prevention, 194
  self-control interventions, 197
    and internalized verbal commands,
      197
    scope, 197
    self-statements, 198
    success, 198
  social problem-solving, 196
    and aggressive children, 196
    dependence on language, 197
    problem-solving sequence, 196
  skill steps, 195
  structured learning method, 194
  student-mediated conflict resolution,
    205
  reinforcements used, 195
social support, 133
  peer/parent specific, 134

social withdrawal, 21, 106
sociometrics,
  and social chaos, 14
  basics of, 111
  classification based on, 113
  ethics in, 116–17
  'last choices' in, 112
  'living sociometrics', 8
  negative consequences of, 117
  number of choices, 113
  peer ratings (vs nominations), 114
  risk management, 117
  social preference, 112
  social impact, 112
  stability of, 114–16
  wording effects, 113
special education classes, 13
spontaneity theory, 4
Sullivan, Harry, 21, 129

'tele', 8
television viewing and aggression, 179
  Finnish children, 179
  in Israeli kibbutzim, 179
temperament,
  adoption studies, 41
    limitations of, 41
  Colorado Adoption Project, 41
  definition, 38
  behavioural genetic methods of
    study, 39
  EAS (emotionality, activity and
    sociability), 39
  limitations of observational methods,
    40
  origins, 37
  nature vs nurture, 37
  parental contrast in sociability, 40
  parental ratings, 40
  shared and non-shared family
    environment, 41–2
  sociability as pre-wired trait, 39
  teacher reports, 41
  twin studies, 39
tracking according to academic ability,
  188
trust, 134–5
twins, 39

Vygotsky, Lev,
  zone of proximal development, 76